Machine Learning for Undergraduate Students

OrangeBooks Publication

1st Floor, Rajhans Arcade, Mall Road, Kohka, Bhilai, Chhattisgarh 490020

Website: **www.orangebooks.in**

First Edition, 2025

ISBN: 978-93-6554-661-3

Price: Rs. 850.00

Printed in India

MACHINE LEARNING

FOR UNDERGRADUATE STUDENTS

DR. A.J.K. PRASAD | DR. REDDAPPA H.N.

OrangeBooks Publication
www.orangebooks.in

About the Cover

The cover of this textbook, *Machine Learning for Undergraduate Students*, has been thoughtfully designed to reflect human learning methodologies and strategies. It visually captures the evolution of human learning and its profound influence on the development of artificial intelligence and machine learning, aligning closely with the themes and content presented in the book.

Human Learning

At its core, incorporation of stages of human growth, highlights the journey of human learning—from infancy to ripened maturity—representing the stages of knowledge acquisition, skill development, and emotional intelligence. Once a new ability is acquired (such as tossing, walking, or reasoning), it becomes a permanent part of the learner's cognitive toolkit. This irreversible advancement mirrors how learning deepens over time, eventually leading to emotional intelligence, creativity, and wisdom. This lifelong continuum of learning forms the very foundation upon which artificial intelligence draws its inspiration.

Learning Strategies: From Human to Machine- Not Just Machines

Above the silhouettes, the cover references core machine learning paradigms: supervised, semi-supervised, unsupervised, and reinforcement learning. These learning strategies directly parallel human learning methods. Just as children learn through guidance, observation, trial-and-error, and rewards or consequences, machines use structured data, pattern recognition, and feedback loops to improve performance. The transition from basic actions to complex reasoning in both humans and machines demonstrates how artificial learning is modelled on biological learning processes.

The term "machine" in *machine learning* refers not to physical robots not computers but to the algorithms and statistical models that learn from data. These systems gain insights and improve over time without needing explicit instructions/programming for every task. The cover reinforces this idea by blending human silhouettes with circuit-like design elements, symbolizing the convergence of natural and artificial learning. Understanding this distinction helps demystify machine learning and positions it as a powerful tool rooted in human-designed logic and data processing.

Artificial Intelligence

Artificial Intelligence draws from key branches of human knowledge—**mathematics**, **computer science**, **neuroscience**, **psychology**, **linguistics**, **philosophy, economics, and ethics**. Each of these disciplines contributes essential insights into how learning, reasoning, and communication occur.

The inclusion of words like "feelings," "emotions," "compassion," and "creativity" on the cover—particularly in the context of humanoid robots and intelligent systems—serves as a reminder that the essence of human cognition remains uniquely complex and deeply nuanced. While AI can simulate certain behaviours and responses, it lacks the real depth of consciousness, empathy, and creative intuition that define human intelligence. These callouts emphasize that, despite significant advancements, current AI research has not yet reached this profound level of human capability.

Preface

It gives us immense pleasure to present the first edition of "Machine Learning for Undergraduate Students", a comprehensive textbook designed to bridge the gap between theoretical foundations and practical applications in the rapidly evolving field of machine learning. This book emerges from our collective experience in teaching machine learning to undergraduate students and our recognition of the need for a resource that balances mathematical rigor with accessibility.

Machine learning has transformed from an academic curiosity to a driving force behind technological innovation across industries. This textbook aims to equip undergraduate students with the fundamental knowledge and practical skills necessary to understand, implement, and innovate in this dynamic field.

The textbook is organized into five carefully structured chapters, each designed to build a strong foundation while gradually introducing advanced topics. Our pedagogical approach emphasizes conceptual understanding supported by mathematical foundations, ensuring that students develop both theoretical knowledge and practical intuition. Special attention has been given by including relevant illustrations and tables that enhance understanding and provide visual clarity to complex concepts. Additionally, each chapter concludes with a set of thoughtfully curated questions, encouraging students to reflect on and apply what they have learned.

Key Features of This Edition:

1. Comprehensive Visual Learning Aids: This first edition includes ***58 figures and 43 tables,*** meticulously designed to simplify complex concepts and support visual learners. We have ensured high-quality visual appeal with clear, informative graphics and simple table formats. Black and white figures are provided in both hard copies and e-books.

2. Structured Learning Framework: Each chapter begins with a concise overview, providing a clear roadmap of the topics covered, and concludes with a comprehensive summary and reflective thoughts to reinforce learning outcomes. This structure helps students navigate complex topics systematically and consolidate their understanding progressively.

3. Active Learning and Reference Features: To support active learning and critical thinking, a comprehensive set of theoretical review questions has been provided, We hope that these questions shall deepen the understanding of the concepts and encourage reflection on the topics covered in the book. Alphabetical index and glossary has been provided for ensuring ease of reference for both students and educators.

Chapter Organization and Content:

Chapter 1: Introduction to Machine Learning (*9 figures and 12 tables*)

This foundational chapter introduces students to the fundamental concepts of machine learning, tracing its historical development and establishing its position within the broader landscape of computer science and artificial intelligence. Students explore what constitutes a "machine" in machine learning, the compelling need for machine learning in modern applications, and the knowledge pyramid that illustrates the progression from data to wisdom. In this chapter the concept of machine is elanorate in that: *What is a "machine" in the context of machine learning?* Contrary to common misconceptions, the term "machine" in machine learning is used figuratively to represent algorithms or statistical models that derive knowledge from data. It does not refer to a physical device or robot. Instead, it describes computational systems capable of learning and improving their performance autonomously over time, without explicit reprogramming. Understanding this distinction is essential to grasping the essence of machine learning as a pivotal branch of artificial intelligence.

The chapter examines machine learning's advantages and limitations and its relationship with related fields such as statistics, data mining, and artificial intelligence, and provides a comprehensive taxonomy of learning paradigms including supervised, semi-supervised, self-supervised, and unsupervised learning methodologies.

Chapter 2: Data Analysis and Feature Engineering (*12 figures and 11 tables*)

Building upon foundational concepts, this chapter delves into the critical aspects of data preparation and analysis that underpin successful machine learning applications. Students learn bivariate and multivariate data analysis techniques, multivariate statistics, and essential mathematical frameworks for understanding complex datasets. The chapter covers feature engineering principles, dimensionality reduction techniques for managing high-dimensional data, learning system design principles, and fundamental modelling and learning theory concepts.

Chapter 3: Similarity-Based Learning and Regression (*11 figures and 05 tables*)

This chapter focuses on intuitive yet powerful machine learning approaches based on similarity measures and regression analysis. Students explore similarity-based learning principles, nearest-neighbour algorithms including weighted K-nearest-neighbor methods, and nearest centroid classifiers. The chapter provides comprehensive coverage of locally weighted regression (LWR), linear regression and its variants including multiple, polynomial, and logistic regression, along with decision tree learning principles and induction algorithms. This chapter mentions that **regressor** refers to the **independent variable(s)** in regression analysis, which are used to predict the **dependent variable** (target outcome).

Chapter 4: Probabilistic Models and Neural Networks (*12 figures, and 08 tables*)

This chapter introduces students to the probabilistic foundations of machine learning and the computational paradigm of neural networks. The content bridges classical statistical approaches with modern computational methodologies, providing students with a comprehensive understanding of both traditional probabilistic models and contemporary neural network architectures.

Chapter 5: Clustering Algorithms and Reinforcement Learning (*14 figures, and 07 tables*)

The final chapter explores unsupervised learning through clustering algorithms and introduces the dynamic field of reinforcement learning. Students gain practical understanding of various clustering techniques and learn the principles of learning through interaction with environments, completing their comprehensive introduction to the major paradigms of machine learning.

A Note to Learners and Instructors

This textbook serves as both a comprehensive learning resource and a practical reference guide. Students are encouraged to engage actively with the material, work through examples, and tackle end-of-chapter questions to deepen their understanding. Instructors will find the structured approach and comprehensive coverage suitable for semester-long courses, with flexibility to emphasize particular topics based on course objectives and student backgrounds.

Machine learning rewards both theoretical understanding and practical experimentation. We encourage readers to complement their study with hands-on programming exercises and real-world applications. The journey into machine learning is challenging but immensely rewarding, opening doors to innovative solutions across diverse domains.

We hope this textbook serves as a valuable companion in your machine learning journey and contributes to your success in this exciting and rapidly evolving field. Constructive suggestions for improvement of the content is welcome form readers and shall be incorporated in subsequent editions.

Authors
First Edition, 2025

Acknowledgement

Firstly, we express our gratitude to the Almighty for blessing us with the opportunity to write this book. We extend our heartfelt thanks to the management of Don Bosco Institute of Technology and the Rajya Vokkaligara Sangha, Bengaluru, for their unwavering support and encouragement.

We would like to sincerely thank **Dr. B.S. Nagabhushana**, Principal of Don Bosco Institute of Technology, and **Dr. Aswath M.U.**, Principal of Bangalore Institute of Technology, Bengaluru, for their guidance and motivation throughout this endeavor.

Dr. Reddappa H.N. expresses his deepest gratitude to his family members, **Mrs. Dharani S.** and **Diganth R.**, for their unending support and encouragement. **Dr. A.J.K. Prasad** is profoundly thankful to **Venkata Lakshmi**, **Aparna**, and **Jyotsna** for their continuous support, encouragement, and understanding throughout this endeavour.

We extend our indebted thanks to our colleagues for their invaluable encouragement and timely support. We also acknowledge Mr. Kushal for his assistance in creating some of the illustrations featured in this book.

We sincerely appreciate the developers and promoters of OpenAI, Sonnet Claude AI, Perplexity AI, Grok AI, DeepSeek AI, and iMathEQ.com for their invaluable tools that significantly aided in clarifying complex concepts, generating SVGs, and providing Python code for visuals and equations. Their contributions have been indispensable to the success of this project, and we extend our heartfelt thanks to all the team members behind these remarkable platforms.

We express our sincere gratitude to Orange Books Publishing (Orangebooks.in) for publishing this book in such an elegant format. Our special thanks go to Madhavi, Kritika, Payal Ghosh, and their team for their editorial support and dedication.

Dr. A.J.K. Prasad
Dr. Reddappa H.N.

Dedication

This book is dedicated to our teachers, whose guidance and wisdom have shaped us, and to our students, whose curiosity and enthusiasm inspire us to remain focused and committed to lifelong learning.

Contents

List of Figures

List of Tables

Chapter - 1

Introduction to Machine Learning

- Introduction to Machine Learning
- Historical Developments
- What is machine in machine learning?
- Need for machine learning
- Knowledge Pyramid
- Machine learning explained advantages and disadvantages
- Maching learning in relation to other fields
- Types of machine learning
- Learning styles Supervised, semi-supervised, self-supervised and unsupervised machine learning, semi-supervised learning.

Chapter Over View

This chapter presents a comprehensive introduction to machine learning, emphasizing its growing significance and usefulness in today's data-rich environment. The chapter delves in the evolution of machine learning as a field, its distinctive position within the broader domains of artificial intelligence and data science, and how it can be applied to complicated/challenging real-world problems. Various kinds of learning (supervised, unsupervised, reinforcement, and emergent paradigms like self-supervised learning) were discussed in detail, providing a solid theoretical foundation. The challenges of ML, such as overfitting, computational constraints, and data quality issues, were highlighted to prepare readers for practical considerations. The machine learning process has been explained, illustrating how data moves through multiple stages to generate meaningful insights. Finally, the chapter discusses big data and its symbiotic relationship with machine learning, demonstrating how contemporary tools tackle the enormous amount and complexity of today's data environments.

1.0 Introduction to Machine Learning

Machine learning is present in numerous areas. This observation appears to become increasingly accurate over time. I struggle to think of any facet of life that could not benefit from in one way or another. For tasks that involve repetition or analyzing data to draw conclusions, machine learning proves beneficial. In recent years, the field of machine learning has experienced significant expansion owing to increased and the widespread availability of data collection to highlight a few uses of machine learning: recommendation systems, image recognition, text processing, autonomous vehicles, spam detection, and medical diagnosis... and many more. Perhaps you have a specific aim or field where you aspire to create a difference (or perhaps you are already doing so!). It is highly probable that machine learning can assist you. The word "machine" in Machine Learning is used in a figurative sense and signifies the algorithm or model that acquires knowledge from data. It does not represent a tangible machine or robot but is instead a collection of computational strategies that enable systems to enhance their efficiency over time without direct programming. This clarification is vital for grasping the nature of Machine Learning as a subset of Artificial Intelligence.

1.1 Need for Machine Learning:

In today's digital age, we are witnessing an unparalleled data explosion, spurred by the growing popularity of digital communications, the internet revolution, and the widespread use of social media platforms like Facebook, X (formerly Twitter). Individuals, organizations, and devices all over the world generate, transfer, and store enormous amounts of data every second! From social media interactions and e-commerce transactions to Internet of Things (IoT) sensor data and corporate operations, the sheer volume of data is astonishing. This data contains significant insights, but manually analyzing and employing it for decision-making is not only impractical, but also nearly impossible!.

Traditional methods of processing and analyzing data depended mainly on manual labor and rule-based programming. While these strategies worked well for small-scale or organized datasets, they struggle to handle the intricacies of modern data streams. Modern datasets are generally unstructured and complex. Moreover, the data is constantly changing, necessitating the adoption of dynamic and scalable strategies for data manipulation. For example, pattern recognition in photos, predicting/forecasting client behavior, and recommending personalized content are beyond the scope of manual or conventional programming. This rising gap between data availability and making useful insights from such big data has necissitated to the development of automated techniques, paving the way for machine learning (ML).

Machine learning addresses the above issue by enabling systems (see explanatory note of machine in machine learning in the following section) to learn from data and improve over time without necessitating explicit programming. Machine learning has democratized data analysis by developing complex algorithms while additionally rendering tools like Python and R more accessible. These technologies allow researchers and businessess to analyze vast datasets, identify trends, and make reliable predictions. Machine learning algorithms can detect fraud in real time, offer products (also services) based on consumer preferences, and even predict diseases using medical images. Machine learning relies on the ability to process, analyze, and provide important conclusions from vast quantities of data, making it extremely important in an information-driven world.

Furthermore, the incorporation of machine learning into modern industries has changed how firms operate. Machine Learning powers/propelles predictive analytics for better informed decision-making, automates repetitive tasks to enhance productivity. On the consumer sector especially I e-commence platforms and entertainment segments such as OTT plataform analyses user behaviour to provide customer-centric solutions.

Whether it is improving supply chains, enhancing cybersecurity, or transforming healthcare diagnostics, the uses of machine learning are reshaping industries. With the rise of big data and technological breakthroughs, machine learning is no longer a luxury; it is a requirement for remaining competitive in a quickly changing digital market.

1.1.1 Evolution of Data-Driven Decision-Making

Development of Data-Driven Decision-Making Historically, organizational decision-making was mainly reliant on intuition, manual analysis, and static reports created from limited datasets. However, with the digital revolution, the volume, variety, and velocity of data grew/swelled tremendously. Modern firms are overrun with data, that includes customer transactions and social media activity to sensor readings and website traffic logs. The abundance of data has paved the way for data-driven decision-making, in which decisions are driven by actionable insights gained through data analysis rather than subjective judgment. Businesses may now use advanced analytics and machine learning to figure out patterns, predicted outcomes, and optimize processes in real time, making decision-making quicker and proactive.

1.1.2 Limitations of Traditional Programming

Traditional programming is based on clearly establishing rules and logic for every possible circumstance, making it rigid and inappropriate for complex, dynamic contexts. This technique suffers with unstructured data tasks including picture recognition, natural language interpretation, and pattern detection in large datasets. Furthermore, manually programming systems to react to new data or changing situations is time-consuming and often impractical. For example, constructing a spam email filter using traditional approaches would necessitate an extensive collection of spam patterns and rules, which would quickly become out of date. making it essential for addressing new, data-intensive challenges, particularly those involving patterns and insights in unstructured data—a key focus of unsupervised learning.

1.2 What is a Machine, in Machine Learning Context?

The phrase **"machine"** in the context of Machine Learning is used figuratively and represents the algorithm or statistical models that acquire knowledge from data. It does not denote a tangible device or a robot; instead, it describes a set of computational methods that enable systems to enhance their efficiency progressively without the need for direct coding. Recognizing this difference is vital for grasping the fundamental nature of Machine Learning as a segment of Artificial Intelligence.

1.3 A Brief Note on Historical Development of Machine Learning

Machine learning (ML) has evolved since the mid-twentieth century, when the foundations of artificial intelligence (AI) began to emerge. Alan Turing's key paper, "Computing Machinery and Intelligence," published in 1950, presented the concept of intelligent computers and proposed the Turing Test as a measure of machine intelligence. In 1959, Arthur Samuel, a pioneer in the field, defined machine learning as computers' ability to learn without being explicitly programmed. His work on checkers-playing platforms was one of the first instances of a machine improving performance through experience.

The 1980s saw the emergence of neural networks, which were inspired by the workings of the human brain. This period witnessed the rise of backpropagation algorithms, enabling artificial neural networks to learn complex patterns. However, development lacked /was hampered due to a lack of computational power and data availability. The 1990s witnessed the introduction of increasingly advanced algorithms such as support vector machines (SVMs) and ensemble approaches, as well as greater availability to digital data.

The early twenty-first century ushered the era of big data, coupled by exponential advances in processing/computational capabilities. Breakthroughs in deep learning, coupled by improved hardware such as GPUs and TPUs, have revolutionized machine learning applications, enabling tasks such as image processing, natural language processing, and autonomous driving. Machine learning is now a cornerstone of AI, continually evolving to address complicated challenges in a number of sectors, including healthcare, finance, entertainment, social media data robotics and consumer product recommendations in e-commerce segment.

This historical trajectory highlights how machine learning has grown from a theoretical concept to a practical tool, driving innovation and transforming industries worldwide.

This historical trajectory highlights how machine learning has grown from a theoretical concept to a practical tool, driving innovation and transforming industries worldwide.

Before we delve into the machine learning concepts, it is important to understand the **knowledge pyramid**. In the following section, detailed understanding of it are presented.

1.4 The Knowledge Pyramid in the Context of Data and Machine Learning

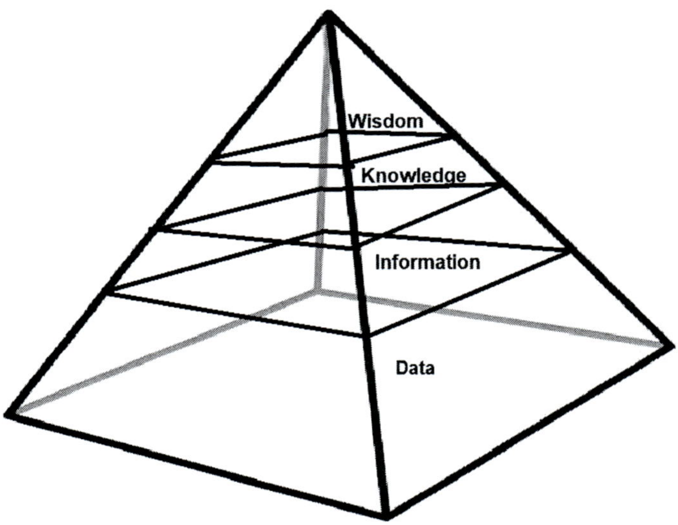

Figure 1.1 the Knowledge Pyramid (Claude AI generated Figure)

The Knowledge Pyramid—also known as the Data, Information, Knowledge, and Wisdowm (DIKW) Pyramid—is a structure with levels that outlines how raw data is transformed into actionable insight. This concept is vital in data science and machine learning (ML), as data is the base and the foundation to develop intelligent systems, Figure 1.1.

Data is the base of the pyramid. Data can be considered/defined as raw, unstructured facts or observations that lack intrinsic meaning or context. It is the primary input for machine learning systems.

Examples: Sensor readings (such as temperature and humidity) from any industrial system are examples of machine learning. User activity records/logs (such as clicks, views, and timestamps) are another example in the context of machine learning. Raw files contain images/photos, audio, and text.

Role in machine learning: Raw data must be pre-processed a pre-requisigte. Data preparation/preprocessing is the initial stage in every machine learning pipeline. Uncleaned/unprocessed data leads to non-reliable predictions.

Information: Data that has been processed or arranged to convey meaning or context. It exposes patterns or relationships within the raw data.

ML instances involve aggregated values, such as the average temperature during a week.

The frequency with which users perform specified tasks. pf a any website who's data analytics is in consideration.

Tagged datasets (for example, labelled photos) are used in supervised learning.

Role In machine learning (ML), data is extracted through preprocessing techniques such as feature engineering and transformation.

Information is the foundation for model training. Definition of Knowledge: Deriving meaningful insights, trends, or patterns from examining information.

Examples pf Knowledge in ML include analyzing the impact of weather on snack sales (e.g., "rain increases bajji sales").

Predicting client attrition/churn out employing past data.

In machine learning, data is extracted using techniques namely employing algorithm s such as regression, classification, and clustering.

Wisdom: The Top of the Pyramid.

Definition: Wisdom is the effective application of knowledge for decision-making, which includes contextual understanding and human judgment.

Some instances of ML include personalized product suggestions (refer to chapter on Recommender System in this book) based on user preferences and contextual data.

Dynamic pricing models for e-commerce.

Self-driving automobiles make autonomous decisions.

The role of machine learning is to apply predictions to real-world issues and gain wisdom. It includes ethical issues, justice, and domain expertise.

In Table 1.1 we present the mapping the knowledge pyramid to machine learning workflow from this table one can grasp the relation between DIKW and ML

Table 1.1: Learning-Based Reflex Agent

DIKW Layer	Machine Learning Workflow Step	Example
Data	Data collection and preprocessing	Collecting images, removing noise, normalizing pixel values.
Information	Feature engineering and exploratory data analysis (EDA)	Extracting edges for image classification.
Knowledge	Model training and evaluation	Training a neural network to classify images as "cat" or "dog."
Wisdom	Model deployment and decision-making	Recommending pet products based on identified user preferences.

Challenges in the DIKW Pyramid

1. **Data Quality**: Raw data is often incomplete, inconsistent, or biased.
2. **Contextual Understanding**: Information without domain knowledge can lead to incorrect inferences.
3. **Model Interpretability**: Black-box ML models hinder understanding and trust.
4. **Ethical Concerns**: Decisions based on ML must align with ethical and societal norms.

Thus, the DIKW Pyramid provides a conceptual framework for understanding how data evolves into actionable insights in the context of machine learning. By leveraging data, extracting information, building knowledge, and applying wisdom, ML systems enable informed decision-making and intelligent automation.

1.5 Machine Learning in Relation to Other Fields

Machine learning (ML) is often viewed as a subset of artificial intelligence (AI), though it has roots with other fields such as statistics and data science. Understanding its relationship with different disciplines provides insight into its breadth and relevance. This section explores these relationships, emphasizing the distinctions, overlaps, and synergies. In figure 1.2 we present a picture depicting the relations between artificial intelligence (AI), Machine Learnings (ML), Deep Learning (DL) and Datas Science (DS)

1.5.1 Machine Learning vs. Artificial Intelligence

Machine learning is an essential component of artificial intelligence. While AI aims to simulate human intelligence in machines, machine learning (ML) focuses on allowing systems to learn from data and improve over time without requiring explicit programming. For example, a chatbot uses machine learning models to interpret and respond to user inputs, but it also relies on other AI techniques, such as rule-based systems, to provide programmed rather predefined responses. Table 1.2 compares the relation between AI and ML.

Table 1.2 Comparison of Artificial Intelligence and Machine Learning

Aspect	Artificial Intelligence	Machine Learning
Scope	Broad, encompassing reasoning, planning, decision-making, etc.	Narrower, focused on data-driven learning.
Techniques	Includes ML, expert systems, rule-based logic, etc.	Primarily algorithms like supervised, unsupervised, and reinforcement learning.
Application	General problem-solving systems like robotics, virtual assistants.	Specific tasks like image recognition, recommendation systems.

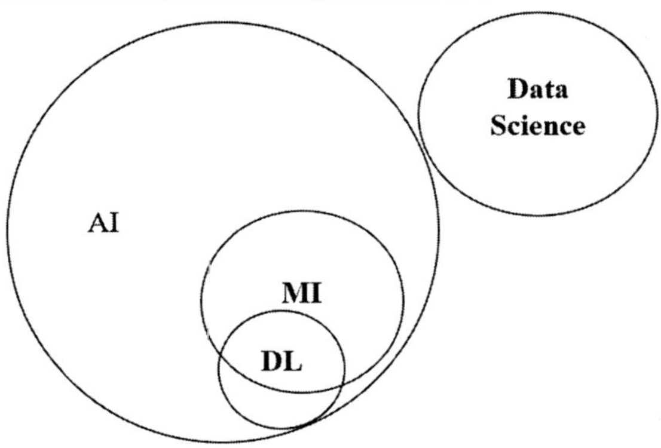

Figure 1.2: A Venn Diagram showing the overlap between Artificial Intelligence, Machine Learning, and Deep Learning.

1.5.2 Machine Learning vs. Data Science

Data science is an interdisciplinary field that focus on data collecting, cleaning, visualization, and analysis. Machine learning is one of the methods used by data scientists to make predictions and derive meaningful insights from data. While data science encompasses business intelligence and exploratory research, machine learning adds value by automating analytical model building/development.

Table 1.3: Comparative of AI, data science, and machine learning.

Aspect	Data Science	Machine Learning
Focus	Data preparation, visualization, statistical analysis.	Developing algorithms to make predictions or automate processes.
Tools Used	Python, R, SQL, Tableau for visualization.	ML libraries like Scikit-learn, TensorFlow, PyTorch.
Outcome	Understanding and interpreting data trends.	Automating and optimizing tasks using data-driven models.

1.5.3 Machine Learning vs. Statistics

Machine learning and statistics share a common foundation in mathematical analysis and data interpretation. However, while statistics stresses inference and hypothesis testing, machine learning focuses on prediction and automation. For example, regression analysis is a statistical method that has been used in machine learning for predictive modelling.

Table 1.4: Comparison and contrasting ML and statistics.

Aspect	Statistics	Machine Learning
Goal	Understanding relationships between variables and testing hypotheses.	Making predictions and improving model performance over time.
Key Techniques	Regression, ANOVA, hypothesis testing.	Decision trees, neural networks, reinforcement learning.
Focus	Interpreting data in a structured framework.	Handling large-scale, often unstructured data.

1.5.4 Synergies Across Fields

These fields are not mutually exclusive; rather, they work highly synergistic was. For example,

- AI applications, such as self-driving cars (autonomous vehicles), rely on statistical principles which form the basis for building machine learning models.
- Machine learning is commonly used in data science workflows to assess and anticipate trends.

  Machine learning abridges theoretical statistical models and actual AI applications, making it important and integral to both disciplines.

Understanding the relation between machine learning, artificial intelligence, data science, and statistics provides valuable insight into how these disciplines complement and strengthen one another. Each plays a crucial role in solving complex, data-driven problems, with machine learning—particularly the selection and application of ML algorithms for specific data forms—serving as the core focal point

1.6 Types of Machine Learning

Machine learning can be classified into different learning styles based on how a model learns from data the input. These learning styles dictate how algorithms process data, adapt, and boost performance over time. The three basic types of learning are (1) supervised learning, (2) unsupervised learning, and (3) reinforcement learning, each designed to address a certain sort of problem. Furthermore, emerging paradigms like semi-supervised learning and self-supervised learning offer novel ways to use partially labelled or totally/ entirely unlabelled datasets.

In supervised learning, models are trained on labelled data with explicit input-output pairings. This approach is commonly used for classification and regression tasks such as recognizing spam emails or predicting house prices. Unsupervised learning, on the other hand, works with unlabelled data, with the goal of uncovering hidden patterns or structures within it. Clustering and dimensionality reduction are excellent examples of unsupervised learning applications.

1.6.1 Supervised, Unsupervised, and Reinforcement Learning

In ***supervised learning***, models are trained on labelled data with explicit input-output pairs. This approach is commonly used for regression and classification tasks such as recognizing spam emails or predicting house prices.

Unsupervised learning, on the contrary, deals with unlabelled data, with the focus of uncovering hidden patterns or structures within the data. Clustering and dimensionality reduction are excellent examples of unsupervised learning applications.

Reinforcement learning adapts a different approach, enabling agents to learn by interacting with the environment and attracting rewards or penalties/punishments for their executed actions. This style of learning is best suited for dynamic, sequential decision-making tasks such as robotics and game playing. Furthermore, semi-supervised learning combines a small amount of labelled data with vast amounts of unlabelled data.

Self-supervised learning leverages inherent structures within data to generate pseudo-labels. These advanced learning approaches push the limits of what machine learning can accomplish, making it more versatile and adaptable to real-world problems.

1.6.2 Supervised Learning

Supervised learning is one of the most widely used machine learning paradigms. In this learning style, models are trained on a labelled dataset where each input is associated with a corresponding output. The objective is to learn a mapping function that predicts the output for new, unseen inputs based on the learned relationships in the training data.

How Supervised Learning Works?

The supervised learning process typically involves:

1. **Data Collection and Preparation:**
    - Collect labelled data with input features (X) and target labels (Y).
    - For example, consider a dataset of house prices with features such as square footage, location, and number of bedrooms, labelled with the price.

2. **Model Training:**
   - Use algorithms to identify patterns in data and minimising errors between predicted and actual outputs.
3. **Model Testing:**
   - Evaluate the model's performance on a separate/new test dataset to ensure it can generalize to new data.

The Iterative Process in Supervised Machine Learning

Supervised machine learning is an iterative process in which the model is refined repeatedly in the training phase. Large datasets usually divide into three subsets: training, testing, and validation. The iterative cycle consists of training the model on the training set, verifying its performance on the test set, validating it on unknown/unseen (meaning not used either in of train, test, validation phases), and repeating the process with new datasets until optimal performance is achieved. When deployed on entirely new, unseen data, a robust model maintains consistent. Figure 1.3 depicts the supervised machine learning workflow.

To understand this iterative nature, lets re-examine the workflow as given below:

Supervised Learning Workflow

1. **Training Dataset:**
   - Example: A dataset containing 1000 emails labelled as "spam" or "not spam."
2. **Learning Algorithm:**
   - Example: Logistic regression learns to assign probabilities for emails being spam.
3. **Trained Model:**
   - Example: The model identifies spam emails with 95% accuracy.
4. **Prediction on New Data:**
   - Example: Classifies a newly received email as "spam" based on its features.

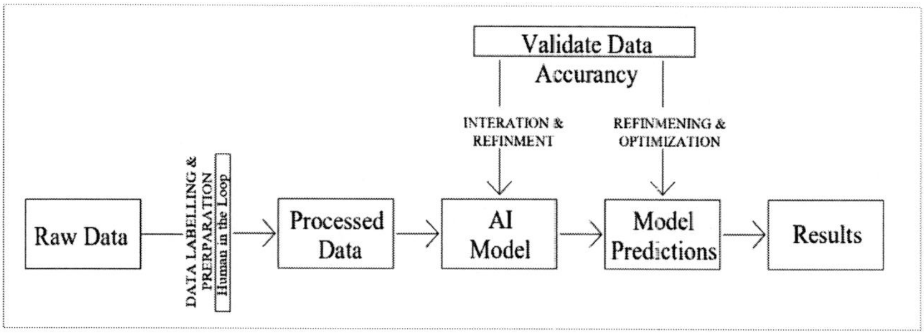

Figure 1.3 Iterative Nature of Supervised Machine Learning

(Flowchart of the supervised learning process (data collection → model training → prediction → evaluation). - Search Images)

Types of Supervised Learning Tasks

1. **Regression**: Regression is a supervised learning technique used to predict continuous outcomes based on input features. It establishes relationships between dependent and independent variables, enabling tasks like forecasting and trend analysis. A detailed explanation can be found in Chapter 3.
    - Used for predicting continuous values.
    - **Example**: Predicting house prices, stock market trends.
    - Algorithms: Linear regression, polynomial regression, decision trees.

In figure 1.4 house price predations using linear regression with area of the house (area/square foot) as one of the variables is presented.

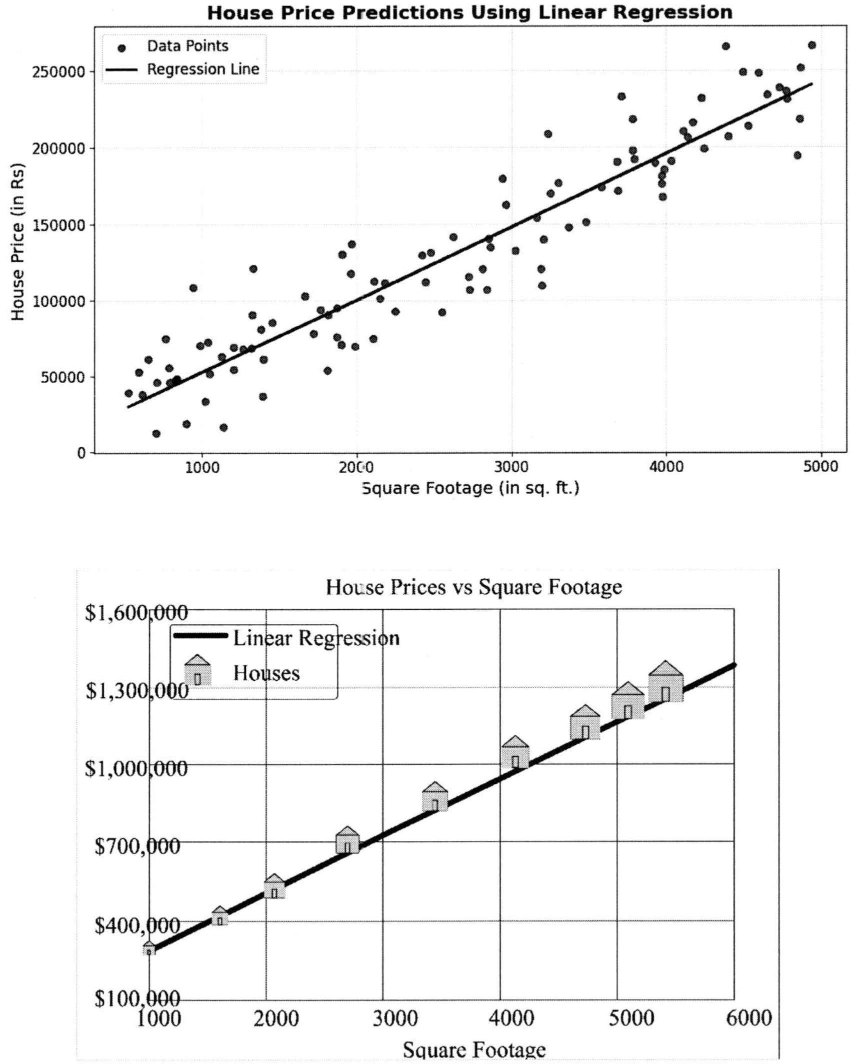

Figure 1.4: House price predations using linear regression with area of the house (area/square foot) as one of the variables

2. **Classification**: Classification is a supervised learning method used to categorize data into predefined classes. It predicts discrete outcomes, such as identifying emails as spam or not spam. For a comprehensive explanation, refer to Chapter 3.
   - Used for categorizing data into discrete classes.

- **Example**: Email classification as spam or not spam.
- Algorithms: Logistic regression, support vector machines (SVM), neural networks.

Advantages of Supervised Learning

- High accuracy when sufficient labelled data is available.
- Direct learning of the relationship between inputs and outputs.

Challenges in Supervised Learning

- Requires large amounts of labelled data, which can be expensive and time-consuming to obtain.
- Overfitting can occur when models memorize training data instead of generalizing.

Table 1.5 Examples of Supervised Learning

Task	Input Features (X)	Output Label (Y)	Algorithm Example
Email Spam Detection	Email content, metadata	Spam or Not Spam	Naïve Bayes, Logistic Regression
House Price Prediction	Size, Location, Number of Bedrooms	Price	Linear Regression
Disease Diagnosis	Patient symptoms, medical history	Disease category	Decision Trees, SVM
Image Recognition	Pixel values of images	Object category (e.g., cat, dog)	Convolutional Neural Networks

Conclusion

Supervised learning remains a cornerstone of machine learning, powering applications across industries. With its ability to predict outcomes from labelled data, it provides actionable insights and automates decision-making. However, the need for labelled data and the risk of overfitting are key challenges that practitioners must address.

1.6.3 Unsupervised Learning

Unsupervised learning involves training models on datasets that do not contain labelled outputs. The goal is to identify hidden structures, patterns, or groupings in the data. Unlike supervised learning, where models are guided by labelled examples, unsupervised learning algorithms work autonomously to uncover insights.

Key Characteristics

- No labelled data is required.
- Focuses on pattern recognition and structure discovery.
- Commonly used for clustering, dimensionality reduction, and anomaly detection.

Examples

1. **Clustering:**
   - Grouping customers based on purchasing behavior (e.g., segmentation for marketing).
   - Algorithms: k-Means, DBSCAN, Hierarchical Clustering.
2. **Dimensionality Reduction:**
   - Reducing features in high-dimensional data for visualization or preprocessing.
   - Algorithms: PCA, t-SNE.

Table 1.6: Comparison of Supervised and Unsupervised Learning

Aspect	Supervised Learning	Unsupervised Learning
Labeled Data	Required	Not Required
Goal	Predict outcomes	Identify patterns
Examples	House price prediction, spam detection	Customer segmentation, fraud detection
Algorithms	Linear regression, decision trees	k-Means, PCA

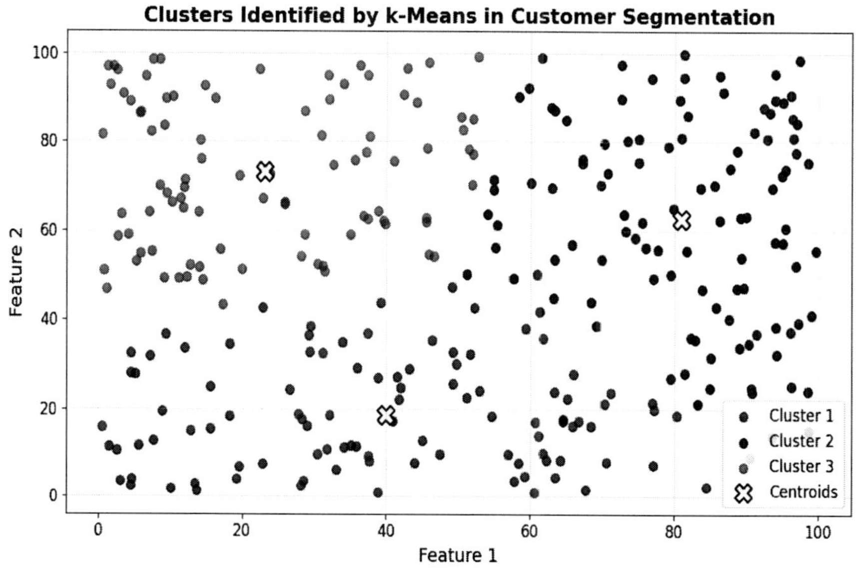

Figure 1.5: A scatterplot showing clusters identified by k-Means in customer segmentation.

1.6.4 Semi-Supervised and Self-Supervised Learning

Semi-supervised and self-supervised learning bridge the gap between supervised and Semi-supervised and self-supervised learning fill the gaps between supervised and unsupervised learning. These approaches use/leverage unlabeled data to increase performance while reducing the reliance on labelled data.

Semi-supervised Learning

Semi-supervised learning involves integrating a small quantity of labelled data with a huge volume of unlabelled data. The labelled data serves as a guide, allowing the model to learn more successfully from unlabelled samples/examples.

Example:

- Predicting diseases using a dataset with few labeled and large unlabeled medical records.
- Algorithms: Label Propagation and Self-Training.

Self-supervised learning

Self-supervised learning generates pseudo-labels from unlabeled data. The model learns by solving pretext tasks, such as predicting missing data or understanding relationships within the data.

Example:

- Natural language processing (NLP), models such as BERT can be trained by predicting masked words in sentences.
- Computer vision involves predicting the orientation of images or sections of them.

In figure 1.6 and in table 1.7 Semi-Supervised Learning Workflow, comparison of Semi-supervised Learning and Self-Supervised Learning are respectively presented.

Table 1.7: Comparison of Semi-Supervised and Self-Supervised Learning

Aspect	Semi-Supervised Learning	Self-Supervised Learning
Labelled Data	Small labelled dataset, large unlabelled dataset	Entirely unlabelled data
Goal	Enhance supervised tasks	Pretrain models for downstream tasks
Examples	Medical diagnosis, sentiment analysis	NLP (BERT), Computer Vision (SimCLR)

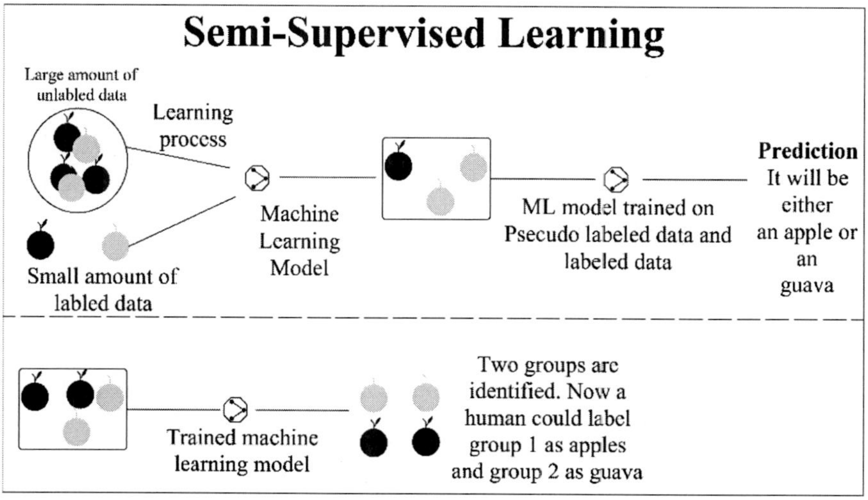

Figure 1.6 (a): Semi-Supervised Learning Workflow

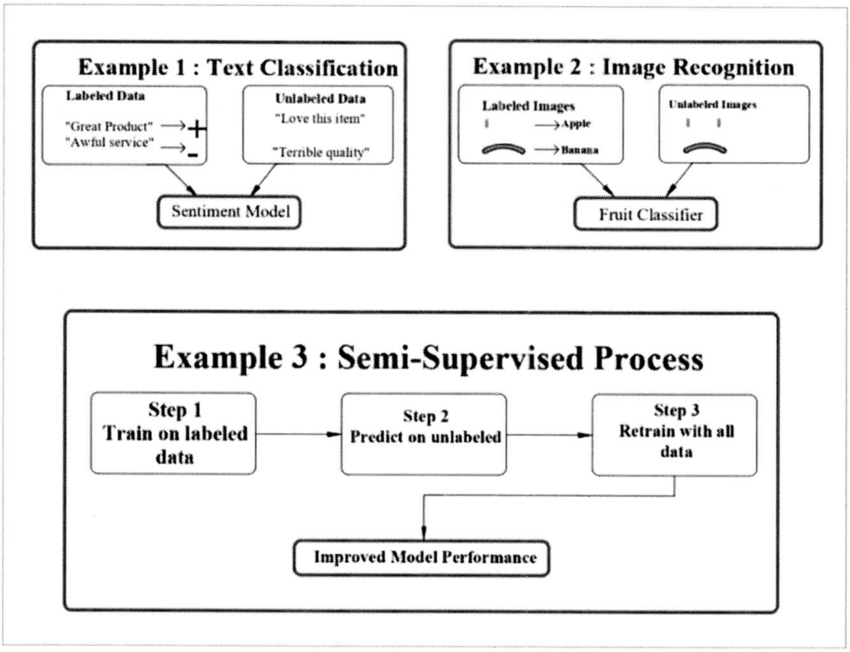

Figure 1.6 (b): Examples of Semi-Supervised Learning Workflow

1.6.5 Reinforcement Learning

Reinforcement learning (RL) is a learning paradigm in which an agent interacts with its environment in order to achieve a certain/sepecific goal. The agent learns through trial and error by receiving rewards or penalties for its actions then adjusting and ultimately optimizing its behaviour to maximize cumulative rewards.

Key Concepts

- Agent: Learner or decision-maker.
- The environment is the system with which the agent interacts.
- Reward: Agent receives feedback on their actions.
- Policy: A strategy the agent uses to determine its action

Examples

1. Game Playing: AlphaGo uses RL to master board games.

2. Robotics: Optimizing robot movements for tasks such as picking and placing goods at designated places

Table 1.8: Characteristics of Reinforcement Learning

Aspect	Reinforcement Learning
Input Data	Observations from the environment
Output	Sequence of actions
Goal	Maximize cumulative rewards
Applications	Autonomous vehicles, game AI

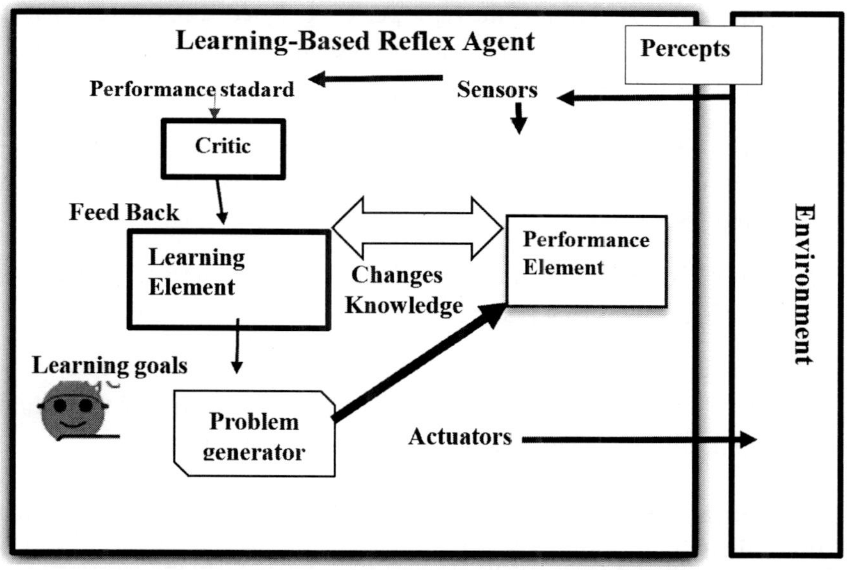

Figure 1.7: Learning-Based Reflex Agent

One of the most critical challenges in machine learning is striking the correct balance between model complexity and generalization.

- **Overfitting** occurs when a model learns the training data too well, including noise and outliers. This leads to high accuracy on the training set but poor performance on unseen data. For example, in polynomial regression, a high-degree polynomial may fit the training data perfectly but not generalize for new samples. Overfitting can also arise with approaches such as k-Nearest Neighbors (kNN) with k=1, where the model memorizes the training points.
- **Underfitting** occurs when a model is overly simplistic and fails to capture underlying patterns in data. This results in low performance across both the training and testing datasets. For example, applying a linear regression model to a nonlinear dataset results in underfitting.
- **The bias-variance trade-off** is a crucial factor in addressing these challenges. High-bias models (e.g., underfitted linear models) fail to account for/capture data complexity, whereas high-variance models (e.g., overfitted complex models) are too sensitive to

training data. Finding the right/perfect balance necessitates careful adjustment Kown as tuning of model parameters, regularization, and the selection of appropriate algorithms.

The concepts of overfitting, underfitting, and bias-variance trade-off are not restricted to regression. They also apply to clustering and kNN.

- In kNN small k values in kNN can produce overfitting, whereas large k values (e.g., near to the dataset size) cause underfitting.
- In clustering overfitting can occur when the number of clusters is too high, capturing noise instead of meaningful groupings, while underfitting occurs when there are too few clusters.

1.7.2 Data Quality, Imbalanced Data, and Computational Constraints

The success of machine learning models is primarily determined on the quality and

QUANTITY OF DATA

- Poor data quality, including missing values, erroneou/incorrect labeling, or noisy data, might negatively impact (degrades) model performance. Preprocessing steps such as imputation, outlier detection, and normalization are crucial for addressing these difficulties.

IMBALANCED DATASETS:

- Imbalanced datasets can result in biased models that benefit the majority but not the minority. For example, in fraud detection, the model may classify most transactions as non-fraudulent due to imbalance. This difficulty can be addressed with techniques like as resampling, SMOTE (Synthetic Minority Oversampling Technique), and cost-sensitive learning.

COMPUTATIONAL CONSTRAINTS:

- Training large models on high-dimensional data demands significant computational resources. This challenge is particularly pertinent for deep learning models, which might take days or weeks to train. Feature selection, dimensionality reduction, and distributed computing are all strategies that can help to ease computational constraints.

In conclusion, we may conclude that difficulties such as overfitting, underfitting, bias, variance Trade-offs, poor data quality, imbalanced datasets, and computational limits need to be addressed effectively for machine learning models to be successful. These ideas will be expanded upon in Chapter 3, specifically in the context of linear, nonlinear, and polynomial regressions, as well as their implications for approaches such as kNN and clustering.

1.7.3 Machine Learning Process: Steps in Machine Learning Pipeline

The machine learning (ML) pipeline is an structure workflow for building, training, and deploying ML models. It consists of a set of interconnected steps that convert (transform) raw data into actionable insights, ensuring that the process is efficient, repeatable, and scalable. Each step in the pipeline is crucial to developing a robust and high-performing model.

Steps in the Machine Learning Pipeline

1. **Problem Definition:**
   - Clearly define the ML project's objective and type of task (e.g., classification, regression, clustering).
   - **Example:** Predicting house prices based on square footage and location.

2. **Data Collection:**
   - Collect relevant data from sources like databases, APIs, and web scraping.
   - Ensure that the dataset being collected is a large and diverse in nature to accurately reflect/predict the problem's complexity.

3. **Data Preprocessing**
   - Clean up missing values, duplicates, and outliers.

- Standardize data by normalizing or scaling features to improve model performance.

4. **Exploratory Data Analysis (EDA).**
    - Analyse data to identify distributions, correlations, and patterns.
    - Use histograms, scatterplots, and correlation matrices to discover relevant trends.

5. **Feature Engineering:**
    - Select or create features that significantly impact model performance.
    - Use dimensionality reduction techniques, such as PCA, to reduce computing complexity.

6. **Model Selection:**
    - Select the right/ appropriate algorithm for the problem type and dataset size (e.g., decision trees for small datasets, neural networks for large datasets).
    - Example: Use logistic regression for binary classification tasks.

7. **Model Training:**
    - Train the model on the training dataset, optimizing its parameters to minimize error.
    - Use techniques like cross-validation to ensure the model generalizes well.

8. **Model Evaluation:**
    - Test the model on a separate validation or test dataset to assess its accuracy, precision, recall, and F1-score.
    - Example: Evaluate a fraud detection model using confusion matrices and ROC curves.

9. **Hyperparameter Tuning:**
    - Fine-tune model parameters like learning rate or number of layers to improve performance.

- Use grid search or random search to systematically find optimal parameters.

10. Model Deployment:

- Deploy the model to a production environment for real-world use.
- Continuously monitor performance and update the model as needed.

In Table 1.9 Steps in a Machine Learning Pipeline and Their Roles are presented. Figure 1.8 depicts a typical machine learning workflow.

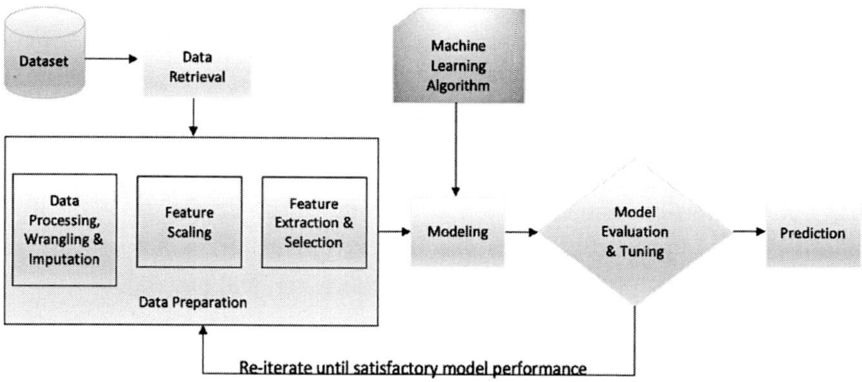

Figure 1.8 Machine Learning Workflow

Table 1.9: Steps in a Machine Learning Pipeline and Their Roles

Step	Role
Problem Definition	Clearly articulate the ML objective and scope.
Data Collection	Gather raw data from various sources.
Data Preprocessing	Clean, normalize, and prepare data for analysis.
Exploratory Data Analysis	Understand patterns and relationships in the data.
Feature Engineering	Create or select impactful features.

Model Selection	Choose the most suitable algorithm for the problem.
Model Training	Optimize the model to minimize error on the training set.
Model Evaluation	Assess model performance on unseen data.
Hyperparameter Tuning	Improve model performance through parameter optimization.
Model Deployment	Integrate the model into production systems for real-world use cases.

1.8 Applications of Machine Learning:

Machine learning (ML) has revolutionized industries by enabling data-driven decision-making and automating complex processes. Its versatility allows it to address challenges and unlock opportunities across various domains, including healthcare, finance, marketing, and beyond.

Applications in Healthcare

1. **Diagnostics and Disease Prediction**:
   - ML models like convolutional neural networks (CNNs) are used in radiology to detect anomalies in X-rays and MRIs.
   - Predictive analytics helps identify the likelihood of diseases like diabetes or cancer based on patient data.
2. **Personalized Medicine**:
   - Analysing genetic and lifestyle data enables customized treatment plans for individual patients.
3. **Drug Discovery**:
   - Accelerates drug discovery by predicting molecule-target interactions using ML algorithms.
4. **Hospital Management**:
   - Optimizing resource allocation and predicting patient admissions.

Example: IBM Watson Health uses ML to assist doctors in diagnosing diseases and suggesting treatment options.

Applications in Finance

1. **Fraud Detection:**
   - ML models assess/ evaluates transaction patterns to detect fraudulent activities in real-time.
2. **Risk Management:**
   - Predictive models evaluate credit risk and predict market trends.
3. **Algorithmic Trading:**
   - Uses real-time data analysis and pattern recognition to make stock trading decisions automatically.
4. **Customer Segmentation:**
   - Clustering algorithms help discover client groupings for specific financial goods. For example, PayPal uses machine learning to combat fraud and improve client security.

Applications in Marketing

1. **Customer Behaviour Analysis:**
   - Conduct sentiment analysis on social media and reviews to identify /understand customer preferences.
2. **Recommendation Systems:**
   - Suggests products or services based on previous purchases and browsing patterns.
3. **Targeted Advertising:**
   - Uses machine learning to optimize ad placement and content for certain demographics.
4. **Churn Prediction:**
   - Identifies customers who are likely to quit and implements retention strategies/tactics.

For example, Amazon's recommendation system suggests things through collaborative filtering.

Applications in Other Fields

1. **Transportation**:
    - Autonomous vehicles powered by reinforcement learning.
    - Traffic flow optimization and route planning.
2. **Manufacturing**:
    - Predictive maintenance of machinery using IoT and ML.
    - Quality control automation.
3. **Energy**:
    - Smart grid optimization and energy consumption prediction.
4. **Education**:
    - Personalized learning systems and automated grading.

Given in table 1.10 is the summary of applications of machine learning in various industries. It may be noted here that, the applications of ML are getting evolved from time to time and the list provided in the table 1.10 is not exhaustive.

Table 1.10: Applications of Machine Learning Across Industries

Field	Applications	Examples
Healthcare	Diagnostics, personalized medicine, drug discovery, hospital management	IBM Watson Health
Finance	Fraud detection, risk management, algorithmic trading, customer segmentation	PayPal, Goldman Sachs
Marketing	Behavior analysis, recommendation systems, targeted advertising, churn prediction	Amazon, Netflix

Transportation	Autonomous vehicles, traffic optimization	Tesla, Google Waymo
Manufacturing	Predictive maintenance, quality control automation	Siemens
Education	Personalized learning, automated grading	Duolingo

1.9 Big Data Analysis Framework

Big data analysis refers to the process of examining large, complex datasets to uncover hidden patterns, correlations, and actionable insights. ML plays a pivotal role in making big data analysis scalable and efficient.

1.9.1 Overview of Big Data

1. **Characteristics of Big Data**:
    - **Volume**: The scale of data is massive, often measured in terabytes or petabytes.
    - **Velocity**: Data is generated and processed in real-time.
    - **Variety**: Data comes in multiple forms—structured (databases), unstructured (videos, text), and semi-structured (JSON, XML).
    - **Veracity**: Ensuring the reliability and accuracy of data is critical.
    - **Value**: Extracting meaningful insights from data is the ultimate goal.
2. **Big Data Architecture**:
    - **Data Sources**: Sensors, IoT devices, transactional data, social media.
    - **Data Storage**: Distributed systems like Hadoop HDFS, Amazon S3.
    - **Data Processing**:
        - **Batch Processing:** Tools like Apache Hadoop.

  - **Real-Time Processing**: Frameworks like Apache Spark, Kafka.
- **Analysis and Visualization**: Tools like Tableau, Power BI, or custom ML models.

1.9.2 Role of Machine Learning in Big Data Analysis

1. **Data Cleaning and Preprocessing**:
   - Automating the detection and correction of errors.
2. **Predictive Analytics**:
   - ML models predict trends and outcomes using big data.
3. **Real-Time Analytics**:
   - Reinforcement learning and streaming algorithms process live data for immediate decision-making.

Table 1.11: Comparison of Batch and Real-Time Processing in Big Data Analysis

Aspect	Batch Processing	Real-Time Processing
Data Handling	Processes data in chunks	Processes data as it arrives
Latency	High latency	Low latency
Tools	Hadoop MapReduce	Apache Spark Streaming, Apache Kafka
Use Cases	Historical analysis, large-scale ETL jobs	Fraud detection, live recommendations

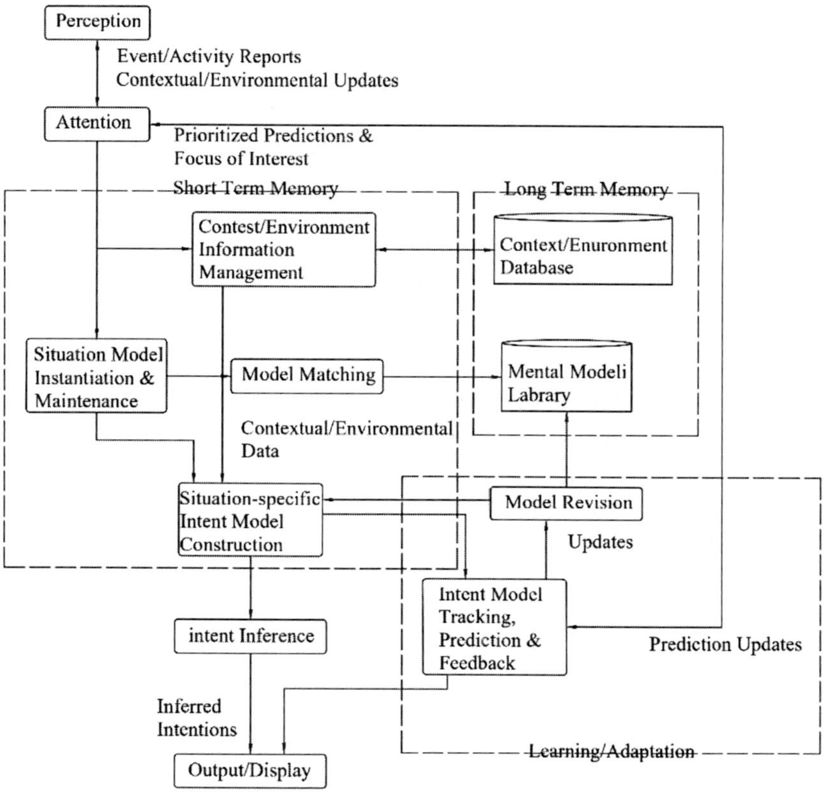

Figure 1.9: Big Data Architecture with Machine Learning Integration

Types of Big Data Architecture

Big data architecture defines the framework and components required to ingest, store, process, and analyze massive datasets efficiently. Depending on the use case, data flow, and processing requirements, big data architecture can be categorized into **batch processing**, **real-time processing**, and **hybrid architectures**.

1. Batch Processing Architecture

Batch processing architecture processes large volumes of data in chunks, typically at scheduled intervals. It is well-suited for scenarios where immediate results are not required.

Key Features:

- Processes data collected over a period.
- High throughput but higher latency.
- Suitable for historical analysis and reporting.

Example:

- Analyzing yearly sales data to identify trends.

Tools Used: Apache Hadoop, Hive, and Amazon EMR.

2. Real-Time Processing Architecture

Real-time (or stream) processing architecture processes data as it arrives, ensuring low latency. It is ideal for time-sensitive applications like fraud detection or stock market analysis.

Key Features:

- Processes data in real-time or near real-time.
- Low latency but may require more resources.
- Suitable for applications requiring immediate action.

Example:

- Detecting fraudulent credit card transactions as they occur.

Tools Used: Apache Spark Streaming, Apache Flink, and Apache Kafka.

3. Hybrid Architecture

Hybrid architecture combines batch and real-time processing to provide flexibility for handling both historical and real-time data.

Key Features:

- Processes historical data in batches and incoming data in real-time streams.
- Balances throughput and latency requirements.
- Suitable for complex systems like recommendation engines or IoT analytics.

Example:

- A recommendation engine that uses batch processing for historical user data and real-time updates for current activity.

Tools Used: Apache Lambda Architecture, Google Cloud Dataflow.

Table 1.12 Comparison of Big Data Architectures

Aspect	Batch Processing	Real-Time Processing	Hybrid Architecture
Data Handling	Processes large data chunks	Processes data as it arrives	Combines batch and stream processing
Latency	High latency	Low latency	Medium latency
Use Cases	Historical analysis, periodic reports	Fraud detection, stock market analysis	Recommendation engines, IoT applications
Tools	Hadoop, Hive, Amazon EMR	Spark Streaming, Kafka, Flink	Lambda Architecture, Google Cloud Dataflow

Benefits of Choosing the Right Architecture

1. **Efficiency**: Matches data processing needs with the system's capabilities.
2. **Scalability**: Ensures the architecture can handle data growth.
3. **Cost-Effectiveness**: Avoids unnecessary resource usage by tailoring architecture to the workload.

Short Answer Questions (2-3 marks each)

1. Define machine learning and explain what the term "machine" signifies in this context.

2. List any five applications of machine learning in today's digital world.

3. What are the limitations of traditional programming approaches in handling modern data challenges?

4. Explain the four levels of the Knowledge Pyramid (DIKW) with one example each.

5. Differentiate between artificial intelligence and machine learning in terms of scope and techniques.

6. What is the difference between supervised and unsupervised learning? Provide one example of each.

7. Define overfitting and underfitting in machine learning models.

8. List the three main characteristics that distinguish big data from traditional data.

9. What is the role of feature engineering in the machine learning pipeline?

10. Explain semi-supervised learning with an example.

Medium Answer Questions (5-7 marks each)

11. Discuss the evolution of data-driven decision-making and its impact on modern businesses.

12. Explain the historical development of machine learning from the 1950s to the present day.

13. Compare and contrast machine learning with statistics in terms of goals, techniques, and focus areas.

14. Describe the iterative process involved in supervised machine learning with a flowchart.

15. Explain the bias-variance trade-off and its significance in model performance.

16. Discuss the challenges associated with imbalanced datasets and computational constraints in machine learning.

17. Describe the complete machine learning pipeline with all ten steps and their importance.

18. Compare batch processing, real-time processing, and hybrid architectures in big data analysis.

19. Explain reinforcement learning with its key concepts and provide two real-world applications.

20. Discuss the role of machine learning in big data analysis framework.

Long Answer Questions (10-12 marks each)

21. Elaborate on the need for machine learning in today's digital age. Discuss how the data explosion has necessitated automated techniques and explain how machine learning addresses these challenges.

22. Provide a comprehensive comparison between supervised learning, unsupervised learning, and reinforcement learning. Include their characteristics, applications, advantages, and challenges.

23. Discuss the relationship between machine learning and other fields (AI, Data Science, Statistics). Explain how these fields complement each other with examples and synergies.

24. Explain the various types of machine learning with detailed examples. Include supervised, unsupervised, semi-supervised, self-supervised, and reinforcement learning paradigms.

25. Describe the applications of machine learning across different industries (Healthcare, Finance, Marketing, Transportation, Manufacturing, Education). Provide specific examples and explain their impact.

Application-Based Questions (8-10 marks each)

26. Design a machine learning solution for email spam detection. Explain which type of learning you would use, the data requirements, algorithm selection, and evaluation metrics.

27. A retail company wants to segment its customers for targeted marketing. Explain the machine learning approach you would recommend, including data collection, preprocessing, and algorithm selection.

28. Discuss how you would implement a house price prediction system. Cover the complete ML pipeline from problem definition to model deployment.

29. Explain how machine learning can be applied to fraud detection in banking. Include the challenges of imbalanced data and how to address them.

30. Design a recommendation system for an e-commerce platform. Explain the type of learning, data requirements, and evaluation approach.

Chapter - 2

Data Analysis and Feature Engineering

- Bivariate and Multivariate Data
- Multivariate Statistics
- Essential Mathematics for Multivariate Data
- Feature Engineering
- Dimensionality Reduction
- Learning System Design
- Modeling and Learning Theory

Chapter Overview

This chapter delves deeply into data analysis and feature engineering techniques, which serve as the foundation for machine learning systems. We begin by looking at various types of data and how they play an important role in machine learning process. The chapter then moves on to descriptive statistics and visualization techniques that can help learners'/practitioners acquire initial insights from data distributions. As we advance, we explore the relationships between variables using bivariate and multivariate analysis, correlation, covariance, and sophisticated visualization techniques. Feature engineering—the process of transforming raw data into more effective representations—is extensively explored, including selection, extraction, and methods for dealing with data imperfections. The chapter also discusses dimensionality reduction approaches for managing high-dimensional data while keeping important information. Finally, we provide the theoretical underpinning of machine learning using basic learning theory ideas. This chapter provides students the analytical skills needed to prepare and understand data before applying sophisticated machine learning algorithms.

2.1 Introduction to Data

2.1.1 Role of Data in Machine Learning

Data provides the core of all machine learning systems, providing the raw material for models to find patterns, correlations, and insights. The quality, quantity and characteristics of the data have a direct impact on the models' performance and capabilities.

Key Aspects of Data in Machine Learning:

- **Training Resource**: Data serves as a training resource, providing instances for algorithms to understand patterns and relationships.
- **Knowledge Repository**: Historical data is a repository (a capsule) for domain knowledge and real-world behaviors.
- **Model Validation**: Validate the model's effectiveness using separate data subsets.
- **Decision Foundation**: data-driven insights serve as the foundation for predictive and prescriptive analytics.

Relationship between Data and the Model:

The relationship between data and models follows a symbiotic pattern:

1. **Data Collection:** Data collection involves collecting useful information from many sources, including web scraping, APIs, public databases, surveys, sensors, IoT devices, social media monitoring, and manual data entry.
2. **Data Processing**: involves transforming raw data into usable formats for analysis. This includes (1) data cleaning to remove duplicates and errors, (2) data integration to combine data from multiple sources, and (3) data transformation to normalize, aggregate, or encode data into the desired format. (4) Data Reduction, achieved by selecting relevant features or using dimensionality reduction techniques like Principal Component

Analysis (PCA); (5) Data Standardization, which scales data to a common format without altering its inherent differences; (6) Data Enrichment, where additional information is added to the dataset for context and insight; and (7) Data Validation, which ensures the dataset adheres to specified rules and constraints, such as correct formats and valid entries.

3. **Model Training**: sing processed data to optimize model parameters.
4. **Insight Generation**: Extracting meaningful patterns and relationships.
5. **Operational Deployment**: Applying learnt patterns to new and unseen data.

As the quality and quantity of data improve, so does the potential of the machine learning models based on it. However, this relationship is not simply linear; there are diminishing returns and potential hazards, such as overfitting/underfitting, that must be carefully avoided.

2.1.2 Types of Data: Structured, Unstructured, and Semi-Structured

Machine learning systems can operate on various types of data, each requiring different handling and processing techniques.

Structured Data:

Structured data follows a rigid format with a predefined schema, typically organized in tabular form.

Characteristics:

- Fixed fields with specific data types
- Clearly defined relationships between elements
- Often stored in relational databases
- Easy to search, analyze, and manipulate

Examples:

- Database tables
- Spreadsheets
- CSV files
- Time series data

Unstructured Data:

Unstructured data lacks a predefined format or organization, making it more challenging to process through traditional methods.

Characteristics:

- No predefined data model
- Irregular or unpredictable organization
- Contains variety in content and format
- Requires specialized processing techniques

Examples:

- Text documents and articles
- Images and photographs
- Audio and video files
- Social media content

Semi-Structured Data:

Semi-structured data combines elements of both structured and unstructured data, containing some organizational features but not conforming to a rigid structure.

Characteristics:

- Contains tags or markers to separate elements
- Follows a loose schema that may evolve
- Hierarchical or graph-based organization
- More flexible than structured but more organized than unstructured

Examples:

- XML and JSON files
- Email messages
- HTML documents
- Graph databases

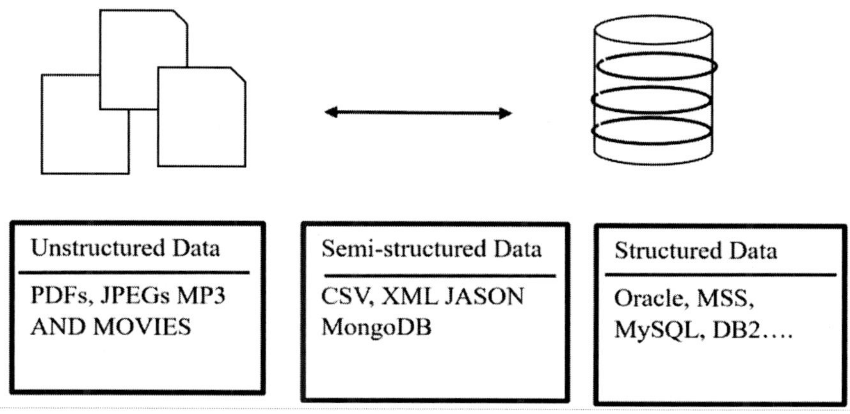

Figure 2.1 Comparison of Data Types

Table 2.1: Comparison of Data Types

Characteristic	Structured Data	Semi-Structured Data	Unstructured Data
Format	Fixed schema	Flexible schema	No schema
Organization	Tabular	Hierarchical/Networked	Variable
Query Ease	High	Medium	Low
Storage	RDBMS	NoSQL, XML databases	Data lakes, file systems
Processing Complexity	Low	Medium	High

ML Preprocessing Needs	Minimal	Moderate	Extensive
Scalability Challenges	Lower	Medium	Higher

2.2 Descriptive Statistics and Visualization

2.2.1 Measures of Central Tendency and Dispersion

Descriptive statistics provide numerical summaries of data distributions, helping data scientists understand the core characteristics of their datasets before applying more advanced techniques.

Measures of Central Tendency:

Central tendency measures identify the "typical" or "central" values in a dataset.

1. **Mean (μ):** The arithmetic average of all values.

$$\mu = \frac{\sum (x)}{n} \quad \ldots\ldots\ldots 2.1$$

    - Sensitive to outliers
    - Appropriate for normally distributed data

2. **Median:** The middle value when data is arranged in order.
    - Robust to outliers
    - Better representation for skewed distributions
    - For even-sized samples, average of two middle values

3. **Mode:** The most frequently occurring value(s).
    - May be multiple modes (multimodal)
    - Useful for categorical and discrete data
    - Not always meaningful for continuous data

4. **Weighted Mean:** Mean where certain values contribute more than others.

   - Formula

$$\mu(wx) = \frac{w_1x_1 + w_2x_2 + w_3x_3 .. + w_nx_n}{w_1 + w_2 + w_3 .. + w_n} = \frac{\sum(w_nx_n)}{\sum w_n} \text{.........}2.2$$

   - Used when observations have different importance

Measures of Dispersion:

Dispersion measures quantify the spread or variability within a dataset.

1. **Range**: Difference between maximum and minimum values.
   - Simple but sensitive to outliers
   - Formula:

$$Range = Max(x) - min(x) \text{.......}2.3$$

2. **Variance (σ^2)**: Average of squared deviations from the mean.
   - Formula: $$\sigma^2 = \frac{\sum(x-\mu)^2}{n} \text{.........}2.3$$
   - Units are squared (makes interpretation challenging)

3. **Standard Deviation (σ)**: Square root of variance.
   - Formula: $$\sigma = \sqrt{\frac{\sum(x-\mu)^2}{n}} \text{.........}2.4$$
   - Same units as original data
   - In normal distributions, ~68% of data falls within ±1σ, ~95% within ±2σ

4. **Interquartile Range (IQR)**: Difference between 3rd quartile (Q_3) and 1st quartile (Q_1).
   - Formula:

$$Interquartile\ Range\ (IQR) = Q_3 - Q_1 \ldots\ldots\ 2.5$$

- Robust to outliers
- Basis for boxplots and outlier detection

5. **Mean Absolute Deviation (MAD)**: Average of absolute deviations from mean.

- Formula: $MAD = \frac{\sum |(x-\mu)|}{n} \ldots\ldots 2.6$
- More robust than variance but less mathematically tractable

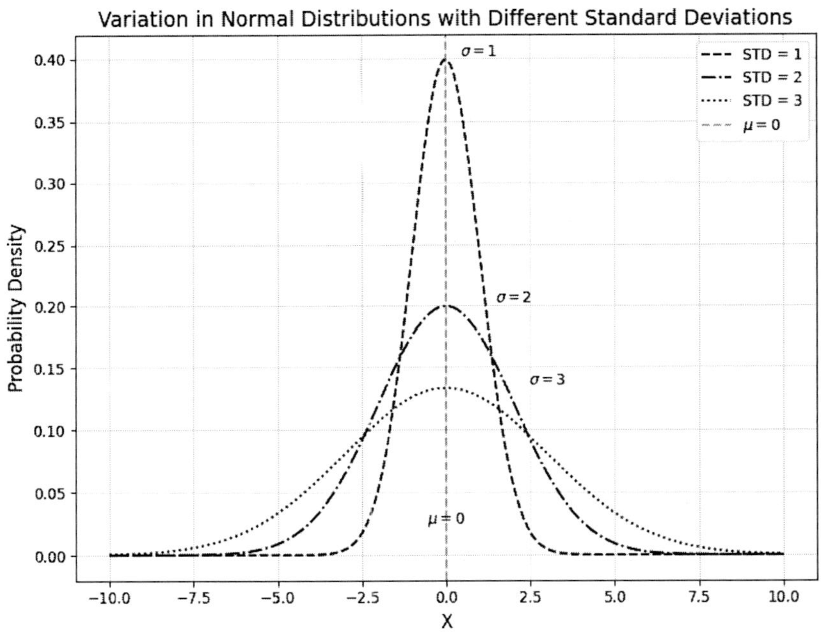

Figure 2.2: Variation in Normal Distributions with Different Standard Deviations

Table 2.2: Relationship Between Standard Deviation and Data Distribution

Distribution Type	Standard Deviation	Interpretation
Small σ	Narrow, peaked	Data points clustered tightly around mean
Large σ	Wide, flat	Data points spread widely from mean
Uniform	$\sigma \approx 0.29 \times$ range	Even probability across values
Normal	68-95-99.7 rule applies	68% within $\pm 1\sigma$, 95% within $\pm 2\sigma$, 99.7% within $\pm 3\sigma$
Right-skewed	Mean > Median	Tail extends toward higher values
Left-skewed	Mean < Median	Tail extends toward lower values

2.2.2 Univariate Data Analysis and Visualization

Univariate analysis focuses at individual variables in isolation, concentrating on their distribution characteristics and trends. It is an important first step in analyzing a dataset because it reveals essential qualities such as central tendency, variability, and the overall shape the data (example balanced/imbalanced). The mean, median, mode, range, variance, and standard deviation are all important statistics to consider when summarizing the variable. This approach also aids in the detection of probable anomalies, outliers, or skewness, which may influence later analysis.

Univariate analysis ensures that any preprocessing, such as addressing missing values or altering data, stems on a full understanding of the data's behaviour. This step establishes the groundwork for more complicated investigations, offering crucial insights before adding correlations between variables or developing predictive models. Visualization methods have been briefly mentioned in the following write-up. Detailed discussions on these are beyond the scope of this book, and readers are advised to consult relevant references.

Numerical Data Visualization:

1. **Histograms**: Bar charts showing frequency distribution across intervals.
    - Reveals shape, central tendency, and spread
    - Bin width selection affects interpretation
    - Useful for identifying modality and skewness
2. **Box Plots (Box-and-Whisker)**: Displays five-number summary.
    - Shows minimum, Q_1, median, Q_3, maximum
    - Identifies outliers beyond whiskers (typically 1.5×IQR)
    - Facilitates comparison between multiple distributions
3. **Violin Plots**: Combination of box plot and kernel density estimation.
    - Shows probability density at different values
    - Width indicates frequency at that level
    - More informative than box plots for complex distributions
4. **Q-Q Plots**: Plots quantiles of data against theoretical distribution.
    - Assesses normality (straight line indicates normal distribution)
    - Identifies deviations from theoretical distributions
    - Useful for distribution assumption verification

Categorical Data Visualization:

1. **Bar Charts**: Displays frequency or proportion for each category.
    - Height proportional to frequency
    - Categories on x-axis, frequency on y-axis

- Can be ordered by frequency for better interpretation

2. **Pie Charts**: Shows proportion of each category as slice of circle.
   - Best for few categories (≤5-7)
   - Total always represents 100%
   - Less precise than bar charts for value comparison
3. **Pareto Charts**: Combines bar chart and line graph.
   - Bars show individual frequencies (descending order)
   - Line shows cumulative percentage
   - Highlights the "vital few" versus "trivial many"

Statistical Tests for Univariate Analysis:

1. **Normality Tests:**

Shapiro-Wilk test: The Shapiro-Wilk test evaluates the null hypothesis that a sample comes from a normally distributed population. It calculates a W statistic that compares the ordered sample values against the expected values from a normal distribution. The test is particularly powerful for small to medium sample sizes ($n < 50$) and rejects normality when the p-value is below a chosen significance level (typically 0.05). Lower W values indicate greater deviation from normality.

Anderson-Darling test: The Anderson-Darling test measures the discrepancy between the empirical cumulative distribution function (ECDF) of the sample data and the cumulative distribution function (CDF) of a normal distribution. It places greater emphasis on the tails of the distribution than other tests, making it particularly sensitive to deviations in these regions. The test calculates an A^2 statistic, with larger values indicating greater departure from normality. It performs well across various sample sizes and is often preferred for detecting non-normality in critical applications.

Kolmogorov-Smirnov test: The Kolmogorov-Smirnov test compares the empirical cumulative distribution function of the sample data with that of a reference normal distribution. The test statistic D represents the maximum vertical distance between these two functions. While it's applicable across various sample sizes, it's generally less powerful than the Shapiro-Wilk or Anderson-Darling tests for detecting departures from normality. The test is distribution-free and can be adapted to test goodness-of-fit for distributions other than normal.

2. Outlier Detection:

Z-score method: The Z-score method standardizes data points by calculating how many standard deviations they are from the mean. Points with absolute Z-scores exceeding 3 are commonly flagged as potential outliers, corresponding to data points beyond the 99.7% probability range in a normal distribution. The method assumes normally distributed data and can be misleading when this assumption is violated. It's straightforward to calculate and interpret but becomes less reliable in the presence of multiple outliers due to their influence on the mean and standard deviation.

Modified Z-score: The modified Z-score improves robustness by using the median absolute deviation (MAD) instead of the standard deviation, and the median instead of the mean. The formula 0.6745(x-median)/MAD produces values comparable to Z-scores but is less influenced by extreme values. Values exceeding 3.5 are typically flagged as potential outliers. This method performs better than traditional Z-scores when dealing with skewed distributions or when multiple outliers are present, as it resists the masking effect where multiple outliers can hide each other.

Tukey's method: Tukey's method (or the boxplot method) defines outliers as points falling beyond 1.5 times the interquartile range (IQR) from the first or third quartiles. Points beyond Q1-1.5×IQR or Q3+1.5×IQR are considered mild outliers, while those beyond 3×IQR are labeled extreme outliers. This non-parametric approach makes no assumptions about the underlying distribution, making it versatile across various data types. The method is visually intuitive when represented in boxplots and balances sensitivity to genuine outliers while limiting false positives.

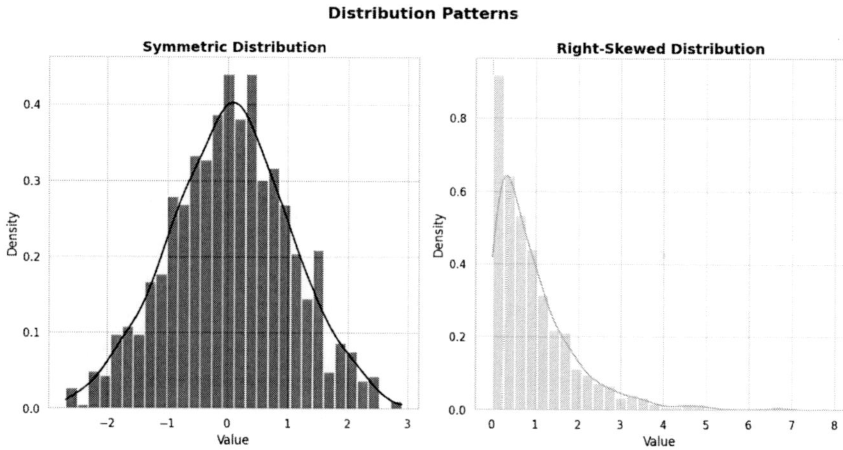

(a)

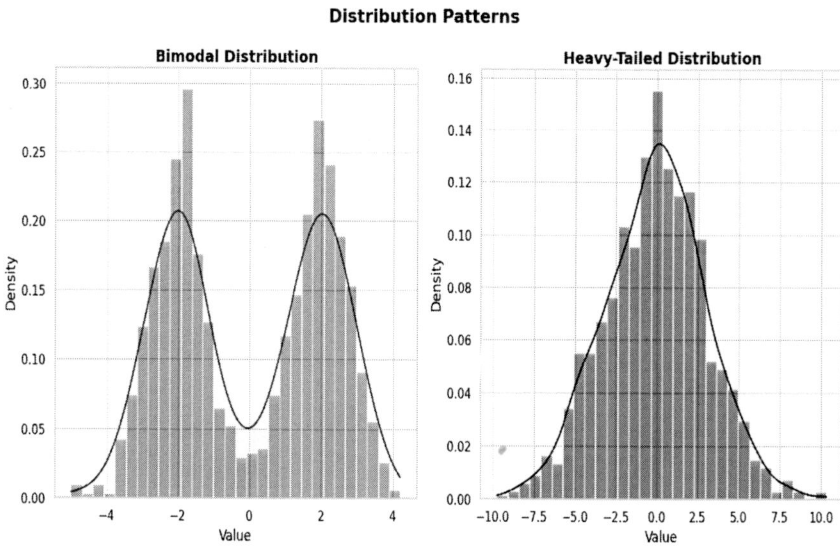

(b)

Figure 2.3. Univariate Distribution Patterns –
(a) Symmetric and Right-Skewed, (b) Bimodal and Heavy-Tailed.

Table 2.3: Interpreting Shape Characteristics in Univariate Distributions

Characteristic	Visual Pattern	Statistical Indicators	ML Implications
Symmetry	Bell-shaped	Mean ≈ Median ≈ Mode	Many algorithms assume this
Right Skew	Long right tail	Mean > Median > Mode	May need transformation
Left Skew	Long left tail	Mean < Median < Mode	May need transformation
Unimodal	Single peak	Single highest frequency	Simpler to model
Bimodal	Two peaks	Two local maxima	May indicate subpopulations
Uniform	Flat, even	Similar frequencies	May indicate lack of signal
Heavy-tailed	Extreme values	Kurtosis > 3	Sensitive to outliers
Light-tailed	Few extreme values	Kurtosis < 3	May miss important patterns

2.3 Bivariate and Multivariate Data Analysis

Bivariate data analysis explores the relationship between two variables, providing crucial insights into their association patterns. This fundamental approach serves as a bridge between basic descriptive statistics and more complex multivariate techniques.

Measures of Association for Bivariate Data

In statistics, bivariate data analysis involves studying the relationship between two variables. Understanding the association between these variables is critical for identifying patterns, making predictions, and deriving meaningful insights. Measures of association quantify the strength and direction of the relationship between two variables and help determine whether changes in one variable are linked to changes in the other.

The choice of a measure depends on the type of data being analysed—categorical, ordinal, or numerical. For example, numerical variables often utilize measures such as correlation coefficients, while categorical variables use measures like contingency tables or chi-square tests. These measures can reveal whether the relationship is positive, negative, or non-existent and provide insight into the linearity or complexity of the association.

Among the most commonly used measures of association for numerical data is Pearson's Correlation Coefficient (r). This measure evaluates the linear relationship between two continuous variables, providing a value between -1 and +1, where -1 indicates a perfect negative correlation, +1 indicates a perfect positive correlation, and 0 implies no linear correlation.

2.3.1 Correlation and Covariance

Correlation quantifies the strength and direction of the linear relationship between two continuous variables. The Pearson correlation coefficient (r) is the most commonly used measure, ranging from -1 (perfect negative correlation) to +1 (perfect positive correlation), with 0 indicating no linear relationship.

Bivariate analysis examines relationships between pairs of variables, quantifying how they vary together and identifying potential dependencies.

Covariance:

Covariance measures the degree to which two variables change together. The formula differs for a population and a sample, as reflected in the denominator. Covariance measures how two variables change together, indicating direction but not strength of relationship.

Population Covariance (Denominator n):

When the entire population is analyzed, the denominator is **n**, the total number of observations. This ensures that the covariance represents the true relationship between the variables without any adjustments since all data points are included.

Sample Covariance (Denominator n−1):

In a sample, the calculation adjusts for the fact that samples tend to underestimate variability compared to the population. The denominator n−1n-1n−1, rooted in the concept of sample variance, corrects this bias, providing a more accurate estimate of population covariance.

- **Formula for population covariance**:

$$COV(X,Y) = \frac{\sum_{1}^{n} X_i - \overline{X}}{n} \quad \ldots\ldots 2.7$$

- **Formulae for sample covariance;**

$$COV(X,Y) = \frac{\sum_{1}^{n} X_i - \overline{X}}{n-1} \quad \ldots\ldots 2.8$$

- **Interpretation**:
  - Positive covariance: Variables tend to increase together
  - Negative covariance: One increases as other decreases
  - Zero covariance: No linear relationship
- **Limitations**:
  - Scale-dependent (affected by units of measurement)
  - Does not standardize relationship strength
  - Difficult to compare across variable pairs

Correlation Coefficients:

Correlation standardizes relationship strength on a scale from -1 to +1.

1. Pearson's Correlation Coefficient (r)

The value of Pearson's correlation coefficient ranges from **-1** to **+1**:

- **-1**: Indicates a perfect negative linear relationship.
- **+1**: Indicates a perfect positive linear relationship.
- **0**: Indicates no linear correlation between the variables.

Pearson's Correlation Coefficient is computed using the formula as given below:

$$R = \frac{\left(\sum_{1}^{n}(x_i-\bar{x})(y_i-\bar{y})\right)}{\sqrt{\sum_{1}^{n}(x_i-\bar{x})^2 \cdot \sum_{1}^{n}(y_i-\bar{y})^2}} \quad \ldots\ldots\ldots\ldots 2.9$$

where

- R: Pearson correlation coefficient.

- x_i,yi: Individual data points of variables X and Y.
- $\overline{x}$ and $\overline{y}$ are the means of the variables.

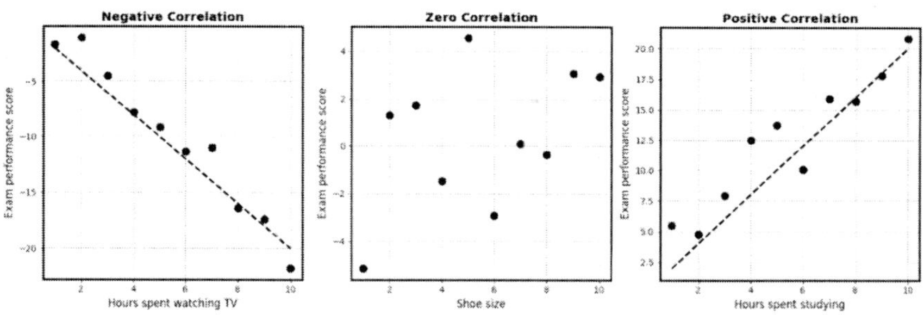

Figure 2.4 Examples of Negative, Zero, and Positive Correlations14

2. Spearman's Rank Correlation (ρ):

For non-normally distributed data or ordinal variables, Spearman's rank correlation $\mathbf{r_s}$ is more appropriate, as it measures monotonic relationships rather than strictly linear ones.

Spearman's Rank Correlation Coefficient (r_s) measures the strength and direction of the monotonic relationship between two variables using their ranks. It is particularly useful for non-linear or ordinal data. The formula for $\mathbf{r_s}$ is calculated using the formula given below:

$$r_s = 1 - \frac{6\sum d_i^2}{n\left(n^2 - 1\right)} \quad \ldots\ldots\ldots\ldots\ldots\ldots\ldots 2.10$$

Where:

- $\mathbf{r_s}$ is Spearman's Rank Correlation Coefficient.
- d_i is the difference between the ranks of corresponding values of the two variables.
- n is the number of paired observations.
- Non-parametric measure that assesses monotonic relationships.
- Less sensitive to outliers than Pearson's coeffiecient.
- Better for detecting non-linear monotonic relationships.

This formula is simple to implement and widely used for ordinal and non-linear data.

3. **Kendall's Tau (τ)**: Measures the strength and direction of the association between two variables based on the relative ordering of data. It ranges from −1 (perfect negative association) to 1(perfect positive association). Kendall's Tau (τ)is calculated using the formula given below:

$$\tau = \frac{C - D}{\frac{1}{2}n(n-1)} \quad \ldots\ldots\ldots\ldots\ldots\ldots\ldots 2.11$$

Explanation:

- C: Number of concordant pairs (where the rank order of two variables matches).
  - D: Number of discordant pairs (where the rank order of two variables does not match).
- n: Total number of data points.

Interpreting Correlation Values:

- **|r| < 0.3**: Weak correlation
- **0.3 ≤ |r| < 0.7**: Moderate correlation
- **|r| ≥ 0.7**: Strong correlation

Important Considerations:

1. **Correlation ≠ Causation**: Strong correlation does not imply causal relationship
2. **Non-linear Relationships**: Traditional correlation may miss non-linear patterns
3. **Outlier Sensitivity**: Pearson's r particularly affected by outliers
4. **Simpson's Paradox**: Correlation can reverse when data is aggregated/disaggregated

In figure 2.5 and table 2.4 the visualization of correlation coefficients and elaboration aspects are presented.

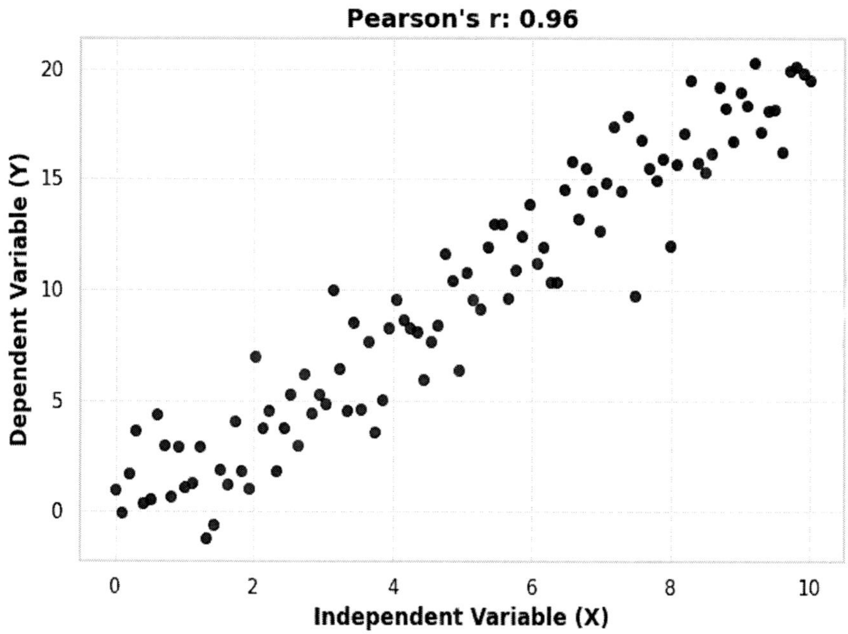

(a) Pearson's Coefficient

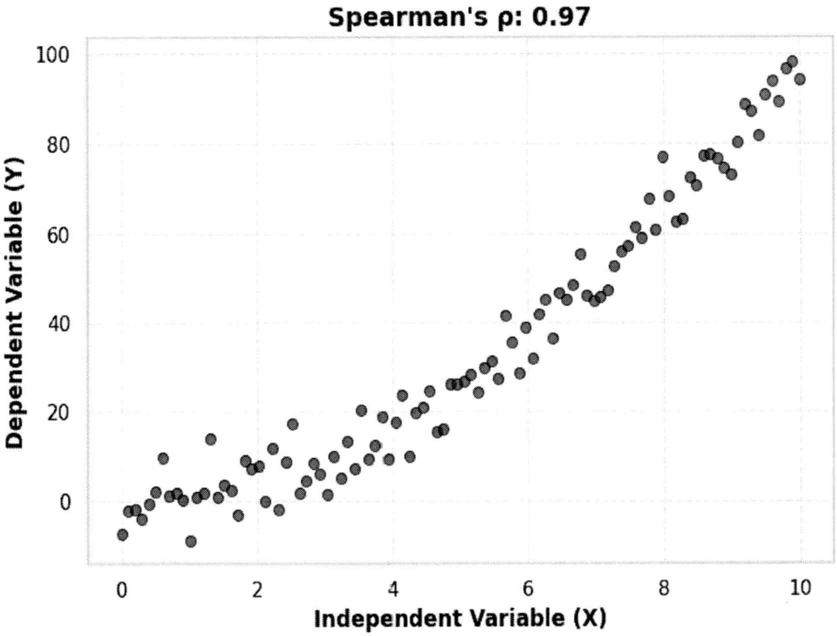

(b) Sperman's Coefficient

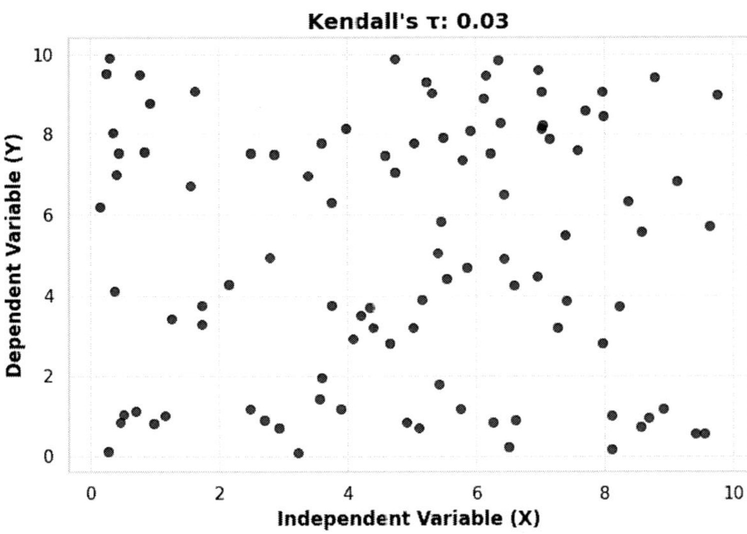

(c) Kenda's Coefficient (τ)

Figure 2.5: Comparison of Correlation Coefficients

Table 2.4: Comparison of Correlation Coefficients

Aspect	Pearson's r	Spearman's ρ	Kendall's τ
Measures	Linear relationship	Monotonic relationship	Concordance of pairs
Data Type	Continuous	Ordinal/Continuous	Ordinal/Continuous
Outlier Sensitivity	High	Moderate	Low
Computational Complexity	O(n)	O (n log n)	$O(n^2)$
Normal Distribution Assumption	Yes	No	No
Ability to Detect Non-linear	Poor	Good	Good
Range	-1 to +1	-1 to +1	-1 to +1

2.3.2 Multivariate Statistics and Visualization Techniques

Multivariate analysis expands the scope of statistical analysis by examining correlations between three or more variables simultaneously. Unlike univariate or bivariate approaches, which only evaluate single variables or pairs of variables, multivariate analysis shows the complicated interdependencies and interactions that are typical of real-world data. This makes it an effective tool for understanding the underlying structure of data and identifying patterns that may not be apparent with simpler methods.

The purpose of multivariate analysis is to discover rather uncover relationships between multiple variables and their combined/collective influence on a certain outcome or event. For example, in a marketing scenario, an organization or business house may examine customer satisfaction in relation to product quality, pricing, and after-sales service. Such investigations frequently use statistical models such as regression analysis, factor analysis, or clustering approaches to extract useful insights from data.

Visualization tools for multivariate data are equally important since they assist comprehend/interpret the results in a more accessible and intuitive manner. Scatterplot matrices, parallel coordinate plots, and heatmaps are common tools for visualizing multivariate relationships. These methods allow analysts to find correlations, clusters, and outliers, which aids in making better choices. Researchers and practitioners get a better grip of multivariate analysis by leveraging statistical rigor with visualization,

Multivariate Statistics: Partial Correlation

1. Definition:

Partial correlation quantifies the relationship between two variables while controlling for the influence of one or more additional variables. This helps isolate the true association between the variables and identify potential spurious correlations caused by the confounding effects of the controlled variables.

2. Importance:

By removing the effects of other variables, partial correlation provides a more accurate assessment of the direct relationship between two variables. It is widely used in fields like economics, social sciences, and biology to control for external influences.

3. Formula:

The formula for calculating the partial correlation between X and Y, controlling for Z, is:

$$r_{XY.Z} = \frac{r_{XY} - r_{XZ} r_{YZ}}{\sqrt{\left(1 - r_{XZ}^2\right)\left(1 - r_{YZ}^2\right)}} \quad \ldots\ldots\ldots\ldots\ldots\ldots 2.12$$

4. Multivariate Statistics: Multiple Correlation:

Definition and Importance:

Multiple correlation quantifies the strength of the association between one dependent variable and two or more independent variables taken together (considered jointly). It extends the concept of simple correlation to situations involving many/multiple explanatory variables, allowing for the evaluation of their combined effect on the dependent variable. This measure is commonly utilized in industries such as finance, social sciences, and engineering, where variables frequently interact in complex ways.

The multiple correlation coefficient (*R*R) indicates how much of the variance in the dependent variable can be explained by the independent variables. A higher *R* value suggests that the independent factors explain more of the variation in the dependent variable. Multiple correlation serves as the foundation for multiple regression models, which seek to predict outcomes or interpret relationships in multidimensional datasets.

The multiple correlation coefficient (*R*) indicates how proportion of variance in the dependent variable explained by the combined set of independent variables. A higher R value indicates that the independent variables collectively provide a stronger explanation for the dependent variable's variation.

Multiple correlation forms the foundation of multiple regression models, which aim to predict outcomes or understand relationships in multidimensional datasets.

Mathematical Representation

The multiple correlation coefficient R is calculated as follows:

$$R = \sqrt{1 - \frac{SSE}{SST}} \quad \ldots\ldots\ldots\ldots\ldots 2.13$$

Where:

- SSE (Sum of Squares for Error): Represents the unexplained variance in the dependent variable.

- SST (Total Sum of Squares): Represents the total variance in the dependent variable.

Alternatively, Rcan be expressed in terms of the simple correlation coefficients when

Alternatively, RRR can be expressed in terms of the simple correlation coefficients when there are two independent variables X_1 and X_2 and a dependent variable Y:

$$R^2 = r^2_{YX1} + r^2_{YX2} - 2r_{YX1} r_{YX2} r_{X1X2} \text{........} 2.14$$

Here:

- r_{YX1}, r_{YX2} : correlations fo Y with X1 and X2
- r_{X1X2} : correlations begween X1 and X2

5. Distance Measures: Introduction and Importance.

Distance measures are crucial in multivariate analysis, notably clustering, (grouping), classification, and similarity analyses. They provide a mechanism to quantify the "closeness" or "similarity" between data points in a multidimensional space. Calculation of these distances allow us to find trends, combine comparable observations, and make predictions. Selecting the appropriate distance metric is critical since it has a direct impact on the analysis's outcome and model accuracy.

Different distance metrics are suitable for different types of data and analytical goals. For example, Euclidean distance is commonly utilized for continuous data in geographical analysis, whereas Manhattan distance is frequently preferred for grid-like data structures. In contrast, Mahalanobis distance takes into account correlations between variables, making it more appropriate for multivariate data with various scales.

Key Distance Measures

Euclidean Distance:

The Euclidean distance is the straight-line distance between two points in a multidimensional space. It is defined as:

$$d_E = \sqrt{\sum_{i=1}^{n} (x_i - y_i)^2} \text{ ....} \qquad 2.15$$

This measure is intuitive and commonly used but may be sensitive to scale differences in the data. It works well in contexts where dimensions are equally important and uncorrelated.

Manhattan Distance:

Also known as the "taxicab" or "city block" distance, the Manhattan distance sums the absolute differences along each dimension:

$$d_M = \sum_{i=1}^{n} \left| x_i - y_i \right| \ldots\ldots\ldots\ldots\ldots 2.16$$

This measure is robust to outliers and is often used for data with a grid-like structure, such as time-series or text data.

Mahalanobis Distance:

The Mahalanobis distance accounts for the correlations between variables and the variability in the data. It is calculated as:

$$d_{Mahalanobis} = \left[\left(X_B - X_A \right)^T \times C^{-1} \times \left(X_B - X_A \right) \right]^{0.5} \ldots\ldots\ldots\ldots\ldots 2.17$$

where

- x_A and x_B are a pair of objects, and
- ***C*** is the sample covariance matrix
- **T** is the transpose operation, which flips a matrix over its diagonal.

Multivariate Normality

Introduction and Significance

Multivariate normality is an extension of the univariate normal distribution into a multidimensional space. In this context, a dataset is said to follow a multivariate normal distribution if any linear combination of its variables also follows a univariate normal distribution. This concept is a cornerstone in many multivariate statistical techniques, such as principal component analysis (PCA), canonical correlation, and linear discriminant analysis, as these methods often rely on the assumption of multivariate normality for validity and interpretability.

The multivariate normal distribution is defined by a mean vector and a covariance matrix. The mean vector provides the central tendency for each variable, while the covariance matrix describes the relationships and variability among the variables. The shape of the distribution is a multidimensional generalization of the familiar bell curve, with the data clustering more densely near the mean vector and tapering off as the distance from the mean increases.

Mathematical Definition

The probability density function (PDF) of a **p**-dimensional multivariate normal distribution is given as:

$$f(x) = \frac{1}{(2\pi)^{p/2}\left|\Sigma\right|^{1/2}} exp\left(-1/2(x-\mu)^T \Sigma^{-1}(x-\mu)\right) \ldots 2.17$$

Where:

- x is the p-dimensional vector of variables.
- μ is the p-dimensional mean vector.
- Σis the p×pcovariance matrix.
- |Σ|| is the determinant of the covariance matrix.

This equation shows that the multivariate normal distribution depends on both the location (mean vector) and spread (covariance matrix) of the data.

Testing Multivariate Normality

Determining whether a dataset follows a multivariate normal distribution is crucial because many statistical methods assume it as a prerequisite. Several statistical tests are available to evaluate multivariate normality:

1. **Mardia's Test:**

   Mardia's test checks for multivariate skewness and kurtosis. It evaluates whether the data's skewness and kurtosis values align with what is expected under a multivariate normal distribution. Large deviations indicate non-normality.

2. **Henze-Zirkler Test:**

   The Henze-Zirkler test is a versatile test for multivariate normality that uses a weighted integral of the empirical characteristic function. It is robust and powerful, even for small sample sizes.

Multivariate Visualization Techniques:

Multivariate visualization techniques help analyze relationships and patterns among multiple variables simultaneously. Common methods include scatter plots, parallel coordinates plots, heat maps, bubble charts, and dimensionality reduction techniques like PCA and t-SNE visualizations.

1. **Scatter Plot Matrix**:
   - Grid of scatter plots showing all pairwise relationships
   - Diagonal often shows univariate distributions
   - Quickly identifies patterns across multiple variable pairs
2. **Parallel Coordinates Plot**:
   - Variables represented as parallel axes
   - Each observation is a line connecting values across axes
   - Good for identifying clusters and patterns in high dimensions
3. **Heatmaps**:
   - Color-coded matrix showing pairwise relationships
   - Often used with hierarchical clustering
   - Effective for correlation matrices and distance matrices
4. **Bubble Charts**:
   - Extension of scatter plots with additional dimension as bubble size
   - Can incorporate fourth dimension with color
   - Useful for multivariate data exploration

5. **Dimension Reduction Visualizations**:
   - PCA plots (first two principal components)
   - t-SNE plots
   - UMAP visualizations
   - Compress high-dimensional data into 2D/3D representation

Interactive Visualization Techniques:

1. **Brushing and Linking**:
   - Selection in one plot highlights same data in other views
   - Allows exploration of multidimensional relationships
   - Helps identify patterns across different projections
2. **3D Rotation and Projection**:
   - Interactive exploration of three-dimensional relationships
   - Useful for identifying clusters and structures
   - Often combined with color for additional dimension

Table 2.5: Multivariate Visualization Techniques Comparison

Technique	Dimensionality	Strengths	Limitations	Best Use Cases
Scatter Plot Matrix	2-15 variables	Shows all pairwise relations	Space-intensive, scales poorly	Exploring correlations among moderate set of variables
Parallel Coordinates	3-20 variables	Scales to many dimensions	Learning curve for interpretation	Identifying patterns and clusters across many variables
Heatmap	10-100+ variables	Compact, scalable	Limited detail on individual relationships	Large correlation matrices,

				clustering results
PCA Plot	Any → 2-3	Preserves global structure	May miss local patterns	Dimensionality reduction, variance exploration
t-SNE	Any → 2-3	Preserves local structure	Computationally intensive, non-deterministic	Cluster visualization, high-dimensional pattern finding
Bubble Chart	4 dimensions	Intuitive	Limited to 4 dimensions	Multivariate relationships with size/importance component

Figure 2.6 illustrates commonly used visualization techniques for analysing multivariate data

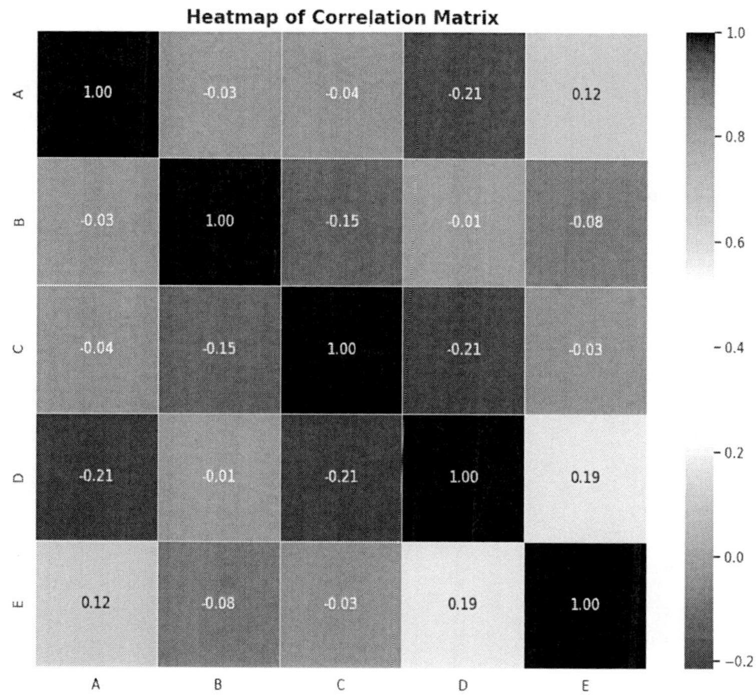

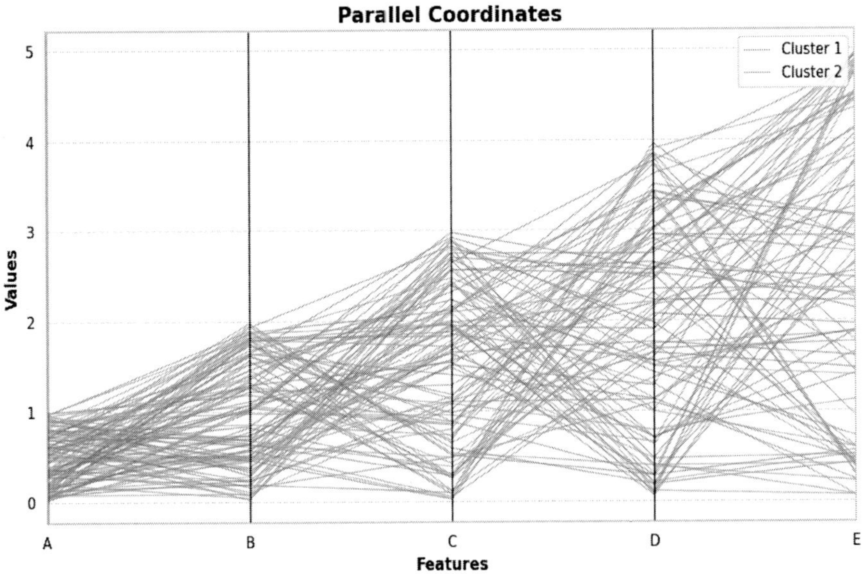
Parallel Coordinates
Cluster 1
Cluster 2
Values
Features
A
B
C
D
E
0
1
2
3
4
5

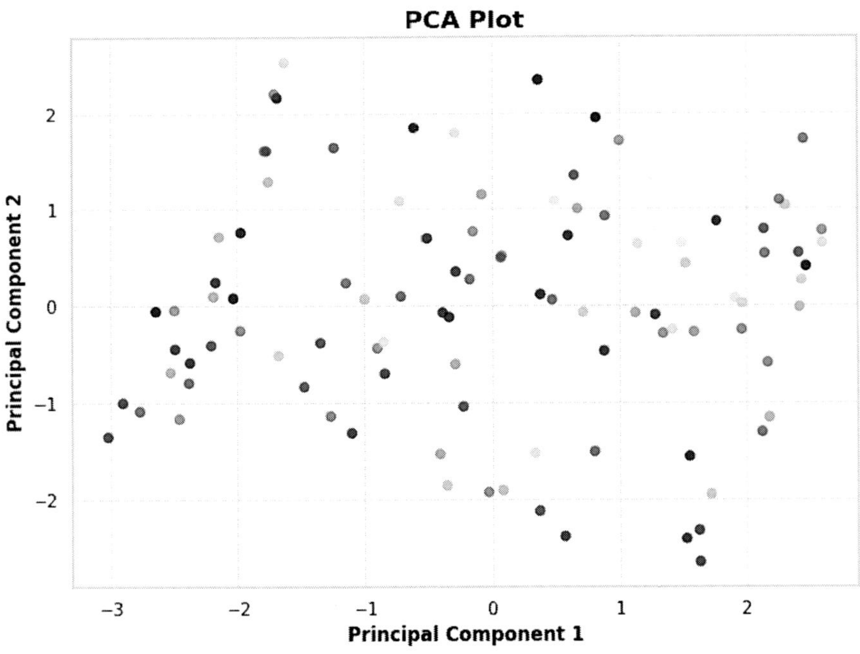
PCA Plot
Principal Component 2
Principal Component 1
−3
−2
−1
0
1
2

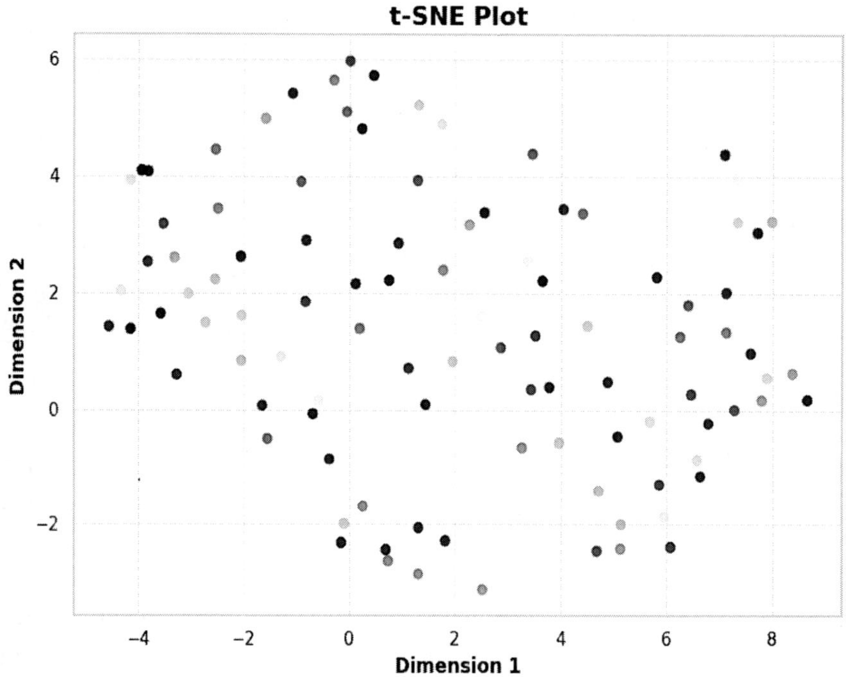

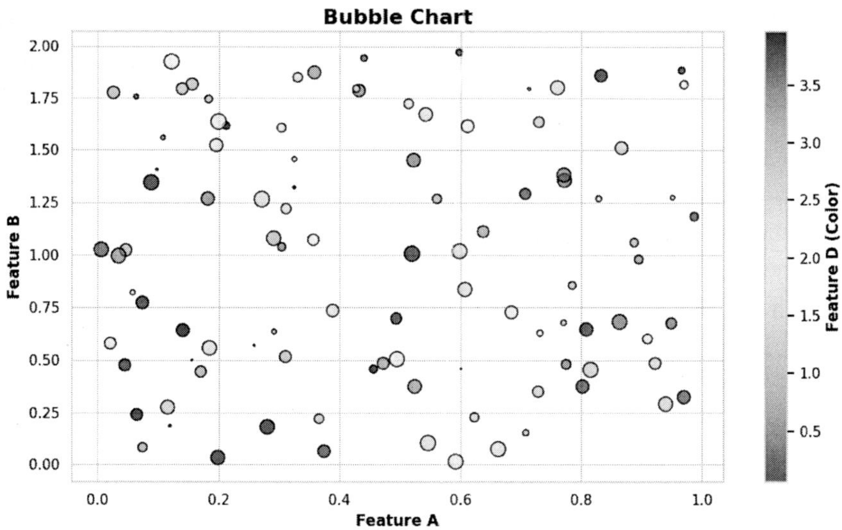

Figure 2.7: Examples of Common Multivariate Visualization Techniques

2.4 Feature Engineering

Feature engineering is a key step in the Machine Learning (ML) workflow that focuses on developing and improving input variables (features) for enhancing the prediction power of ML models. By extracting useful/meaningful information from raw data, feature engineering transforms unstructured or high-dimensional datasets into a format that algorithms can effectively process. This step is typically critical to the success of a machine learning model since the quality and relevance of features have a substantial impact on the model's accuracy and generalization capacity.

Different techniques, like feature extraction, transformation, and selection, are used in the context of machine learning to engineer features. Raw data, for example, could consist of time series data, images, or categorical information. Raw data is transformed into useful features using techniques such as normalization, polynomial expansion, and domain-specific feature extraction. Examples include translating timestamps into cyclical features such as "day of the week" and identifying shapes by extracting edges from images. Furthermore, feature selection techniques such as Recursive Feature Elimination (RFE) or mutual information are employed to keep only the most important features, lowering complexity and increasing computational efficiency.

Effective feature engineering necessitates a combination of subject knowledge and technological proficiency. It bridges the gap between raw data and machine learning algorithms, ensuring that models are not only accurate but also interpretable and robust. As a result, feature engineering remains a critical technique for realizing machine learning's full potential across an extensive spectrum of applications.

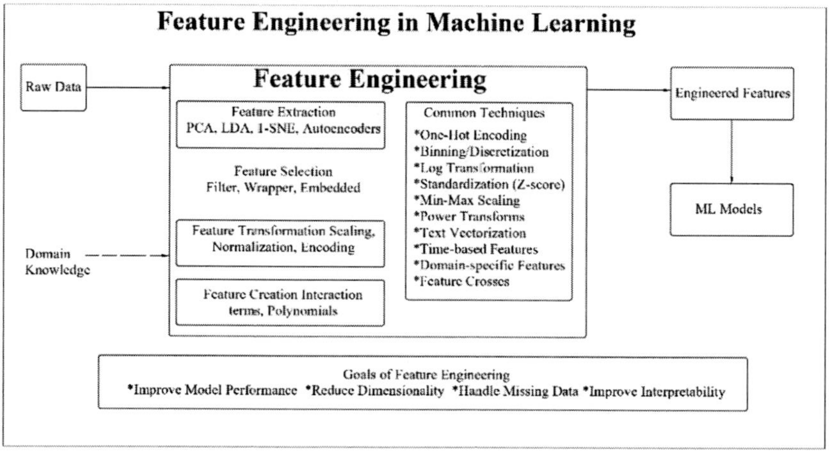

Figure 2.8 Feature Engineering in Machine Learning

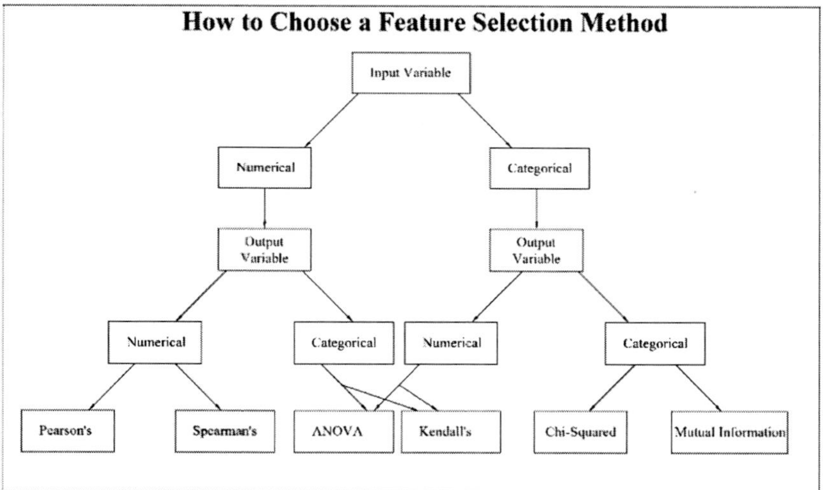

Figure 2.9: Feature selection methods based on the nature of input and output variables

Figure 2.6 illustrates the key components of feature engineering in machine learning, emphasizing the processes of feature extraction, selection, transformation, and creation. These steps bridge raw data and machine learning models, with techniques like PCA, one-hot encoding, scaling, and feature crosses ensuring that data is both meaningful and suitable for model training. The diagram highlights how domain knowledge and common preprocessing methods can significantly enhance the quality of features, improving model performance, interpretability, and efficiency.

In parallel, figure 2.7 provides a decision tree for selecting appropriate feature selection methods based on the nature of input and output variables. It categorizes input variables as numerical or categorical and links them to the corresponding target variable type, guiding the user to methods like Pearson's correlation, ANOVA, or Chi-Squared tests. Together, these visuals demonstrate how a systematic approach to feature engineering and selection ensures that only the most relevant and impactful features are utilized, creating a strong foundation for robust machine learning models.

2.4.1 Feature Selection and Feature Extraction

Feature engineering plays an essential role in transforming raw data into forms that machine learning algorithms can process effectively. By refining and improving/optimising the input variables, this approach improves predictive model performance, efficiency, and interpretability. Feature selection is the process of determining the most relevant variables that contribute to the model's prediction power. It reduces dimensionality, reduces overfitting, and improves computational efficiency by focusing on the most important features. Statistical tests, recursive feature removal, and tree-based feature importance rankings are popular methods for determining the most important characteristics otherwise most impactful features in a dataset.

On the other hand, feature extraction involves creating new features by combining or manipulating existing variables to provide more meaningful representations. This step is especially critical when working with high-dimensional or noisy datasets. Principal Component Analysis (PCA), Singular Value Decomposition (SVD), and autoencoders are all techniques that can extract latent patterns and compress/reduce the feature space while retaining essential data. Feature extraction improves model performance by converting information into a lower-dimensional representation. It also facilitates in the visualization and interpretation of complex data. Feature selection and extraction are the foundations of effective feature engineering, bridging the gap between raw data and machine learning models.

Feature Selection:

Feature selection identifies the most relevant subset of original features, reducing dimensionality while preserving information.

1. Filter Methods:

- Select features based on statistical measures.
- Independent of learning algorithm.
- Examples of filter methods include:
  - **Chi-square test**: Used for categorical features to test the independence between variables.
  - **ANOVA F-test**: Evaluates numerical features by analyzing the variance between groups to identify significant features.
  - **Correlation coefficients**: Measure the linear relationship between numerical variables (e.g., Pearson or Spearman correlation).
  - **Information gain**: Measures the reduction in entropy when a feature is used to split data, commonly used in decision trees.
  - **Variance threshold**: Removes features with low variance that do not contribute significantly to the model.

2. Wrapper Methods: An Overview:

Wrapper approaches are a more advanced approach to feature selection that involves training and testing a machine learning model on subsets of the features. Unlike filter approaches, which rely on statistical metrics, wrapper methods evaluate characteristics in terms of the target learning algorithm's predictive power. These methods iteratively search for the best subset of features, using the model's performance (for example, accuracy or error rate) as an evaluation metric. While computationally expensive owing to repetitious model training, wrapper approaches are often more accurate since they account for feature relationships and interactions.

Wrapper approaches include many methods, such as Recursive Feature Elimination (RFE), forward selection, and backward elimination. RFE removes features recursively depending on their importance, keeping only the most important subset remains. Forward selection begins with an empty feature set and adds one feature at a time to optimize model performance. Backward elimination, on the other hand, starts with all features and systematically eliminates the ones that are least important. Another method, exhaustive search, assesses all possible feature subsets but is computationally impractical for high-dimensional datasets. Despite their computational requirements, wrapper methods are often utilized when attaining the best model performance is critical, particularly in situations where accuracy assumes prime importance pver computational time (computational complexity).

- Examples:
    - Recursive Feature Elimination (RFE)
    - Forward/backward selection
    - Exhaustive search
- Computationally expensive but predictions of the model are more accurate

3. **Embedded Methods:** Embedded methods combine the advantages of filter and wrapper methods by performing feature selection as part of the model training process. These methods are integrated into the learning algorithm itself, which allows them to evaluate the importance of features while minimizing computational overhead. Techniques like Lasso (L1 regularization) and Ridge (L2 regularization) regression are common examples, where irrelevant or less important features are penalized and their coefficients are reduced or set to zero during training. Decision trees and ensemble methods, such as Random Forests, also inherently rank feature importance based on their contribution to reducing prediction error. Embedded methods are particularly effective in high-dimensional datasets, as they balance computational efficiency with model accuracy, making them a popular choice in practical machine learning workflows.

    - Feature selection integrated into model training

- Examples:
    - LASSO regularization (L1)
    - Decision tree importance
    - Elastic Net
- Balance between filter and wrapper approaches

Feature Extraction:

Feature extraction creates new features by transforming or combining original features.

1. **Dimensionality Reduction Techniques**: (please refer section 2.5 for elaboration of the concepts mentioned below)
    - Principal Component Analysis (PCA)
    - Linear Discriminant Analysis (LDA)
    - t-SNE
    - UMAP
    - Autoencoders
2. **Mathematical Transformations**:
    - Logarithmic transformation: log(x)
    - Power transformation: x^p
    - Box-Cox transformation
    - Polynomial features: x^2, x^3, xy, etc.
    - Trigonometric transformations: sin(x), cos(x)
3. **Domain-Specific Techniques**:
    - Text: TF-IDF, word embeddings
    - Images: Edge detection, HOG features
    - Audio: Spectral features, MFCCs
    - Time series: Rolling statistics, Fourier transforms

Evaluation Metrics for Feature Selection:

1. **Performance-based**:
   - Model accuracy with/without feature
   - Cross-validation score improvement
   - Information criteria (AIC, BIC)
2. **Information-based**:
   - Mutual information
   - Information gain
   - Entropy reduction
3. **Statistical**:
   - p-values from statistical tests
   - False discovery rate
   - Effect size

Table 2.6 provides a comparative analysis, helping readers appreciate the trade-offs and applications of different approaches. Combined, these resources offer a comprehensive framework for making informed decisions in feature selection.

Table 2.6: Comparison of Feature Selection Methods

Method Type	Computational Cost	Model Independence	Handles Feature Interactions	Handles Redundancy	Example Algorithms
Filter	Low	Yes	No	Partial	Variance threshold, Chi-square, Correlation
Wrapper	High	No	Yes	Yes	RFE, Sequential selectio, Genetic algorithms

Embedded	Medium	No	Yes	Yes	LASSO, Decision trees, Neural network pruning

2.4.2 Handling Missing Data and Outliers

Missing data and outliers must be handled properly during data preprocessing because they can significantly impact model performance and lead to erroneous/inaccurate predictions. Missing data originates as a result of missing observations, sensor malfunctions, or human errors, and if not dealt with it can introduce bias or lower statistical power in analysis. There are various solutions for dealing with missing values, ranging from basic deletion to advanced imputation methods. Deletion, while simple, risks losing crucial information, particularly in datasets with few observations. Imputation methods, such as substituting missing values with the mean, median, or mode, are widely employed for numerical data. Advanced techniques, such as k-Nearest Neighbors (k-NN) imputation, multiple imputations, and model-based imputation, preserve data associations and are more effective with larger, complex data sets.

In contrast, outliers are extreme data points that differ/deviate significantly from the majority of observations. These could be the consequence of measurement errors, data entry issues, or natural variations in data. Outliers, if not managed properly, can skew statistical metrics and machine learning models, resulting in overfitting or misleading/incorrect interpretations. Outliers are detected using statistical approaches such as the Z-score, Modified Z-score, or Tukey's IQR method, as well as visualization techniques like box plots or scatter plots. Outliers, once identified, can be handled by capping, removing, or transforming them, depending on their nature and the analysis' context. Robust algorithms, such as RANSAC or Huber regression, are better suited for coping with noisy datasets since they naturally handle outliers. dealing Addressing missing data and outliers effectively guarantees that the machine learning models yield reliable and accurate results.

Missing Data Mechanisms:

1. **Missing Completely at Random (MCAR)**:
    - Missing values occur entirely by chance
    - No relationship between missingness and any values
    - Example: Random equipment failure during measurement
2. **Missing at Random (MAR)**:
    - Missingness related to observed variables
    - Can be accounted for using other variables
    - Example: Older people less likely to answer income questions
3. **Missing Not at Random (MNAR)**:
    - Missingness related to unobserved factors or missing value itself
    - Systematic pattern that cannot be fully accounted for
    - Example: People with high incomes less likely to report income

Missing Data Handling Techniques:

1. **Deletion Methods**:
    - Listwise deletion (remove entire rows)
    - Pairwise deletion (use available data for each analysis)
    - Advantages: Simplicity, no bias introduction
    - Disadvantages: Loss of information, reduced statistical power
2. **Imputation Methods**:
    - Mean/median/mode imputation
    - k-Nearest Neighbours imputation
    - Regression imputation
    - Multiple imputation (MICE, Amelia)

- Matrix factorization methods
- Advantages: Preserves data volume
- Disadvantages: May introduce bias or reduce variance

3. **Model-Based Methods**:
    - Expectation-Maximization (EM) algorithm
    - Deep learning approaches (denoising autoencoders)
    - Advantages: Theoretical foundations, uncertainty quantification
    - Disadvantages: Computational complexity, assumptions
4. **Special Value Approach**:
    - Treat missing values as separate category
    - Create indicator variables for missingness
    - Advantages: Captures "missingness" as information
    - Disadvantages: Increases dimensionality

Outlier Detection and Handling:

1. **Statistical Methods**:
    - Z-score (>3 standard deviations)
    - Modified Z-score using median
    - Tukey's method (1.5×IQR)
    - Grubbs' test
2. **Proximity-Based Methods**:
    - k-Nearest Neighbours distance
    - Local Outlier Factor (LOF)
    - DBSCAN clustering
    - Isolation Forest

3. **Model-Based Methods**:
    - One-class SVM
    - Autoencoders reconstruction error
    - Robust covariance estimation
    - Gaussian mixture models

Outlier Handling Strategies:

1. **Remove**: Delete outlier observations
2. **Transform**: Apply log or other transformations to compress range
3. **Cap**: Winsorizing (capping at percentile thresholds)
4. **Separate Models**: Build separate models for outlier vs. non-outlier data
5. **Robust Methods**: Use algorithms less sensitive to outliers

Algorithms commonly considered robust to outliers:

1. **Robust Regression Techniques**
    - RANSAC (Random Sample Consensus): Iteratively fits a model by using subsets of the data, excluding outliers, and determining the best fit for the majority of data points.
    - Theil-Sen Estimator: A non-parametric method for linear regression that calculates the median of slopes of all lines connecting pairs of points.

2. **Robust Classification Algorithms**
    - Support Vector Machines (SVM) with Soft Margin: Uses slack variables to tolerate outliers while maintaining a robust decision boundary.
    - Robust Logistic Regression: Adds regularization or modifies the loss function to reduce sensitivity to outliers.

3. **Robust Clustering Techniques**
    - DBSCAN (Density-Based Spatial Clustering of Applications with Noise): Identifies outliers as points that do not belong to any cluster.
    - K-Medoids: Uses medoids instead of means, which are less sensitive to extreme values.
4. **Robust Dimensionality Reduction**
    - Robust PCA (Principal Component Analysis): A variation of PCA that identifies and isolates outliers in the dataset.

These algorithms adapt to the presence of outliers and focus on capturing the underlying structure of the data without being disproportionately influenced by extreme values.

Missing Data Handling: Strategies and Trade-offs

Handling missing data is a critical step in data preprocessing, as missing values can significantly impact the performance and reliability of machine learning models. The choice of a missing data handling method depends on the nature of the missing data, computational resources, and the specific needs of the analysis.

The **Figure 2.7** visually outlines various missing data handling approaches, categorizing them based on their applicability to different missing data mechanisms—MCAR (Missing Completely at Random), MAR (Missing at Random), and MNAR (Missing Not at Random)—and their key characteristics. The Table 2.7 complements the figure by providing a detailed comparison of popular techniques, highlighting their appropriate scenarios, advantages, limitations, and computational costs.

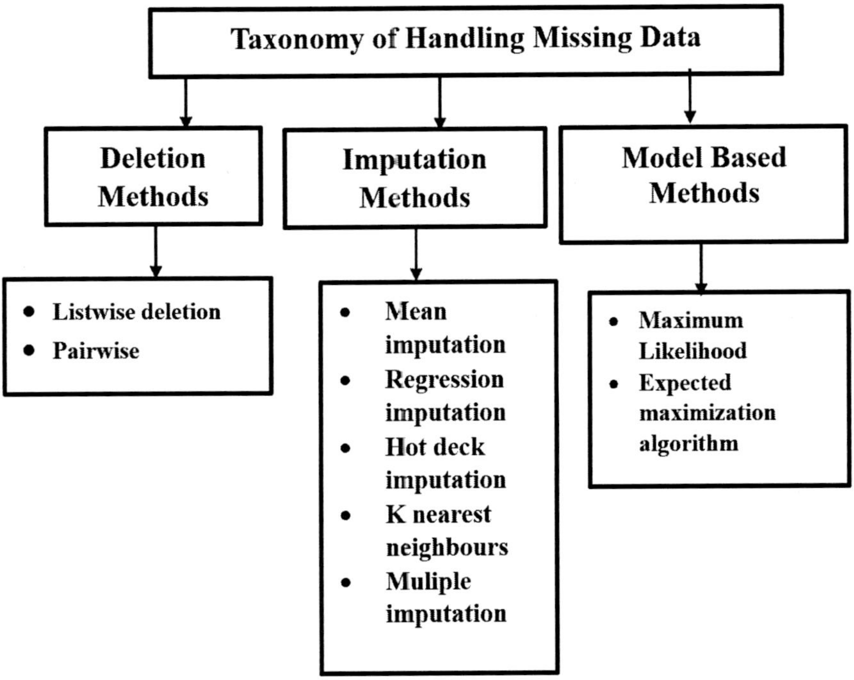

Figure 2.10: Approaches for Handling Missing Data

Table 2.7: Comparing Missing Data Handling Approaches

Method	Appropriate When	Advantages	Disadvantages	Computational Cost
Listwise Deletion	MCAR, small % missing	Simple, unbiased under MCAR	Loss of information, biased under MAR/MNAR	Low
Mean/Median Imputation	MCAR, quick solution needed	Simple, preserves mean	Reduces variance, ignores relationships	Low

KNN Imputation	MAR, relationships exist	Preserves relationships	Computationally expensive	Medium-High
MICE	MAR, complex relationships	Handles multiple variable types, uncertainty	Computationally intensive	High
EM Algorithm	MAR, parametric assumptions valid	Statistical foundation, efficient	Requires distribution assumptions	Medium
Deep Learning	Complex patterns, large datasets	Captures non-linear relationships	Requires large data, black box	Very High

2.5 Dimensionality Reduction Techniques:

Dimensionality reduction extends beyond traditional structured data represented in matrices to encompass more complex data formats such as tensors, graphs, and networks. Matrices, which are two-dimensional representations of data, often serve as the starting point for dimensionality reduction techniques like Principal Component Analysis (PCA) or Singular Value Decomposition (SVD). However, real-world datasets frequently involve higher-order relationships, which are better captured using tensors—multi-dimensional generalizations of matrices. Tensor decomposition methods, such as Canonical Polyadic Decomposition (CPD) and Tucker Decomposition, are specifically designed to reduce the dimensionality of tensor data while preserving its inherent multi-dimensional structure. These methods find applications in areas like recommendation systems, video processing, and spatiotemporal data analysis, where relationships span multiple dimensions.

For more complex data structures such as graphs and networks, dimensionality reduction focuses on preserving the relationships and topology of nodes and edges. Techniques like graph embedding map nodes in a high-dimensional graph to a lower-dimensional vector space while retaining the graph's structural information. Methods such as Node2Vec, DeepWalk, and Graph Convolutional Networks (GCNs) are instrumental in simplifying graph data for downstream tasks like clustering, classification, and link prediction. When dealing with multimodal data, where information comes from diverse sources like images, text, and audio, dimensionality reduction combines modalities into a unified lower-dimensional representation. Techniques like multimodal embeddings and autoencoders effectively integrate heterogeneous data, enabling applications in areas such as sentiment analysis, medical diagnosis, and cross-modal retrieval. These advanced approaches demonstrate the adaptability of dimensionality reduction techniques to modern, complex datasets, enhancing their relevance in cutting-edge research and practical applications. complex data types used in dimensionality reduction in running matter:(1) Graphs and Networks, (2) Multimodal Data, (3) Sparse and High-Dimensional Data, (4) Sequential Data, (5) Hierarchical and Tree-Like Data, (6) Images and Video Data, (7) Textual Data, (8) Audio and Signal Data, (9) Spatial Data, (10) Tabular Data.

2.5.1 Principal Component Analysis (PCA)

Principal Component Analysis (PCA) is a fundamental dimensionality reduction technique that transforms correlated variables into a smaller set of uncorrelated variables while maximizing variance.

Core Concepts:

1. **Principal Components**:
    - Linear combinations of original features
    - Orthogonal to each other (uncorrelated)
    - Ordered by amount of variance explained
    - First PC captures maximum variance, second PC captures maximum remaining variance, etc.

2. **Mathematical Foundation**:
    - Based on eigenvectors and eigenvalues of covariance matrix
    - Each PC is an eigenvector
    - Corresponding eigenvalue represents variance explained
    - Transformation: Y = XW (where W contains eigenvectors)
3. **Implementation Process**:
    - Standardize data (zero mean, unit variance)
    - Compute covariance matrix
    - Calculate eigenvectors and eigenvalues
    - Sort eigenvectors by eigenvalues (descending)
    - Project data onto selected eigenvectors

Applications of PCA:

1. **Dimensionality Reduction**:
    - Reduce number of features while preserving information
    - Combat curse of dimensionality
    - Improve computational efficiency
2. **Visualization**:
    - Project high-dimensional data to 2D/3D space
    - Identify clusters and patterns
    - Understand feature relationships
3. **Noise Reduction**:
    - Lower-ranked PCs often capture noise
    - Reconstruction using top PCs reduces noise
    - Signal extraction in image/audio processing

4. **Multicollinearity Handling**:
    - Transform correlated features to uncorrelated PCs
    - Improves stability of regression models
    - Addresses variance inflation in statistical models

PCA Variations:

Let us dwell on this concept. Principal Component Analysis (PCA) has evolved into a number of variations designed that address specific issues in dimensionality reduction and data analysis. Kernel PCA extends classic PCA by applying it to a transformed feature space using kernel functions, enabling the identification of nonlinear patterns in data. This is especially beneficial for datasets with complex, nonlinear interactions, which standard PCA cannot handle well. In contrast, incremental PCA is intended for big datasets that cannot be stored in memory all at once. It processes data in pieces, making it ideal for real-time or streaming data analysis while preserving accuracy.

Sparse PCA applies sparsity constraints to the main components, resulting in interpretable components with fewer original variables. This approach is useful in applications where interpretability and feature selection are crucial. Finally, Robust PCA is intended to manage data with outliers or noise by decomposing the dataset into a low-rank approximation and a sparse component that isolates the outliers. This makes robust PCA especially useful for tasks that involve distorted or missing data. Together, these PCA versions offer adaptable techniques for dimensionality reduction that may be adapted to a variety of data challenges. In figure 2.9 and table 2.8, detailed visualization and consolidated

1. **Kernel PCA:**
    - Extends PCA to non-linear relationships
    - Uses kernel trick to implicitly map to higher dimensions
    - Common kernels: RBF, polynomial, sigmoid
2. **Incremental PCA**:
    - Processes data in batches
    - Suitable for large datasets

- Updates PCA model incrementally

3. **Sparse PCA**:
   - Encourages sparsity in loading vectors
   - Improves interpretability
   - Uses regularization techniques
4. **Robust PCA**:
   - Less sensitive to outliers
   - Decomposes data into low-rank and sparse components
   - Applications in background subtraction, recommender systems

Limitations and Considerations:

1. **Linear Assumptions**:
   - Only captures linear relationships
   - Ineffective for complex non-linear structures
2. **Feature Scaling**:
   - Sensitive to feature scales
   - Standardization is typically required
3. **Interpretability**:
   - PCs often lack clear real-world meaning.
   - Loading vectors can be difficult to interpret
4. **Variance ≠ Relevance**:
   - High variance doesn't guarantee relevance to target
   - Supervised variations (like PLS) may be more appropriate

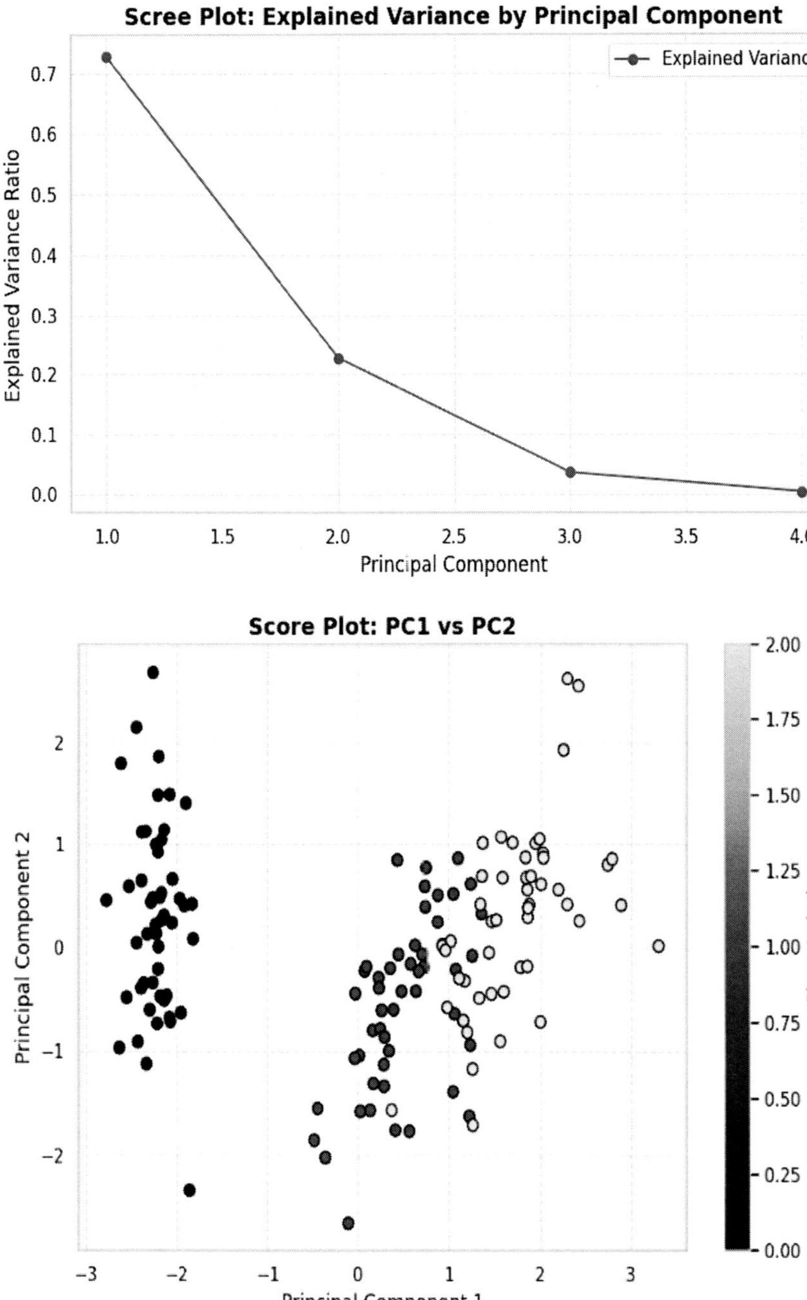

Figure 2.11: PCA Analysis (a) Explained Variance Scree Plot (b) Score Plot of PC1 vs. PC2

Table 2.8: Key Metrics for PCA Interpretation

Metric	Description	Interpretation	Usage
Eigenvalues	Variance explained by each PC	Larger = more information	Determine number of PCs to retain
Explained Variance Ratio	Proportion of total variance	Higher = more important	Feature importance, scree plot
Cumulative Explained Variance	Running sum of explained variance	Threshold (e.g., 95%)	Decide cutoff for dimensionality.
Loading Vectors	Coefficients of original variables	Magnitude indicates importance	Feature contribution to each PC
Score Plot	Data projected onto PCs	Clusters indicate patterns	Visualization, pattern identification
Biplot	Combined score and loading plot	Shows relationships between samples and variables	Complex relationship visualization

2.5.2 t-SNE and Other Dimensionality Reduction Methods

While PCA focuses on preserving global structure, other techniques offer alternative approaches for specific dimensionality reduction challenges.

t-Distributed Stochastic Neighbor Embedding (t-SNE):

1. **Core Concept**:
    - Non-linear technique focusing on preserving local structure

- Converts similarities to joint probabilities
- Minimizes KL divergence between high- and low-dimensional distributions
- Uses t-distribution in low-dimensional space to address crowding problem

2. **Key Parameters**:
   - Perplexity: Balance between local and global structure (5-50)
   - Learning rate: Affects optimization speed and quality
   - Early exaggeration: Encourages cluster formation
   - Number of iterations: Controls convergence quality
3. **Strengths**:
   - Exceptional at revealing clusters
   - Preserves local similarities
   - Works well for high-dimensional data visualization
   - Handles non-linear relationships
4. **Limitations**:
   - Non-deterministic results
   - Computationally expensive ($O(n^2)$)
   - No out-of-sample extension
   - Can distort global structure
   - Different runs produce different results

Other Important Dimensionality Reduction Techniques:

1. **Uniform Manifold Approximation and Projection (UMAP)**:
   - Based on Riemannian geometry and algebraic topology
   - Faster than t-SNE with similar quality
   - Better preserves global structure

- Provides theoretical framework
- Supports supervised dimension reduction

2. **Linear Discriminant Analysis (LDA)**:
   - Supervised technique maximizing class separability
   - Projects data to maximize between-class variance and minimize within-class variance
   - Useful for classification pre-processing
   - Limited to C-1 dimensions (C = number of classes)

3. **Multidimensional Scaling (MDS)**:
   - Preserves pairwise distances between data points
   - Classical MDS equivalent to PCA for Euclidean distances
   - Non-metric MDS preserves rank order of distances
   - Useful for similarity/dissimilarity data

4. **Autoencoders**:
   - Neural network approach to dimensionality reduction
   - Encoder compresses data, decoder reconstructs
   - Hidden layer(s) form bottleneck representing reduced dimensions
   - Variations include denoising, variational, and contractive autoencoders
   - Can capture complex non-linear relationships

5. **Locally Linear Embedding (LLE)**:
   - Preserves local neighborhood relationships
   - Reconstructs each point from its neighbors
   - Solves sparse eigenvalue problem
   - Computationally efficient for certain datasets

6. **ISOMAP**:
   - Extends MDS using geodesic distances
   - Constructs neighborhood graph
   - Computes shortest paths as geodesic approximations
   - Preserves global structure of non-linear manifold

Selection Criteria for Dimensionality Reduction:

1. **Data Characteristics**:
   - Size: t-SNE/UMAP struggles with >100K points.
   - Dimensionality: Autoencoders excel for very high dimensions.
   - Linearity: PCA for linear, t-SNE/UMAP for non-linear relationships
2. **Task Requirements**:
   - Visualization: t-SNE/UMAP typically superior
   - Pre-processing: PCA more stable for downstream Modellig
   - Classification: LDA leverages class information
3. **Computational Constraints**:
   - Time: PCA < UMAP < t-SNE < Autoencoders
   - Memory: ISOMAP/t-SNE have quadratic complexity
4. **Interpretability Needs**:
   - PCA components have direct relationship to original features
   - Factor Analysis designed for interpretable factors
   - t-SNE/UMAP focus on visualization, not interpretation

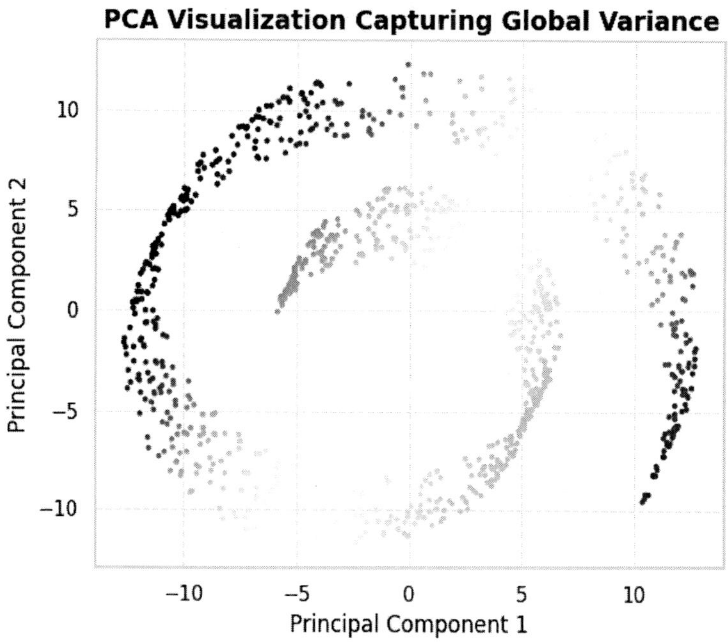
PCA Visualization Capturing Global Variance
Principal Component 2
Principal Component 1

(a)

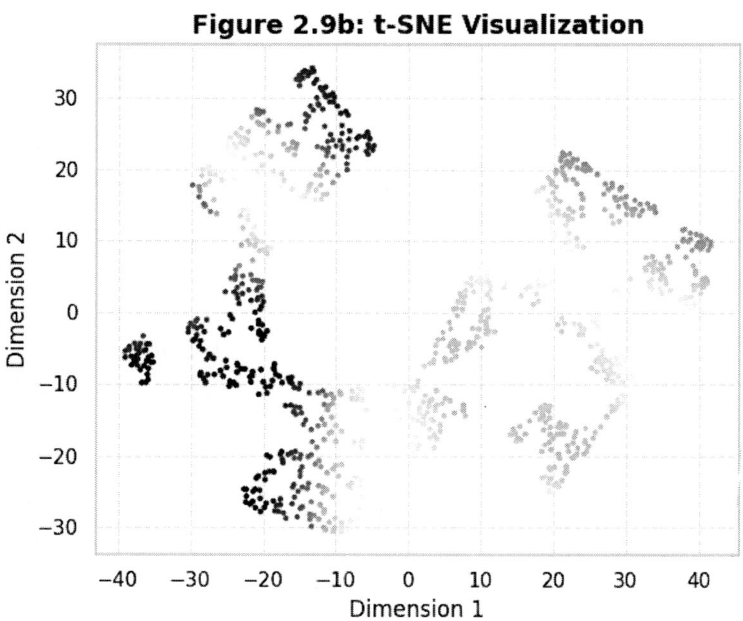
Figure 2.9b: t-SNE Visualization
Dimension 2
Dimension 1

(b)

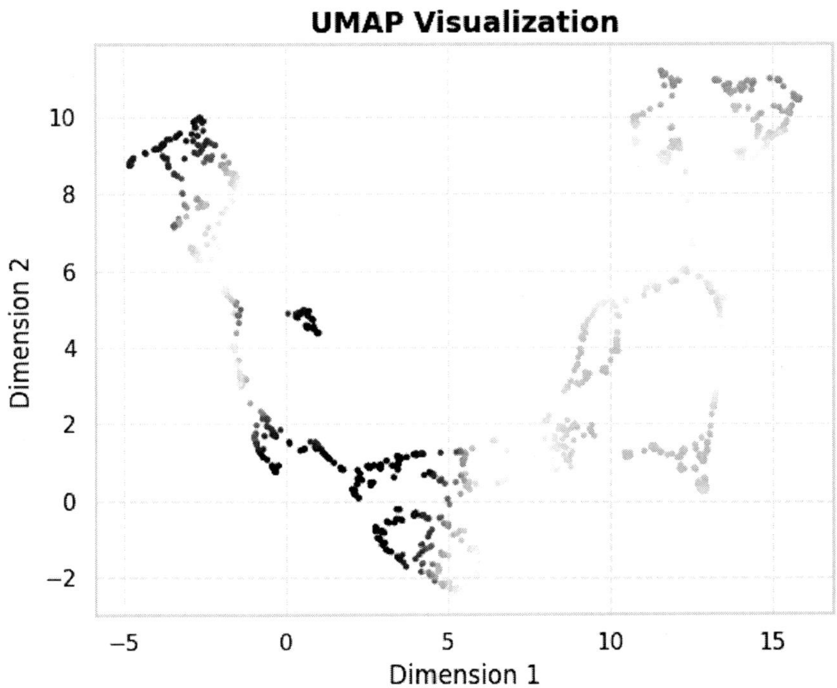

(C)

Figure 2.12: Visualization of Dimensionality Reduction Techniques (a) PCA Visualization – Capturing Global Variance, (b) t-SNE Visualization – Preserving Local Similarities, (c) UMAP Visualization – Balancing Local and Global Structure

Table 2.9: Comparative Analysis of Dimensionality Reduction Techniques

Technique	**Algorithm Type**	**Preserves**	**Computation Complexity**	**Out-of-Sample Extension**	**Best For**
PCA	Linear	Global variance	$O(p^3)$ or $O(n^3)$	Yes	Linear relationships, noise reduction

t-SNE	Non-linear	Local similarities	$O(n^2)$	No	Visualization, cluster identification
UMAP	Non-linear	Local & some global	O(n log n)	Yes	Faster alternative to t-SNE with better global structure
LDA	Linear, supervised	Class separation	$O(np^2)$	Yes	Classification preprocessing
Autoencoders	Non-linear	Reconstructability	O(n) per iteration	Yes	Complex non-linear patterns, large datasets
ISOMAP	Non-linear	Geodesic distances	$O(n^3)$	With approximation	Data on manifold, preserving global structure
LLE	Non-linear	Local neighborhoods	$O(dn^2)$	With approximation	Manifold learning, preserving local properties

2.6 Basic Learning Theory

2.6.1 Design of Learning Systems

Learning theory provides the theoretical foundation for machine learning systems, explaining how algorithms learn from data and generalize to new, unseen examples. This framework helps us understand both the capabilities and limitations of machine learning approaches.

Theoretical Foundations:

The design of effective learning systems draws upon various mathematical and statistical principles:

1. **Statistical Learning Theory**:
   - Formalizes the learning process as statistical estimation
   - Provides bounds on generalization error
   - Examples: Vapnik-Chervonenkis (VC) theory, Probably Approximately Correct (PAC) learning
2. **Information Theory**:
   - Quantifies information content and entropy
   - Guides feature selection via mutual information
   - Provides formal basis for decision tree splitting criteria
3. **Optimization Theory**:
   - Addresses the mathematical techniques for finding optimal parameters
   - Includes gradient-based, evolutionary, and probabilistic approaches
   - Deals with challenges like local minima and saddle points
4. **Computational Learning Theory**:
   - Analyzes algorithmic efficiency and learnability
   - Studies sample complexity (data needed for reliable learning)
   - Establishes computational complexity of learning algorithms

Core Learning Paradigms:

1. **Supervised Learning**:
   - Learning from labeled examples (input-output pairs)

- Objective: Approximate mapping function from inputs to outputs
- Performance measured by prediction accuracy on unseen data
- Examples: Classification, regression, sequence labeling
- Key challenge: Balancing fit to training data vs. generalization

2. **Unsupervised Learning**:
    - Learning from unlabeled data without explicit guidance
    - Objective: Discover inherent structure or patterns in data
    - Performance often subjective or application-dependent
    - Examples: Clustering, dimensionality reduction, density estimation
    - Key challenge: Defining meaningful objectives without labels

3. **Semi-supervised Learning**:
    - Learning from both labeled and unlabeled data
    - Typically, small amount of labeled data, large amount unlabeled
    - Leverages unlabeled data to improve supervised tasks
    - Examples: Self-training, co-training, graph-based methods
    - Key challenge: Effectively utilizing unlabeled data without introducing bias

4. **Reinforcement Learning**:
    - Learning through interaction with environment
    - Objective: Maximize cumulative reward over time
    - Balances exploration (trying new actions) and exploitation (using known good actions)

- Examples: Game playing, robotics, resource allocation, recommendation systems
- Key challenge: Delayed feedback and credit assignment problem

Components of Learning Systems:

1. **Data Collection and Preprocessing**:
    - Gathering relevant data from various sources
    - Cleaning, normalization, and standardization
    - Feature engineering and selection
    - Train/validation/test splitting
    - Data augmentation when appropriate
2. **Model Selection**:
    - Algorithm choice based on problem characteristics
    - Architecture design (for neural networks)
    - Prior knowledge incorporation
    - Computational constraints consideration
    - Interpretability requirements
3. **Learning Process**:
    - Optimization algorithm selection (SGD, Adam, etc.)
    - Hyperparameter tuning strategies
    - Regularization techniques to prevent overfitting
    - Batch size and learning rate scheduling
    - Early stopping criteria.
4. **Evaluation Framework**:
    - Appropriate metrics selection for specific tasks
    - Cross-validation strategies for robust assessment
    - Statistical significance testing of results

- Interpretability and explainability analysis
- Fairness and bias evaluation

5. **Deployment and Monitoring**:
    - Production integration considerations
    - Performance monitoring over time
    - Concept drift detection mechanisms
    - Retraining strategies and triggers
    - Feedback loops for continuous improvement

Learning System Design Principles:

1. **Modularity**:
    - Divide system into independent, interchangeable components
    - Allows focused optimization of each part
    - Facilitates testing and debugging
    - Enables incremental improvements
2. **Robustness**:
    - System should handle noise, outliers, and edge cases
    - Performance should degrade gracefully under stress
    - Should account for distributional shifts
    - Multiple validation methods ensure reliable performance
3. **Scalability**:
    - Architecture should accommodate growing data volumes
    - Computational efficiency for both training and inference
    - Distributed processing capabilities when needed
    - Resource utilization optimization

4. **Adaptability**:
    - o System should evolve with changing data patterns
    - o Should incorporate new knowledge efficiently
    - o Continuous learning capabilities
    - o Active learning for efficient data acquisition

Table 2.10: Design Considerations for Learning Systems

Component	**Key Questions**	**Considerations**	**Impact on Performance**
Data	How much data is needed? What quality?	Quantity, quality, bias, balance, representation	Foundation for all performance; garbage in, garbage out
Features	Which attributes matter? How to represent them?	Relevance, correlation, transformations, domain knowledge	Direct impact on model capacity and learning efficiency
Algorithm	Which learning approach best suits the problem?	Inductive bias, scalability, interpretability, complexity	Determines fundamental learning capability and limitations
Evaluation	How to measure success?	Metrics alignment with goals, generalization assessment	Guides optimization and selection decisions
Regularization	How to prevent overfitting?	Complexity control, prior knowledge incorporation	Balances bias-variance trade off for optimal generalization
Optimization	How to efficiently find	Learning rate, batch size,	Affects training speed and

	optimal parameters?	convergence criteria	quality of solution
Infrastructure	What compute resources are required?	Memory requirements, parallelization, hardware acceleration	Enables handling of larger models and datasets
Ethics	What are the societal implications?	Fairness, transparency, privacy, security	Ensures responsible deployment and usage

2.6.2 Modelling in Machine Learning

Machine learning Modelling involves selecting appropriate algorithms, optimizing parameters, and evaluating performance to solve specific problems effectively. This process requires both theoretical understanding and practical know-how.

Fundamental Concepts:

1. **Inductive Bias:**
   - Assumptions made by learning algorithm to generalize beyond training data
   - Examples: Smoothness, sparsity, hierarchical structure, locality
   - Stronger bias: More constrained models, potentially better generalization with less data
   - Weaker bias: More flexible models, potentially higher variance requiring more data
   - Appropriate bias selection crucial for problem domain match

2. **Capacity and Complexity:**
   - Model capacity: Ability to fit diverse functions and complex patterns

- Higher capacity: Can fit more complex patterns but risk overfitting
- Lower capacity: More constrained but potentially more robust with limited data
- Formal measures: VC dimension, Rademacher complexity, parameter count
- Practical control: Regularization, architecture constraints, pruning

3. Bias-Variance Trade-off:

- Bias: Error from incorrect assumptions or simplified model
- Variance: Error from sensitivity to training data fluctuations
- Total expected error = bias^2 + variance + irreducible error
- Sweet spot: Minimize total error by balancing bias and variance
- Relationship to model complexity: Simpler models (higher bias, lower variance), complex models (lower bias, higher variance)

4. Generalization:

- Ability to perform well on previously unseen data
- Gap between training and test performance indicates generalization quality
- Influenced by model complexity, data quantity and quality, noise level
- Generalization bounds from theory: PAC learning, VC theory
- Regular empirical evaluation via cross-validation crucial

Modelling Process Framework:

1. **Problem Formulation:**
    - Define objectives precisely
    - Determine appropriate learning paradigm
    - Establish evaluation criteria
    - Set performance targets
    - Understand constraints (computational, time, interpretability)
2. **Data Preparation:**
    - Exploratory data analysis to understand distributions
    - Feature engineering and selection
    - Data cleaning and normalization
    - Handling class imbalance if present
    - Creating appropriate train/validation/test splits
3. **Model Selection and Training:**
    - Choose candidate algorithms based on problem characteristics
    - Start with simpler models as baselines
    - Implement progressive model complexity
    - Perform hyperparameter optimization
    - Employ regularization techniques as needed
4. **Model Evaluation and Refinement:**
    - Assess performance using appropriate metrics
    - Diagnose overfitting or underfitting
    - Perform error analysis on misclassified instances
    - Iterate on feature engineering and model selection
    - Consider ensemble methods to improve performance

5. **Deployment and Monitoring:**
    - Translate model to production environment
    - Establish monitoring systems for performance
    - Implement feedback mechanisms
    - Plan for model updates and maintenance
    - Monitor for concept drift and data distribution shifts

Characteristics of Learning Algorithms:

Learning algorithms are defined by their ability to generalize from data, adapt to changing patterns, and complete tasks with minimal human interaction. Scalability allows algorithms to efficiently manage big datasets; flexibility allows for adaptation to varied data kinds and challenges; and robustness ensures reliable performance even in the face of noise or outliers. Furthermore, algorithms are frequently evaluated using the bias-variance tradeoff, which defines the balance of underfitting and overfitting. Another key component is interpretability, which allows stakeholders to understand how the model makes decisions. Finally, computational complexity and resource efficiency are important considerations when selecting an algorithm, especially for real-time or large-scale applications.

1. **Linear Models:**
    - Strong bias toward linear relationships between features and targets
    - Low variance, high interpretability, computationally efficient
    - Examples: Linear regression, logistic regression, SVMs with linear kernels
    - Best for: Problems with many features, limited data, interpretability requirements
    - Limitations: Cannot capture complex non-linear relationships

2. **Tree-Based Models:**
   - Capture non-linear relationships through recursive partitioning
   - Handle mixed data types naturally without preprocessing
   - Inherently perform feature selection
   - Examples: Decision trees, random forests, gradient boosting machines
   - Best for: Tabular data, mixed feature types, capturing feature interactions
   - Limitations: Can overfit without proper pruning, struggle with smooth functions

3. **Neural Networks:**
   - Flexible function approximators with variable capacity
   - Hierarchical representation learning from raw features
   - Strong in perceptual domains with spatial or temporal structure
   - Compute-intensive training but efficient inference possible
   - Best for: Computer vision, NLP, speech, complex pattern recognition
   - Limitations: Data hungry, black box nature, optimization challenges

4. **Probabilistic Models:**
   - Model uncertainty explicitly
   - Incorporate prior knowledge through Bayesian approaches
   - Provide confidence intervals and distributions rather than point estimates
   - Examples: Naive Bayes, Bayesian networks, Gaussian processes

- Best for: Small data settings, risk-sensitive applications
- Limitations: Assumptions about data distributions, computational complexity

Model Selection and Evaluation:

Model selection and evaluation are key processes in the machine learning process that ensure the chosen model is both effective and right for the task at hand. Model selection entails evaluating various methods and configurations to determine which one best balances performance and complexity for the given dataset. In contrast, assessment evaluates the ability of a model to generalize to previously unseen data using metrics such as accuracy, precision, recall, F1-score, or area under the ROC curve. Cross-validation methods, like as k-fold validation, are widely used to avoid overfitting and offer a reliable estimate of model performance. Together, these procedures ensure that the final model is not only accurate, but also reliable and adaptive to real-world scenarios.

1. **Cross-Validation Techniques:**
   - k-fold: Split training data into k parts, train on k-1, validate on remainder
   - Stratified: Preserves class distribution in each fold
   - Leave-one-out: Extreme case with k = n (sample size)
   - Time series split: Respects temporal ordering
   - Benefits: Mitigates overfitting to validation set, provides variance estimate

2. **Hyperparameter Optimization Approaches:**
   - Grid search: Exhaustive search over parameter space
   - Random search: Randomly sample from parameter space
   - Bayesian optimization: Model-based sequential optimization
   - Genetic algorithms: Evolutionary approach to parameter search

- Trade-off between exploration and exploitation

3. **Performance Metrics Selection:**
    - Classification: Accuracy, precision, recall, F1, AUC-ROC, AUC-PR
    - Regression: MSE, MAE, R^2, RMSE, MAPE
    - Ranking: NDCG, MAP, MRR
    - Clustering: Silhouette coefficient, Davies-Bouldin index, V-measure
    - Multi-objective: Weighted combinations for balanced evaluation

4. **Diagnostic Tools:**
    - Learning curves: Plot performance vs. training set size
    - Validation curves: Plot performance vs. hyperparameter value
    - Confusion matrices: Detailed view of classification errors
    - Residual plots: Identify patterns in regression errors
    - Feature importance: Understand model decision factors

Advanced Modelling Considerations:

Advanced modeling considerations aim to improve the performance, interpretability, and robustness of machine learning models in complex situations. These include dealing with imbalanced datasets, enhancing/optimizing hyperparameters using approaches such as grid or random search, and integrating domain knowledge to improve model relevance. Furthermore, optimizing computational efficiency for large-scale datasets and applying regularization approaches to avoid overfitting are critical. Ethical considerations such as fairness, accountability, and transparency are also important in promoting responsible development of models. By addressing these advanced issues, practitioners can develop more effective and trustworthy models that meet real-world requirements.

1. **Ensemble Methods:**
    - Bagging: Reduce variance through parallel training (e.g., Random Forest)
    - Boosting: Reduce bias through sequential training (e.g., AdaBoost, XGBoost)
    - Stacking: Combine multiple models through meta-learner
    - Benefits: Improved performance, robustness, reduced overfitting
    - Costs: Increased complexity, computation, potential interpretability loss

2. **Transfer Learning:**
    - Leverage knowledge from related tasks/domains
    - Fine-tune pre-trained models for specific applications
    - Particularly powerful in deep learning contexts
    - Reduces data requirements for new tasks
    - Examples: ImageNet pre-trained models, language model fine-tuning

3. **Automated Machine Learning (AutoML):**
    - Automates pipeline creation and optimization
    - Handles feature selection, model selection, hyperparameter tuning
    - Reduces manual effort and expertise requirements
    - Examples: Auto-sklearn, TPOT, Google AutoML
    - Limitations: Black box approach, may miss domain-specific optimizations

4. **Explainable AI (XAI):**
    - Techniques to understand model decisions
    - Global explanations: Feature importance, rule extraction

- Local explanations: LIME, SHAP values
- Counterfactual explanations: "What would change the outcome?"
- Essential for high-stakes applications and regulatory compliance

Table 2.11 provides an overview of common machine learning algorithms, highlighting their characteristics, typical applications, and suitability for various types of data and tasks. This comparison serves as a quick reference for selecting appropriate algorithms based on problem requirements.

Table 2.11: Common Machine Learning Algorithms and Their Characteristics

Algorithm	Inductive Bias	Strengths	Weaknesses	Typical Applications
Linear Regression	Linearity	Interpretable, stable, efficient	Limited capacity for complex patterns	Trend analysis, simple prediction, baseline Modellig
Decision Trees	Axis-parallel splits	Handles mixed data types, interpretable	High variance, prone to overfitting	Rule extraction, classification with clear decision boundaries
Random Forests	Ensemble of trees	Robust, handles high dimensionality, few parameters	Black box, computationally intensive	General-purpose supervised learning, feature importance analysis
SVM	Maximum margin	Effective in high dimensions, kernel flexibility	Sensitive to parameters and scaling	Text classification, image recognition, small-to-medium datasets

k-Means	Spherical, equal-sized clusters	Simple, scalable, intuitive	Requires k specification, sensitive to initialization	Customer segmentation, image compression, anomaly detection
Neural Networks	Hierarchical representations	Flexible, handles complex patterns, automatic feature learning	Data hungry, black box, parameter tuning challenges	Computer vision, NLP, complex pattern recognition, deep learning applications
Naive Bayes	Conditional independence	Fast, probabilistic, works well with small data	Oversimplified independence assumption	Text classification, spam detection, real-time prediction
Gradient Boosting	Sequential error correction	High performance, handles mixed data, good with imbalanced classes	Can overfit, parameter sensitive, sequential nature limits parallelization	Competitions, tabular data problems, predictive analytics
kNN	Local similarity	Non-parametric, simple, adaptable	Computationally expensive for large datasets, curse of dimensionality	Recommendation systems, pattern recognition, imputation
DBSCAN	Density-based clusters	Discovers arbitrary shapes, no cluster count needed	Sensitive to parameter settings, struggles with varying densities	Spatial clustering, anomaly detection, noise identification

This section on Basic Learning Theory establishes the theoretical foundations and practical approaches for designing effective machine learning systems. Understanding these principles allows practitioners to make informed decisions throughout the Modelling process, from algorithm selection to evaluation and deployment. The interplay between data characteristics, model properties, and learning objectives forms the core of successful machine learning applications.

Chapter Summary and Concluding Thoughts

This chapter has explored the critical components of data analysis and feature engineering that form the foundation of successful machine learning systems. We began by examining the fundamental nature of data—structured, unstructured, and semi-structured—and its essential role in machine learning. Through descriptive statistics and visualization techniques, we learned how to extract initial insights from data distributions and identify key patterns that inform further analysis.

The exploration of bivariate and multivariate relationships revealed how variables interact, with correlation and covariance providing quantitative measures of these relationships. Advanced visualization techniques like scatter plot matrices, parallel coordinates, and heatmaps enable data scientists to comprehend complex multidimensional patterns that would otherwise remain hidden. Feature engineering emerged as a crucial step that transforms raw data into more effective representations through selection, extraction, and transformation techniques.

We addressed the common challenges of missing data and outliers, presenting systematic approaches to handle these issues without compromising data integrity. Dimensionality reduction techniques—particularly PCA, t-SNE, and UMAP—provide powerful tools for managing high-dimensional data while preserving essential information. Finally, our examination of basic learning theory established the theoretical framework that underpins all machine learning systems, highlighting the importance of inductive bias, the bias-variance tradeoff, and generalization in model design and evaluation.

The concepts covered in this chapter demonstrate that data analysis and feature engineering are not merely preliminary steps but rather integral, ongoing processes that significantly impact model performance. The quality of data preparation often determines the ultimate success of machine learning applications more than the choice of algorithm itself. As machine learning continues to evolve, the principles outlined in this chapter remain fundamental—understanding your data deeply, transforming it thoughtfully, and designing learning systems with clear theoretical foundations will continue to be essential skills for any practitioner in the field. The next chapters will build upon these foundations, exploring specific algorithms and more advanced techniques that leverage the well-prepared data that results from applying the methods presented here.

Conceptual Questions:

1. Define and differentiate between structured, unstructured, and semi-structured data. Provide examples of each type.
2. Explain the importance of feature engineering in machine learning. How does it improve model performance?
3. Discuss the role of descriptive statistics in data analysis. What are the key measures of central tendency and dispersion?
4. Describe the process and significance of dimensionality reduction. How do PCA and t-SNE differ in their approaches?
5. What are the major differences between correlation and covariance? Provide examples where each would be useful.
6. Summarize the key techniques for handling missing data and outliers during preprocessing.
7. Explain the bias-variance tradeoff in the context of machine learning model design.
8. Discuss multivariate visualization techniques and their role in understanding complex datasets.

Application-Based Questions:

9. Given a dataset with numerical and categorical features, outline the steps for feature selection and extraction.
10. Design a preprocessing pipeline for a dataset with missing values, outliers, and high-dimensional features.

11. Create a scenario where univariate, bivariate, and multivariate analysis would be necessary. Justify the choice of techniques.
12. Explain how you would choose between PCA, t-SNE, and UMAP for dimensionality reduction in a given dataset.

Critical Thinking Questions:

13. Why is data quality considered more critical than algorithm selection in machine learning projects?
14. Discuss the ethical implications of improperly handling outliers in datasets.
15. Propose a method for integrating domain knowledge into feature engineering for a healthcare dataset.

Chapter - 3

Similarity Based Learning and Regression

- Similarity-Based Learning
- Nearest-Neighbor Learning
- Weighted K-Nearest-Neighbor Algorithm
- Nearest Centroid Classifier
- Locally Weighted Regression (LWR)
- Regression Analysis
- Linear Regression and Variants (Multiple, Polynomial, Logistic Regression)
- Decision Tree Learning
- Decision Tree Models and Induction Algorithms

Chapter Overview

This chapter explores similarity-based learning methods and regression techniques that form essential components of the machine learning toolkit. We begin by examining how algorithms can make predictions based on the similarity between data points, focusing on k-Nearest Neighbors (k-NN) and its variants. The chapter then transitions to regression analysis, covering linear, polynomial, and logistic regression methods. Finally, we introduce decision tree learning as another powerful approach to both classification and regression tasks. Throughout the chapter, we emphasize the theoretical foundations, practical implementations, advantages, and limitations of each technique.

3.1 Introduction to Similarity-Based Learning

Similarity-based learning is an essential concept of machine learning which suggests that objects with similar features are likely to belong to the same category or produce comparable/similar results. An intuitive method mimics the way humans categorize and perceive things around them-the world. For instance, we could classify an unknown fruit as an apple because it shares attributes such as color, size, and form with previous apples we've seen. This concept is formalized in machine learning by comparing data points with a similarity measure like Euclidean distance, cosine similarity, or other domain-specific metrics.

The k-Nearest Neighbors (k-NN) method exemplifies/epitomizes similarity-based learning. It classifies a given data point by examining its k nearest neighbors in the feature space and assigns it to the majority class among those neighbors. This algorithm is simple yet powerful, as it makes predictions directly from stored data without the need for explicit training. In addition to classification, similarity-based algorithms are employed in regression, recommendation systems, and clustering tasks, showing their versatility. These methods' strength lies in their ability to adapt to complex patterns and relationships in data while staying interpretable and simple to implement.

While similarity-based learning is apparent/intuitive it does have disadvantages/chllanges. When a dataset has noise, irrelevant features, or uneven distributions, the performance of such algorithms suffers. In addition, they frequently necessitate careful parameter tuning/adjustments, such as the number of neighbors (k), to prevent underfitting or overfitting. Notwithstanding these challenges, similarity-based learning has become an important concept in machine learning, providing as a foundation for more complex models and methodologies.

3.1.1 Nearest Neighbour Learning Concepts

Nearest Neighbour (NN) learning is one of the most intuitive machine learning algorithms, using a similarity principle to develop predictions. When presented with a new instance, the algorithm finds the closest comparable example in the training dataset and assigns it a label to new instance. This strategy is based on the assumption that similar data points are likely to have the same label or output. Its simplicity, lack of a formal training phase, and flexibility to adapt to different types of data input make NN learning a fundamental idea in machine learning.

Three important factors determine Nearest Neighbor Learning's performance. First, a distance metric is used to measure the similarity of data points, with prominent choices being Euclidean distance, Manhattan distance, and cosine similarity. Second, a set of labelled training examples is necessary to compare to the new instance. These instances describe the knowledge basis from which predictions are arrived at. Finally, a decision rule is employed to assign a label, usually by selecting the label from the nearest training example. This simple strategy can be expanded to include multiple neighbors, as demonstrated in k-Nearest Neighbor (k-NN), to improve robustness and noise reduction. While NN learning is computationally expensive for big datasets, its simplicity and effectiveness have made it a key component of instance-based learning systems.

1. **A distance metric**: A method to quantify similarity between data points
2. **Training examples**: A collection of labelled instances
3. **A decision rule**: How to assign a label based on nearest neighbours

The most common distance metrics include: Euclidean and Manhattan distances metrics were discussed in chapter-2. For the sake of recapturing, these concepts have been presented below:

Euclidean distance: The Euclidean distance is the straight-line distance between two points in a multidimensional space. It is defined as:

$$d_E = \sqrt{\sum_{i=1}^{n} (x_i - y_i)^2} \text{........2.15}$$

- **Manhattan distance**: The Manhattan distance, also known as the **L1 norm** or **taxicab distance**, measures the total absolute difference between the coordinates of two points in a multi-dimensional space. This distance metric is particularly useful when measuring distances in grid-like paths, such as city blocks or pixels in images.

$$d_M = \sum_{i=1}^{n} |x_i - y_i| \text{..........} \mathbf{2.16}$$

- **Minkowski distance**: Minkowski Distance Minkowski distance is a generalized metric for measuring the distance between two points in a multi-dimensional space. It is a parameterized distance metric that includes both Euclidean distance (when p=2) **Manhattan distance** (when p=1p = 1p=1) as special cases.

$$d(x, y) = (\sum_{i=1}^{n} |x_i - y_i|^p)^{1/p} \text{......} \mathbf{3.1}$$

Where:

- x and yare two points in nnn-dimensional space,
- p is the order parameter, determining the type of distance metric.
- **Cosine similarity**: Cosine similarity measures the similarity between two vectors by calculating the cosine of the angle between them. It evaluates how aligned two vectors are, regardless of their magnitude, making it especially useful in text analysis and high-dimensional data.

$$\textit{Cosine similarity} = \frac{A.B}{\square A \square\square B \square} \text{......} \mathbf{3.2}$$

Where:

- A·B is the dot product of vectors A and B,
- ‖A‖ and ‖B‖ are the magnitudes of A and B respectively.

The choice of distance metric significantly influences the performance of nearest neighbor algorithms and should be selected based on the specific characteristics of the data.

Advantages of Nearest Neighbor methods:

- Simple to understand and implement
- No explicit training phase required
- Can model complex decision boundaries
- Adapts easily as new training data becomes available

Disadvantages:

- Computationally expensive during prediction
- Sensitive to irrelevant features
- Requires careful feature scaling
- Memory-intensive (must store entire training set

Illustration of Nearest Neighbour classification in a 2D feature space is presented in fiture 3.1

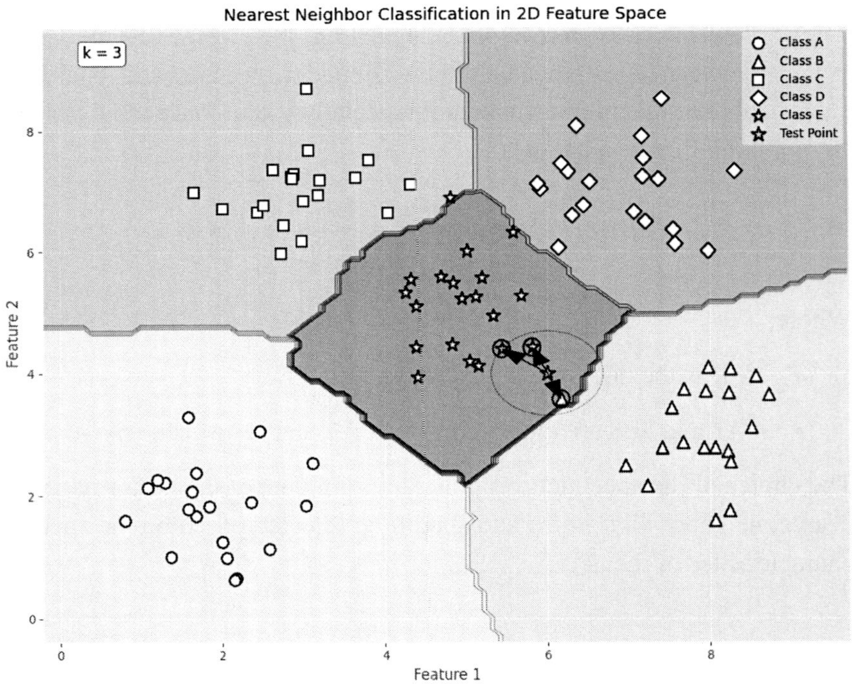

Figure 3.1: Illustration of Nearest Neighbour classification in a 2D feature space

3.1.2 k-Nearest Neighbour (k-NN) Algorithm

The k-Nearest Neighbor (k-NN) approach is a non-parametric, instance-based learning to classify a data point based on the labels of its k nearest neighbors in the feature space. Unlike single-nearest neighbor techniques, which rely exclusively on the closest data point for prediction, k-NN uses information from multiple neighbors to make a decision. This aggregation is resistant to noise and outliers, as consensus from numerous points frequently leads to better predictions. The hyperparameter k has a substantial impact on model performance. A little k could lead to overfitting, whereas a large $k$can smooth out crucial information.

The algorithm operates in three stages. The distance between the query point and all data points in the training set is first calculated using a distance metric, such as the Euclidean, Manhattan, or Minkowski distance. The query point's neighborhood is formed by identifying the k nearby points. Finally, for classification tasks, the query point is assigned the class label that appears the most frequently among its neighbors, and for regression tasks, the algorithm predicts the average or weighted average of the neighbors' results. This simplicity and versatility make k-NN a crucial building component for machine learning applications ranging from image categorization to anomaly detection.

While k-NN is easy to implement and interpret, it is computationally intensive, particularly for large datasets. Its reliance on distance metrics makes it sensitive to feature scale and distribution, necessitating normalization or standardization. In addition, irrelevant or highly correlated features might skew/distort distance forecasts, necessitating feature selection or dimensionality reduction as preprocessing steps. Despite these challenges, k-NN is still commonly used due to its versatility, ease of implementation, and ability to handle classification and regression problems.

Algorithm steps:

1. Choose a value for k and a distance metric
2. For a new instance x: a. Calculate distance between x and all training examples b. Select the k training examples closest to x c. Assign the most common class among these k neighbours (for

classification) d. Calculate the average of the k neighbours' target values (for regression)

Selecting k:

- Small k values: More sensitive to noise but can capture fine-grained patterns
- Large k values: Smoother decision boundaries but may miss important patterns
- Common practice: Use odd values of k (to avoid ties in binary classification)
- k can be optimized using cross-validation

Algorithmic complexity:

$$Time\,Complexity = O(nd + n\log n) \ldots\ldots 3.3(a)$$

$$Space\,complexity = O(nd) \ldots\ldots\ldots\ldots\ldots 3.3(b)$$

Pseudocode for k-NN classification:

```
function k_NN_Classify(training_set, x_new, k):
  distances = []
  for each example (x_i, y_i) in training_set:
    d = distance(x_new, x_i)
    distances.append((d, y_i))
  sort distances in ascending order
  neighbors = first k elements of distances
  return most_frequent_class(neighbors)
```

In figure 3.2 effect of different k values on decision boundaries is presented.

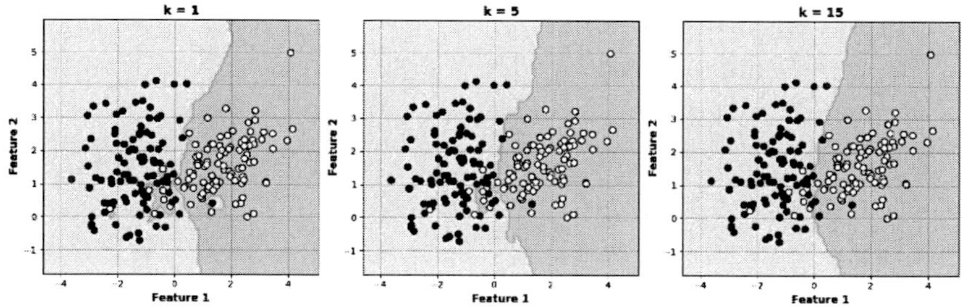

Figure 3.2: Effect of different k values on decision boundaries

3.2 Extensions to k-NN

While the basic k-NN algorithm is powerful, several extensions have been developed to address its limitations and enhance its performance across different scenarios.

3.2.1 Weighted k-NN

In standard k-Nearest Neighbour (k-NN), all neighbours contribute equally to the classification or regression decision, regardless of distance from the query position. This equal weighting can often result in inadequate/suboptimal predictions, particularly when closer neighbors better match the query point's true class or value. Weighted k-NN overcomes this limitation by weighting neighbours according to their distance from the query point. Closer neighbors are typically given higher weights, indicating that they are more relevant to the prediction. This adjustment can increase the model's sensitivity to local trends while reducing the impact of outliers or less important distant points.

In weighted k-NN, the inverse of the distance is commonly used as a weighting system. For example, $\boldsymbol{w_i = 1 / d_i}$. The distance between the query point and the i-th neighbor is denoted by di Other versions, such as Gaussian or exponential decay functions, are also employed to highlight proximity while smoothing out the effect of weight discrepancies. By incorporating these weights, weighted k-NN enhances its ability to handle datasets with varying density or noise levels, resulting in more robust and accurate predictions. This flexibility makes weighted k-NN an important expansion of the traditional k-NN algorithm, especially in complex real-world situations where local context is vital for decision-making.

Common weighting schemes:

1. **Inverse distance weighting**: The weight decreases inversely with the distance between the query point xxx and its neighbor x_i

$$x_i = \frac{1}{d(x, x_i)} \text{.......3.4}$$

Exponential weighting: Exponential weighting assigns weights to neighbors based on an exponential decay function, where closer neighbors receive higher weights.

$$w_i = e^{-d(x, x_i)} \text{...........3.5}$$

Where:

- W_i is the weight assigned to the ith neighbour,
- $d(x,x_i)$ is the distance between the query point x and the ith neighbour.

2. **Kernel weighting**: Kernel weighting, particularly using the Gaussian kernel, assigns weights based on the squared distance between the query point and its neighbours, scaled by a parameter σ which controls the spread of the weights.

$$w_i = e^{-\frac{d(x, x_i)^2}{2\sigma^2}} \text{...........3.6}$$

- W_i is the weight assigned to the ith neighbour,
- $d(x,x_i)$ is the distance between the query point x and the ith neighbour.
- σ i s the bandwidth parameter that influences the smoothness of the weights.

Algorithm modification:

- For classification: Instead of counting votes equally, sum the weights associated with each class
- For regression: Calculate a weighted average of target values

Advantages:

- Reduces the influence of distant neighbors
- Smoother transition between decision regions
- Often better performance than standard k-NN

Implementation considerations:

- Weight normalization: o normalize the weights so they sum to 1, the following equation is used. This normalization ensures that the weights are proportional and their total contribution is uniformly scaled.

$$\mathbf{w}' = \frac{\mathbf{w}^{\mathbf{i}}}{\sum_{\mathbf{j}=1}^{\mathbf{k}} \mathbf{w}_{\mathbf{j}}} \text{.........}\mathbf{3.7}$$

Where:

- w_i' is the normalized weight for the iii-th neighbor,
- W_i is the original weight assigned to the i-th neighbour,
- $\sum_{j=1}^{k} w_j$ is the sum of the weights of all k neighbours.
- Kernel bandwidth selection (for kernel weighting)
- Computational overhead slightly higher than standard k-NN

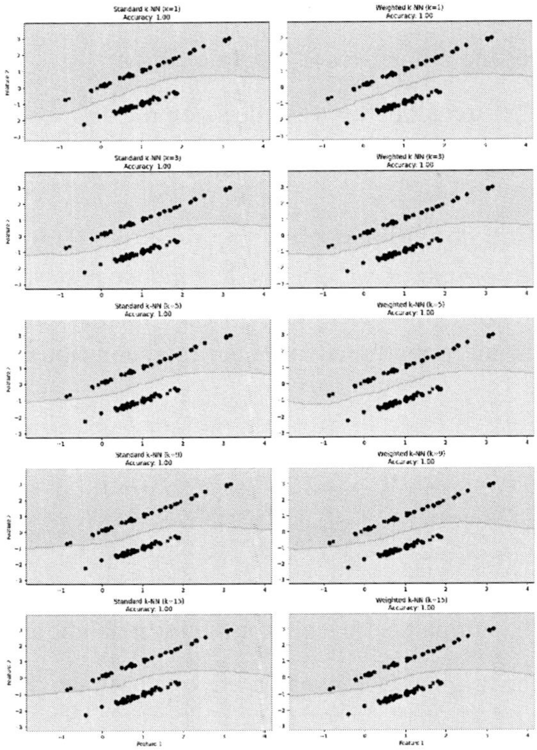

Figure 3.3: Comparison of standard k-NN and weighted k-NN decision boundaries

Figure 3.3 illustrates the impact of varying k-values on the decision boundaries of **standard k-NN** and **weighted k-NN** classifiers. The left column shows decision boundaries for standard k-NN, where all neighbours contribute equally, while the right column demonstrates weighted k-NN, which assigns higher importance to closer neighbours using distance-based weights. As k increases (from k=1 to k=15k), the decision boundaries become smoother. Smaller kkk values lead to more detailed and jagged boundaries, making the model highly sensitive to noise and prone to overfitting. On the other hand, larger kkk values result in smoother boundaries, reducing noise sensitivity but risking underfitting by oversimplifying the decision regions.

The comparison highlights the strengths of weighted k-NN, where closer neighbours influence the decision more than distant ones, leading to refined decision boundaries. Weighted k-NN performs better in scenarios with imbalanced or noisy data by reducing the impact of less-relevant points. Standard k-NN relies solely on the majority vote among k neighbours, making it more susceptible to outliers and distant points. Figure 3.3 emphasizes the importance of selecting an appropriate k-value and showcases how weighted k-NN can provide more reliable classifications in complex or unevenly distributed datasets.

3.2.2 Nearest Centroid Classifier

The Nearest Centroid Classifier is a lightweight alternative to k-NN that lessens computational complexity while retaining good classification performance. Instead of saving all training examples, this algorithm computes the centroid (or mean vector) of each class during training. A centroid is the geometric center of all data points from that class in the feature space. During prediction, a new instance is classified by calculating its nearest centroid using a distance metric, such as Euclidean or Manhattan distance. The Nearest Centroid Classifier uses significantly fewer memory and computing resources than k-NN since it summarizes each class with a single representative point.

This strategy is more effective when classes are linearly separable or the data points in each class are distributed symmetrically around a central mean. It may struggle with non-linear boundaries or datasets with overlapping classes, though, because the centroid does not capture complex distributions or intra-class shifts/variations. Despite its simplicity, the Nearest Centroid Classifier is widely employed in applications such as text classification, which frequently have sparse and high-dimensional information. Its interpretability, efficiency, and ease of implementation make it a useful tool for situations requiring quick and approximate classifications.

Algorithm steps:

1. **Training phase:**
    - Calculate the centroid for each class:
    - Store only these centroids

2. **Prediction phase:**
    - Assign the new instance to the class with the closest centroid

Key characteristics:

- Significantly faster prediction time than k-NN
- Much lower memory requirements
- Less sensitive to individual noisy examples
- Unable to model complex decision boundaries
- Works best when classes are well-separated and roughly spherical

Variations:

The Regularized Nearest Centroid classifier modifies the traditional technique by reducing the class centroids to the global centroid of all training data points. This regularization reduces the effects of noisy or sparsely distributed data, particularly when individual class centroids are affected/skewed by outliers. In moving the centroids closer to the global center, the model becomes more robust/resilient to minor variations in the data and achieves higher generalization. This approach is especially useful when dealing with small datasets or datasets with highly skewed class distributions, as class-specific centroids may not properly represent the underlying data structure.

- **Regularized Nearest Centroid**: Shrinks class centroids toward the global centroid

The Soft Nearest Centroid classifier utilizes a probabilistic methodology, assigning new examples to classes based on their relative distances from all centroids. Instead of making a hard decision-making based merely on the nearest centroid, the algorithm considers/computes probabilities for each class, frequently employing a softmax function. These probabilities represent the likelihood that a new instance will belong to each class. This soft decision-making approach yields more nuanced predictions and is especially beneficial in cases involving high uncertainty or large data point overlap between classes. Both of these enhancements will increase the

Nearest Centroid Classifier's versatility and applicability, allowing it to handle a greater range of real-world datasets effectively.

- **Soft Nearest Centroid**: Uses probabilistic assignments based on distances

Table 3.1 provides a comprehensive comparison of three k-NN variants—Standard k-NN, Weighted k-NN, and Nearest Centroid—across critical metrics including computational efficiency, performance characteristics, and practical implementation considerations. This comparative analysis highlights the trade-offs between these algorithms, illustrating how Standard k-NN offers complex decision boundaries but poor scalability, Weighted k-NN improves handling of imbalanced data while maintaining flexibility, and Nearest Centroid dramatically reduces computational requirements at the expense of modelling capability.

Table 3.1: Comparison of k-NN variants across different metrics

Feature	Standard k-NN	Weighted k-NN	Nearest Centroid
Training time	O(1) - No explicit training	O(1) - No explicit training	O(n) - Computing centroids
Prediction time	O(nd + n log k)	O(nd + n log k)	O(cd) - c = number of classes
Memory requirements	High - Entire training set	High - Entire training set	Low - Only centroids
Decision boundary complexity	Complex, non-linear	Complex, non-linear	Linear
Sensitivity to noise	High with small k	Moderate	Low
Sensitivity to irrelevant features	High	High	Moderate

Handling of imbalanced classes	Poor with standard k	Better with distance weighting	Poor without adjustments
Interpretability	High - Based on similar examples	High - Based on similar examples	High - Based on class prototypes
Hyperparameter tuning	k value	k value and weighting function	Few or none
Scalability to large datasets	Poor	Poor	Good
Handling of missing values	Requires imputation	Can incorporate in distance metric	Robust if few missing values
Adaptability to new data	Excellent - Just add examples	Excellent - Just add examples	Requires recomputing centroids
Optimal application scenarios	Small to medium datasets with clear local patterns	Problems where distance is meaningful for similarity	Well-separated classes with roughly spherical distributions

3.3 Locally Weighted Regression (LWR)

Locally Weighted Regression (LWR) is a versatile extension of similarity-based learning created to solve regression problems. Unlike global regression models, which apply a single function to an entire dataset, LWR creates localized models that are tailored to a specific region of the feature space near the query point. This is accomplished by giving higher weights to nearby data points while decreasing the influence of ones farther away. weighing is usually carried out using a kernel function, such as a Gaussian kernel, with weights determined by the distance between the query and data points. This approach enables LWR to adapt its predictions to local patterns and variations, making it especially useful in situations involving non-linear relationships or heterogeneous data distributions.

The procedure involves using a simple model, typically a linear regression, on a weighted subset of data points around the query point. The model is recalculated for each query point, focusing on local data while ignoring distant portions of the feature space. This localized method makes LWR extremely adaptable, capturing complicated patterns without assuming a set global structure. In contrast to traditional linear regression, LWR is capable of modelling deviations in relationships between features and output across regions.

However, the benefits of LWR are offset by higher computational costs. Since the model must recompute weights and train a local regression for each query point, it can be computationally expensive for big/large datasets or high-dimensional feature spaces. Choosing the appropriate kernel function and bandwidth parameter (σ) is essential for optimal performance. Despite these problems, LWR remains a powerful tool for regression tasks demanding great flexibility and adaptation, particularly in domains like as robotics, economics, and medical diagnostics, where localized patterns are prevalent.

3.3.1 Non-Parametric Regression Techniques

Non-parametric regression methods are a type of method which relies on few assumptions about the underlying data distribution, providing a flexible approach to modelling complex relations. Unlike parametric methods, which use a predefined functional form (such as a linear or polynomial connection), non-parametric methods let the data "speak for itself" by generating the model structure directly from the observed data. These methods are particularly useful when the data has nonlinear relationships or heterogeneity that a fixed global model cannot fully reflect. Kernel regression, smoothing splines, and Locally Weighted Regression (LWR) are among the most used nonparametric regression methods.

Locally Weighted Regression (LWR) is an example for the non-parametric method by fitting localized models to specific a part/region of the feature space. By weighting data points based on their closeness to the query location, LWR successfully adapts to local trends while preventing a rigid global structure. This makes it appropriate for datasets with complicated/complex relationships between regions, where standard parametric models would fail. Non-parametric regression techniques are more flexible, but they demand more processing resources namely computationally complexity because the model must modify dynamically for each prediction. Despite this, their ability to simulate complicated, real-world phenomena with few assumptions has made them useful in domains such as machine learning, environmental modelling, and finance.

Key characteristics of non-parametric regression:

- No fixed number of parameters
- Greater flexibility in capturing complex relationships
- Typically requires more data than parametric approaches
- Often computationally intensive
- Risk of overfitting without proper regularization

Locally Weighted Regression principles:

1. For each query point, construct a local regression model
2. Weight nearby points more heavily than distant ones
3. Discard the local model after making the prediction
4. **Mathematical Formulation for Locally Weighted Regression**

The goal of Locally Weighted Regression (LWR) is to minimize a weighted error term for a query point xxx, as shown in Equation (3.8):

$$\sum_{i=1}^{n} K(d(x, x_i))(y_i - f(x_i))^2 \qquad (3.8)$$

Where:

- K is the **kernel function** that determines weights based on the distance d(x,xi)d(x, x_i)d(x,xi),
- y_i is the actual value of the iii-th training point,

- $f(x_i)$ is the predicted value at the iii-th training point,
- $d(x,x_i)$is the distance between the query point x and the ith training point.

Common Kernel Functions

- **Gaussian Kernel**:

  The Gaussian kernel assigns weights based on the squared distance, scaled by a bandwidth parameter σ:

$$K(d) = e^{-\frac{d^2}{2\sigma^2}} \text{ ....3.9}$$

- Tricube: The Tricube kernel reduces the weight to zero for points beyond a unit distance and assigns weights within the range using a cubic function:

$$\text{Tricube} K(d) = \left(1 - |d|^3\right)^3 \text{ for } |d| < 1,\ 0 \text{ otherwise......3.10}$$

- Epanechnikov: The Epanechnikov kernel uses a quadratic function to assign weights within the range |d|<1:

$$K(d) = \frac{3}{4}\left(d^2\right) \text{for } |d| < 1, 0 \text{otherwise......3.11}$$

Figure 3.4 illustrates the difference between Global Linear Regression (top) and Locally Weighted Regression (LWR) with different bandwidth parameters (bottom). The top plot shows a single linear model trying to fit non-linear data, resulting in higher error (MSE: 6.7814). Tau (τ) is the bandwidth parameter in LWR that controls the "locality" of the regression - smaller values (τ=0.5) create very local models that fit the data more closely, while larger values (τ=2.0) result in smoother but less accurate fits. As shown in the bottom plots, the smallest τ value produces the lowest error (MSE: 0.1979) because it most precisely follows the non-linear pattern in the data.

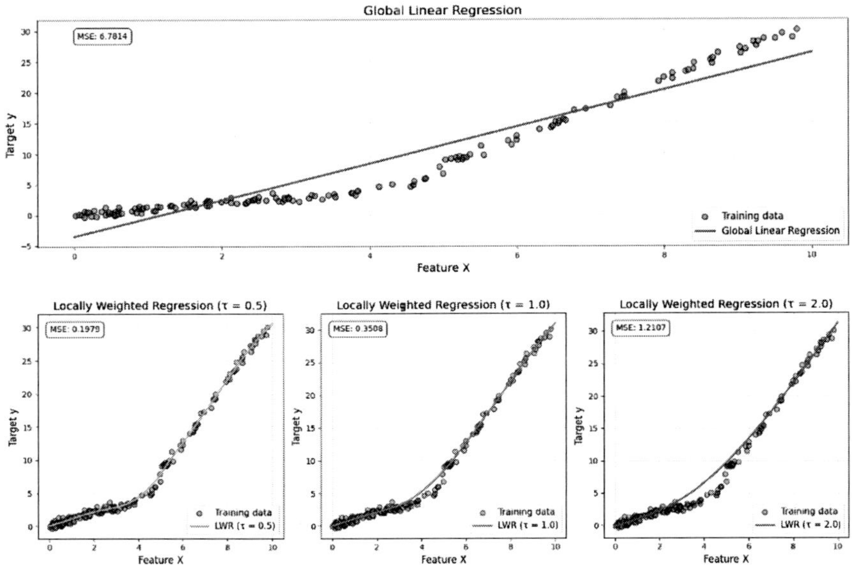

Figure 3.4: Comparison of global linear regression and locally weighted regression

3.3.2 Applications and Limitations

Locally Weighted Regression (LWR) is a versatile technique that has found applications in a number of domains. In time series prediction, LWR can adapt to changing trends and local patterns, making it useful for forecasting instances/problems where variable relationships change over time. In computer vision, it is used for tasks such as image smoothing and augmentation by approximating pixel intensities based on their surroundings. LWR enhances adaptability in control systems and robotics by allowing robots to make decisions based on localized data patterns, such as altering motor control or trajectory planning. Additionally, recommender systems benefit from LWR's ability to model user preferences locally, providing individualized recommendations depending on user behavior. Spatial data analysis also use LWR for tasks such as mapping and geographic modelling, which require localized interactions.

Applications of LWR:

- Time series prediction
- Computer vision (image smoothing and enhancement)

- Control systems and robotics
- Recommender systems
- Spatial data analysis

Limitations: Despite its usefulness, LWR has some significant limits. The computational cost of LWR is considerable for large datasets since the model must recompute weights and solve a local regression problem for each query point. This renders it less suitable for real-time applications involving vast amounts of data. LWR performance is highly dependent on the kernel function and bandwidth parameter (τ), which must be carefully tuned to avoid overfitting or underfitting. LWR also fails in high-dimensional spaces because to the curse of dimensionality, in which data points become sparse and the concept of "locality" loses significance. Finally, it is vulnerable to noisy data, as outliers might disproportionately affect local models unless robust weighting mechanisms /schemes are used. Despite these problems, LWR is nevertheless an effective tool for applications that rely heavily on localized, non-linear associations/relations.

Computational complexity: Must perform a new regression for each prediction

1. **Curse of dimensionality**: Performance degrades in high-dimensional spaces
2. **Bandwidth selection**: Critical parameter that affects bias-variance tradeoff
3. **Boundary effects**: May perform poorly near the edges of the feature space
4. **Data sparsity issues**: Requires sufficient local data density

Implementation considerations:

- Fast neighbour lookup structures (KD-trees, ball trees)
- Approximate methods for large datasets
- Adaptive bandwidth selection techniques
- Feature selection or dimensionality reduction as preprocessing

Table 3.2 compares various regression approaches based on their training and prediction complexity, memory requirements, scalability, and real-time applicability. Although linear and polynomial regression are computationally easy/efficient and scale well to big datasets, non-parametric techniques such as k-NN regression and locally weighted regression (LWR) are computationally expensive and thus unsuitable for real-time or large-scale applications. The decision tree regression strikes a decent cbalance between moderate scalability and efficient prediction in applications of real time.

Table 3.2: Comparison of computational requirements between regression techniques

Technique	Training Complexity	Prediction Complexity	Memory Requirements	Scalability to Large Datasets	Real-time Applicability
Linear Regression	$O(nd^2)$	O(d)	O(d)	Good	Excellent
Polynomial Regression	$O(nd^2)$	O(d)	O(d)	Good	Excellent
k-NN Regression	O(1)*	O(nd + n log n)	O(nd)	Poor	Poor
Locally Weighted Regression	O(1)*	$O(nd^2 + nd)$	O(nd)	Poor	Poor
Decision Tree Regression	O(nd log n)	O(log n)	O(nodes)	Moderate	Good

3.4 Introduction to Regression Analysis

Regression analysis represents a fundamental approach to modelling relationships between variables, focusing on predicting continuous outputs rather than discrete categories.

Regressor

The **regressor** refers to the **independent variable(s)** in regression analysis, which are used to predict the **dependent variable** (target outcome).

Regressor Examples:

- **In predicting house prices:**
    - Regressors: Number of bedrooms, square footage, location
    - Dependent variable: House price
- **In predicting stock prices**:
    - Regressors: Historical stock prices, trading volume, economic indicators
    - Dependent variable: Future stock price
- **In estimating student performance**:
    - Regressors: Study hours, attendance, previous test scores
    - Dependent variable: Final exam score

Key concepts in regression:

- **Dependent variable**: The target value we want to predict
- **Independent variables**: Features used to make predictions
- **Residuals**: Differences between predicted and actual values
- **Fitted values**: The model's predictions on the training data

- **Regression coefficients**: Parameters that quantify relationships between variables

3.4.2 Types of Regression Problems

Regression problems can be categorized based on several dimensions:

By relationship type:

- **Simple regression**: Single independent variable
- **Multiple regression**: Multiple independent variables
- **Linear regression**: Linear relationship between variables
- **Nonlinear regression**: Nonlinear relationships modeled

By regression task:

- **Univariate regression**: Predicting a single output variable
- **Multivariate regression**: Predicting multiple output variables simultaneously
- **Ordinal regression**: Predicting ordered categorical variables
- **Count regression**: Predicting count data (e.g., Poisson regression)

By statistical approach:

- **Parametric regression**: Fixed form with finite parameters
- **Non-parametric regression**: Flexible form with unlimited parameters
- **Bayesian regression**: Incorporating prior distributions on parameters
- **Frequentist regression**: Maximum likelihood estimation approach

Figure 3.5 illustrates the relationship between a regressor (independent variable) and the dependent variable using a simple regression model. The data points represent observed values, while the dashed red line shows the fitted regression line. The text box highlights that the **regressor (X)** serves as the input feature used to predict the **dependent variable (y)**.

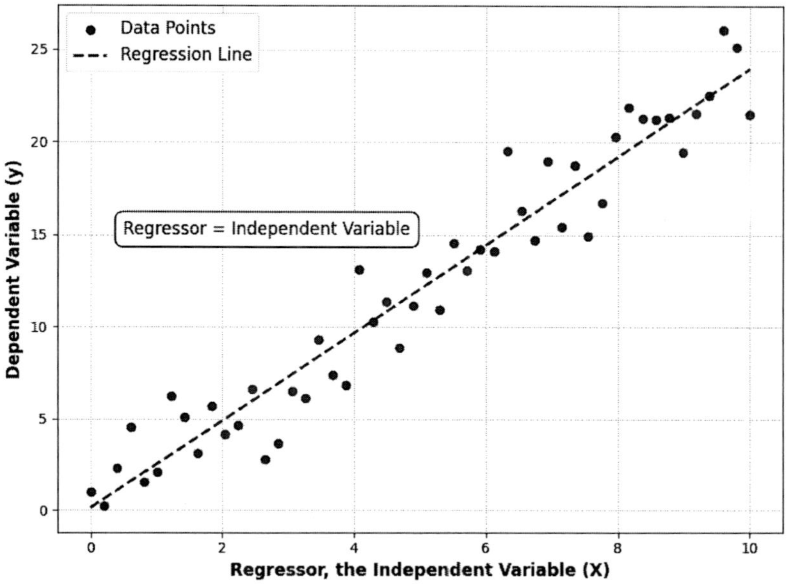

Figure 3.5: Illustrating the Relationship Between Regressor and Dependent Variable

3.5 Linear and Polynomial Regression

3.5.1 Simple Linear Regression

Simple Linear Regression

Simple linear regression establishes a relationship between one independent variable (X) and one dependent variable (Y) using a linear equation.

The Model:

$$Y = \beta_0 + \beta_1 X + \varepsilon \text{..............} \mathbf{3.12}$$

Where

- Y: Dependent variable
- X: Independent variable (Knowmn as Regressor
- β_0: Y-intercept (value of Y when X=0)
- β_1: Slope (change in Y for a unit change in X)

- ε: Error term (random variation not explained by the model)

Assumptions:

1. **Linearity:** The relationship between X and Y is linear
2. **Independence:** Observations are independent of each other
3. **Homoscedasticity**: Variance of residuals is constant across all X values
4. **Normality**: Residuals follow a normal distribution

Linear regression provides the foundation for many regression techniques, while polynomial regression extends this approach to capture non-linear relationships.

3.5.1 Linear Regression: Assumptions and Implementation

Linear regression models the relationship between a dependent variable y and one or more independent variables X using a linear combination:

$$y = \beta_0 + \beta_1 x_1 + \beta_2 x_2 + ... + \beta_n x_n + \epsilon$$

Where:

- β_0 is the intercept
- $\beta_1, \beta_2, ..., \beta_n$ are coefficients
- ϵ represents random error

Key assumptions:

1. **Linearity**: The relationship between X and y is linear
2. **Independence**: Observations are independent of each other
3. **Homoscedasticity**[a]: Constant variance of errors [see Heteroscedasticity footnote [b]]
4. **Normality**: Errors are normally distributed
5. **No multicollinearity**: Independent variables are not highly correlated

a. Homoscedasticity: Refers to the condition where the variance of residuals is constant across all levels of the independent variable.2Heteroscedasticity: **heteroscedasticity** refers to **varying variance** of residuals, not necessarily always increasing. The variance could increase, decrease, or fluctuate irregularly across the independent variable.

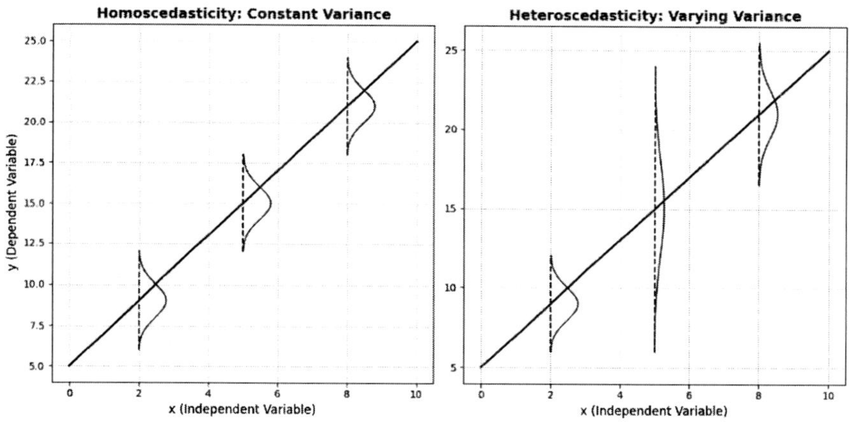

Figure 3.6 Illustration of the concepts of homoscedasticity and heteroscedasticity

Figure 3.6 contrasts the difference between homoscedasticity and heteroscedasticity in regression. In the first plot, residuals exhibit constant variance (homoscedasticity), fulfilling a key regression assumption. In contrast, the second plot shows increasing variance in residuals (heteroscedasticity), which violates this assumption and may impact the reliability of regression inferences.

Ordinary Least Squares (OLS) estimation: The coefficients are estimated by minimizing the sum of squared residuals:

Objective Function (Least Squares)

$$\textbf{minimize}\sum_{i=1}^{n}\left(y_i-\left(\beta_0+\beta_1x_1+\ldots..+\beta_px_p\right)\right)^2 \ldots..\mathbf{3.13}$$

Matrix formulation is $y = \boldsymbol{X\beta} + \boldsymbol{\varepsilon} \ldots\ldots\ldots \mathbf{3.14}$

Where:

- $\mathbf{y} = \begin{bmatrix} y_1 \\ y_2 \\ \vdots \\ y_n \end{bmatrix}$ (response vector)
- $\mathbf{X} = \begin{bmatrix} 1 & x_{11} & x_{12} & \cdots & x_{1p} \\ 1 & x_{21} & x_{22} & \cdots & x_{2p} \\ \vdots & \vdots & \vdots & \ddots & \vdots \\ 1 & x_{n1} & x_{n2} & \cdots & x_{np} \end{bmatrix}$ (design matrix)
- $\boldsymbol{\beta} = \begin{bmatrix} \beta_0 \\ \beta_1 \\ \vdots \\ \beta_p \end{bmatrix}$ (parameter vector)

Implementations:

1. **Closed-form solution**: Direct computation using matrix operations
2. **Gradient descent**: Iterative optimization for large datasets
3. **Stochastic gradient descent**: Processing one example at a time
4. **Ridge and Lasso regularization**: Adding penalty terms to prevent overfitting

Evaluation metrics:

- **Mean Squared Error (MSE)**:

$$\text{MSE} = \sum_{i=1}^{n} (y_i - \hat{y}_i)^2 \text{.....3.15}$$

- **Root Mean Squared Error (RMSE)**:

$$\text{RMSE} = \sqrt{\text{MSE}} = \sqrt{\sum_{i=1}^{n} (y_i - \hat{y}_i)^2} \text{......3.16}$$

- **Mean Absolute Error (MAE)**:

$$\text{MAE} = \frac{1}{n} |y_i - \hat{y}_i| \text{........3.17}$$

- **Coefficient of Determination (R^2)**: Proportion of variance explained by the model

$$(\mathbf{R}^2) = \mathbf{1} - \frac{\sum_{i=1}^{n} (y_i - \hat{y}_i)^2}{\sum_{i=1}^{n} (y_i - \bar{y})^2} \quad \text{.......}\mathbf{3.18}$$

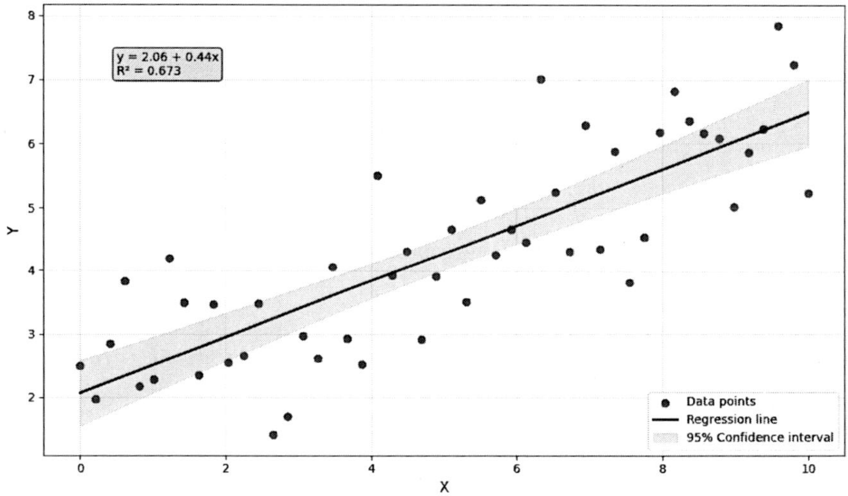

Figure 3.7: Linear regression with confidence intervals.

Figure 3.7 depicts linear regression analysis, with the red line representing the best-fit linear relationship among X and Y variables and the shaded grey region indicating the 95% confidence interval around the regression line. The confidence interval reflects the range of uncertainty in the predictions; it is broader at the extremes of the data range and narrower toward the center, signifying greater uncertainty when extrapolating beyond the observed data points.

Polynomial Regression:

Polynomial regression extends linear regression by adding polynomial terms of the independent variables to capture non-linear relationships. Polynomial regression analyses the relationship between an independent variable (x) and a dependent variable (y) using an n-degree polynomial. Unlike linear regression, which assumes a straight-line relationship, polynomial regression may represent curved patterns in data, making it suited for capturing non-linear relationships. This flexibility is especially valuable in cases where data points depart from a linear trend and exhibit peaks, troughs, or other deviations.

The model equation for polynomial regression is given as in equation 3.19.

$$Y = \beta_0 + \beta_1 X + \beta_2 X^2 + \beta_3 X^3 + \ldots. \beta_p X^p + \varepsilon \ldots\ldots 3.19$$

The Model:

- Y: Dependent variable
- X: Independent variable
- X^2, X^3, ..., X^p: Polynomial terms
- β_0, β_1, ..., β_p: Regression coefficients
- ε: Error term

For example, a quadratic regression (n=2) models a parabolic curve, while a cubic regression (n=3) can capture inflection points. Polynomial regression involves transforming the original independent variable into additional features that indicate its powers (e.g., $x^2, x^3, \ldots$). These features are subsequently used as inputs into a linear regression model. Despite the non-linear relationship between $x$and y, the transformed regression problem stays linear in the model coefficients, making it computationally efficient to solve.

However, care must be used while selecting the degree of the polynomial. Higher-degree polynomials can fit the training data extremely well, resulting in overfitting and poor generalization for new data. Conversely, an insufficient degree may fail to capture the underlying patterns. Cross-validation techniques can help determine the polynomial's appropriate degree in order to strike a balance between underfitting and overfitting.

Implementation Approach:

1. Create polynomial features by raising X to different powers
2. Use these polynomial features as independent variables in a standard linear regression model
3. OLS can still be used for parameter estimation

Choosing the Polynomial Degree:

- Higher degrees offer more flexibility but risk overfitting
- Lower degrees may not capture the true relationship (underfitting)
- Cross-validation can help determine the optimal degree

Implementation approach:

1. Generate polynomial features (x^2, x^3, etc.)
2. Treat these as additional independent variables
3. Apply standard linear regression techniques

Degree selection: Choosing the right degree for a polynomial regression model is essential for striking a fair balance between model complexity and generalizability. The degree determines the model's flexibility, with higher degrees capturing more detailed patterns but increasing the risk of overfitting. Lower degrees, on the other hand, may result in underfitting, which occurs when the model fails to capture the underlying trends in the data. The following bulleted points reveals the mechanism of choosing.

- Higher degree → More flexible model → Risk of overfitting
- Lower degree → Less flexible model → Risk of underfitting
- Cross-validation typically used to select optimal degree

Advantages:

- Simple extension of linear regression
- Can capture non-linear relationships
- Well-understood statistical properties
- Standard software implementations available

Limitations:

- Sensitive to outliers
- May oscillate between data points (high variance)
- Poor extrapolation beyond the range of training data
- Curse of dimensionality with interaction terms

Table 3.3 provides examples of polynomial regression models with varying degrees and their respective equations, R^2, and RMSE values. It demonstrates how increasing the degree of the polynomial improves model fit (higher R^2 and lower RMSE), but with diminishing returns beyond a certain degree.

Table 3.3 Example of Polynomial Regression Models.

Model	Equation	R^2	RMSE
Linear (p=1)	$Y = 10 + 5X$	0.75	12.5
Quadratic (p=2)	$Y = 8 + 3X + 2X^2$	0.89	8.2
Cubic (p=3)	$Y = 7 + 2X + 1.5X^2 + 0.5X^3$	0.94	6.1
Quartic (p=4)	$Y = 7 + 2X + 1.5X^2 + 0.5X^3 + 0.1X^4$	0.95	5.8

Regularization Methods in Regression

Regularization methods serve as vital tools in regression analysis for addressing the problem of overfitting, especially in models with high complexity or multicollinearity. Overfitting takes place when a model captures noise in training data, resulting in poor generalization to new/unseen/untrained data. Regularization addresses this issue by including penalty terms in the loss function, successfully restricting the model's complexity and reducing the size of its coefficients.

Ridge Regression (L2 Regularization):

Ridge regression, or L2 regularization, applies a penalty equal to the squared magnitude of the coefficients to the loss function. This penalty term discourages large coefficient values, increasing the model's resistance to multicollinearity and overfitting. The updated loss function for ridge regression is given in the following equation:

$$\textit{Ridge Regression}(L2)\,\textit{Loss} = \sum_{i=1}^{n}(y_i - \hat{y}_i)^2 + \lambda\sum_{j=1}^{p}\beta_i^2 \text{......3.20}$$

Here, λ is the regularization parameter controlling the strength of the penalty. As λ increases, the model coefficients shrink toward zero but

never become exactly zero. This makes ridge regression particularly suitable in situations where all predictors contribute to the outcome, but their impact varies in magnitude.

- **Objective function**: Minimize RSS + $\lambda \sum \beta^2_i$
    - RSS: Residual sum of squares is $\sum_{i=1}^{n}(y_i - \hat{y}_i)^2$
    - λ: Regularization parameter (controls penalty strength)
    - $\sum \beta^2_i$: Sum of squared coefficients
- Shrinks coefficients toward zero but rarely makes them exactly zero
- Particularly useful when dealing with multicollinearity

Lasso Regression (L1 Regularization):

least absolute shrinkage and selection operator; also Lasso, LASSO or L1 regularization

Lasso regression, or L1regularization, introduces a penalty term proportional to the absolute value of the coefficients. The loss function for lasso regression is:

$$\textbf{\textit{Lasso Regression}}(\textbf{\textit{L}}1)\,\textbf{\textit{Loss}} = \sum_{i=1}^{n}(y_i - \hat{y}_i)^2 + \lambda \sum_{j=1}^{p}|\beta_i| \text{.....}\mathbf{3.21}$$

- **Objective function**: Minimize RSS + $\lambda \sum |\beta_i|$
    - $\sum |\beta_i|$: Sum of absolute values of coefficients
- Can shrink some coefficients exactly to zero, performing feature selection
- Good for high-dimensional data with many irrelevant features

Elastic Net: Elastic Net Regression Elastic Net combines the penalties of ridge and lasso regression, making it a hybrid approach. The loss function for elastic net is:

$$\textbf{\textit{ElasticNetLoss}} = \sum_{i=1}^{n}\left(y_i - y_i\right) + \lambda_1 \sum_{J=1}^{P}|\beta_j| + \lambda_2 \sum_{j=1}^{P}\beta_j^{\,2} \text{...}\mathbf{3.22}$$

- Combines both L1 and L2 penalties
- **Objective function**: Minimize RSS + $\lambda_1\sum|\beta_i| + \lambda_2\sum\beta^2_i$
- Balances the benefits of Ridge and Lasso

Selecting λ (Lambda):

- Cross-validation is typically used to find the optimal λ value
- $\lambda = 0$ corresponds to ordinary least squares
- As λ increases, the penalty effect becomes stronger

3.6 Logistic Regression

What is Logistic Regression?

Logistic Regression is an algorithm for supervised machine learning that is frequently used to model the likelihood of a given class or occurrence. It is most effective when the data is linearly separable, and the output variable is binary or dichotomous. This makes logistic regression suitable for binary classification problems which require predicting an output variable with two distinctive classes.

Binary classification involves foreseeing distinct outcomes such as Yes/No, Pass/Fail, Win/Loss, and Cancerous/Non-cancerous. Logistic regression is widely used in a variety of fields, including health, economics, and social sciences, for purposes such as disease diagnosis, credit risk assessment, and user behaviour modelling.

Despite its name, logistic regression is essentially a classification procedure, not a regression approach. It is used to predict whether an observation belongs to one of two classes (binary classification). Logistic regression produces probabilities on a continuous scale between 0 to 1, which can be threshold to provide a certain class label. This makes it ideal for applications such as spam identification, medical diagnosis, and binary decision-making tasks.

3.6.1 Classification Using Logistic Regression

The logistic regression model is expressed as: 3.23

$$P\left(y = 1/X\right) = \frac{1}{1+e^{-(\beta_0+\beta_1 X_1+\beta_2 X_2+...+\beta p Xp)}} ......3.23$$

Here:

- $P\left(y = 1/X\right)$ represents the probability of the target variable y being 1 given the input features X.
- β_0 is the intercept term, and $\beta_1, \beta_2, \beta_p$, are the coefficients for the features.
- $X_1, X_2, \ldots$, are the independent variables (features).
- e is the base of the natural logarithm.

The decision boundary is determined by a threshold, typically 0.5. For example, if $P\left(y = 1/X\right) > 0.5$, the observation is classified as belonging to class 1: therwise, it is classified as belonging to class 0.

The logistic regression model is trained by maximizing the likelihood of the observed data. This involves finding the coefficients (β\betaβ) that maximize the likelihood function: eqn3.24

$$L(B) = \prod_{1}^{n} P\left(y_i \mid 1/X\right)^{y_i} \left(1 - P\left(y_i \mid 1/X\right)^{1-y_i}\right) ......3.24$$

Likelihood is often used to simplify computation

$$\log L(B) = \sum_{i=1}^{n} \left| y_i \log P\left(y_i \mid 1/X\right) + (1-y_i)\log\left(1 - P\left(y_i \mid 1/X\right)\right) \right| .....3.25$$

The coefficients are typically estimated using optimization techniques like gradient descent. Logistic regression's simplicity, interpretability, and probabilistic framework make it a popular choice for binary classification tasks.

Decision boundary:

- Classify as positive if $P\left(y_i \mid \frac{1}{X}\right)$ > threshold (typically 0.5)
- This creates a linear decision boundary in the feature space

Types of Logistic Regressions:

There are two types of logistic regression. They are (1) **Simple Logistic Regression** utilizes a single independent variable to predict a binary result, and (2) **Multiple Logistic Regression**: Utilizes multiple independent variables to predict a binary outcome, allowing for more complex relationships between predictors and target variables.

Multi-class logistic regression:

- **One-vs-Rest**: Train binary classifiers for each class
- **Multinomial logistic regression**: Direct generalization using softmax function.

Logistic regression is an extension of linear regression tailored for classification problems. It applies the sigmoid (logistic) function to linearly predicted values, transforming them into probabilities within the range of 0 and 1. A threshold value, typically 0.5, is then used to classify the predictions into binary outcomes. Figure 3.8 contrasts the key difference between linear and logistic regression for binary classification. While linear regression can produce predictions beyond the range of 0 and 1, logistic regression uses the sigmoid function to constrain predictions within this range, making it more suitable for classifying binary outcomes with a threshold, typically set at 0.5.

Logistic regression models the relationship between independent variables (X) and the probability of an outcome (P) using the logistic (or sigmoid) function. The logistic function converts any real-valued input into a value between 0 and 1, guaranteeing that expected probability are correct.

Figure 3.9 depicts the sigmoid function used in logistic regression, showing how it maps input values to probabilities between 0 and 1. The decision boundary at x=0 and the classification threshold at P=0.5 highlight the separation of binary classes.

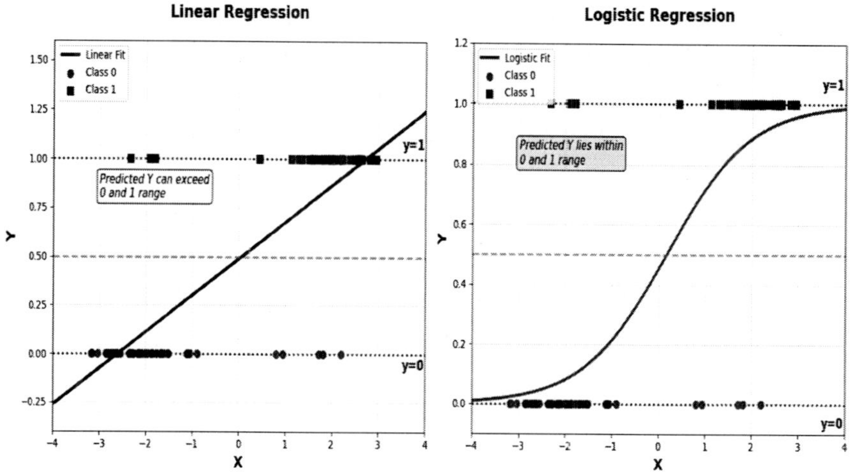

Figure 3.8: Comparison of Linear Regression and Logistic Regression for Binary Classification

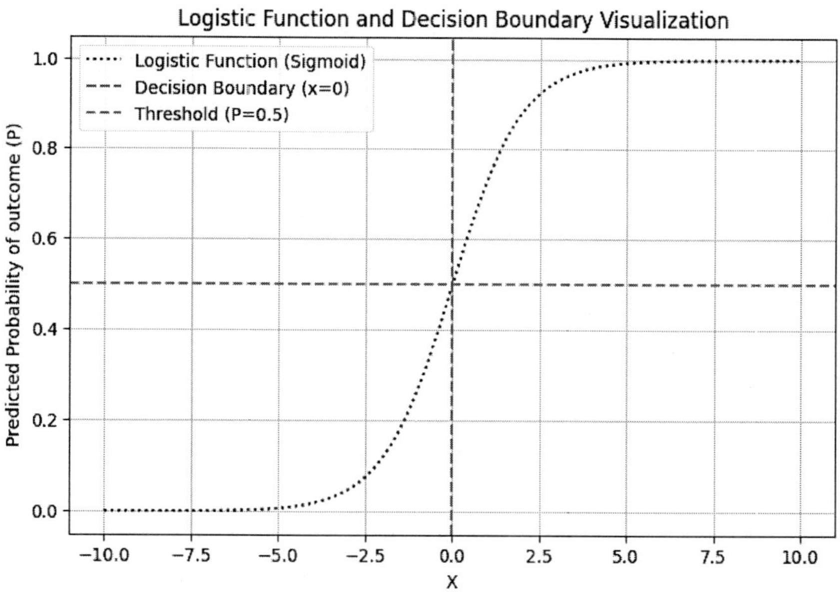

Figure 3.9: Logistic function and decision boundary visualization

3.6.2 Performance Evaluation Metrics

Proper evaluation of logistic regression models requires metrics that provide deeper insights into the model's performance beyond simple accuracy. These metrics assess the balance between true positives, false positives, and false negatives, helping to evaluate the model's effectiveness in various classification scenarios. The following are commonly used evaluation metrics in logistic regression:

Confusion matrix components:

- True Positives (TP): Correctly predicted positive cases
- True Negatives (TN): Correctly predicted negative cases
- False Positives (FP): Incorrectly predicted positive cases
- False Negatives (FN): Incorrectly predicted negative cases

Common evaluation metrics:

1. **Accuracy**:

$$Accuracy = \frac{TP}{TP + TN + FP + FN} \quad ..3.26$$

2. **Precision**:

$$Precision = \frac{TP}{TP + FP} \quad ..3.27$$

3. **Recall (Sensitivity)**:

$$Recall = \frac{TP}{TP + FN} \quad .....3.28$$

4. **F1-Score**:

$$\mathrm{F1Score} = 2\frac{Precision.Recall}{Precision + Recall} \quad ....3.29$$

AUC-ROC: Area under the Receiver Operating Characteristic curve

5. **Log loss**:

$$\mathrm{Log\,Loss} = -\frac{1}{n}\sum_{i=1}^{n}\left|y_i \log(p_i) + (1 - y_i)\log(1 - (p_i)\right| ...3.30$$

These metrics collectively provide a comprehensive assessment of logistic regression model performance, guiding improvements and comparisons across models.

Threshold selection:

- Different thresholds prioritize precision vs. recall
- ROC curve and precision-recall curve help visualize tradeoffs
- Domain-specific considerations guide threshold selection

Table 3.3 outlines the strengths, limitations, and ideal use cases of various evaluation metrics for logistic regression. It provides guidance on selecting the most appropriate metric based on the problem context and data characteristics.

Table 3.4: Advantages and Disadvantages of Different Evaluation Metrics

Metric	Advantages	Disadvantages	Best Used When
Accuracy	Simple, intuitive	Misleading with imbalanced data	Classes are balanced
Precision	Focuses on false positive rate	Ignores false negatives	False positives are costly
Recall	Focuses on false negative rate	Ignores false positives	False negatives are costly
F1-Score	Balances precision and recall	Still affected by class distribution	Need balance between precision/recall
AUC-ROC	Threshold-independent	Less intuitive	Need probability estimates
Log Loss	Sensitive to probability calibration	Hard to interpret directly	Well-calibrated probabilities matter

MAE	Less sensitive to outliers	May underestimate error impact	Outliers should have less weight
RMSE	Penalizes large errors	Sensitive to outliers	Large errors should be penalized more

Regression predicts numerical outcomes, like prices or yields, while classification assigns inputs to predefined categories, such as spam or not-spam. Their differences are evident in output type, evaluation metrics, and the loss functions used during training**.** Table 3.4 Illustrates the key aspects of regression and classification

Table 3.5 Aspects of Regression and Classification

Aspect	Regression	Classification
Output type	Continuous values	Discrete categories
Loss function	Typically squared error	Log loss, 0-1 loss, etc.
Evaluation metrics	RMSE, MAE, R^2	Accuracy, F1-score, AUC
Example applications	Price prediction, yield forecasting	Spam detection, disease diagnosis

3.7 Decision Tree Learning

Decision tree learning is a powerful yet straightforward and intuitive machine learning technique that can be applied to both classification and regression tasks. This works by recursively partitioning the feature space into regions based on feature values, leading to a tree-like structure in which each internal node represents a feature-based decision, each branch represents the outcome of that decision, and each leaf node corresponds to a final output (such as a class label for classification or a numerical value for regression). The procedure starts at the root node, where the algorithm chooses a feature and a threshold to separate/splits the data into subsets, with the goal of maximizing the homogeneity of the groups. This homogeneity is frequently quantified in classification using metrics such as Gini impurity or entropy, whereas in regression, variance reduction is commonly utilized. The recursive splitting process continues until a stopping requirement is satisfied, such as a maximum tree depth or a minimum number of samples per node, resulting in an easy-to-understand and visualize model.

A decision tree is built by picking the optimum feature and threshold at each node in order to optimize a specific criterion. For instance, in classification, the algorithm may use the Gini impurity, which assesses the likelihood of incorrectly classifying a randomly selected element in a node and prioritize splits that lower this impurity. In regression, the goal is to minimize the variance in the target variable within each node. CART (Classification and Regression Trees) algorithms are frequently employed to construct decision trees by greedily selecting the split that maximizes the improvement in the specified metric. However, this greediness can result in overfitting, in which the tree grows excessively complex and gathering noise in the training data. To address this, approaches such as pruning (removing branches with minimal predictive significance/power) and constraint setting (for example, minimum samples per leaf) are used to balance model complexity with generalization.

Decision trees have various advantages, including interpretability and the ability to handle both numerical and categorical data with minimal preprocessing. They are capable of modeling nonlinear interactions and are robust to irrelevant features because the algorithm automatically selects the most informative ones. However, they are sensitive to slight changes in the data, which can result in completely different trees, and they may struggle with imbalanced datasets or tasks that need smooth predictions, such as regression over continuous surfaces. Ensemble approaches, such as Random Forests or Gradient Boosting, frequently use decision trees to improve robustness and accuracy by integrating several trees and reducing variance or bias. These attributes make decision trees an essential tool in machine learning, with applications ranging from medical diagnosis to forecasting finances.

Despite its advantages, decision trees have limitations that must be overcome in reality. Their tendency to overfit is accentuated with high-dimensional datasets, where the tree can grow overly complex in order to catch false patterns. Furthermore, decision trees may be biased toward features with multiple categories, which generate more potential splits. Methods such as feature significance analysis, which is based on the decrease of impurity or variation across splits, aid in determining which features drive the model's decisions. By recognizing these trade-offs and combining decision trees with ensemble approaches or careful tuning, practitioners can take utilize of their intuitive structure to achieve robust and effective predictive modeling.

3.7.1 Introduction to Decision Tree Models

A decision tree is a hierarchical model that makes decisions by following conditions from the root to the leaves:

Key components:

- **Root node**: The starting point of the tree
- **Internal nodes**: Represent tests on attributes
- **Branches**: Outcomes of the tests
- **Leaf nodes**: Final predictions (class labels or values)

Advantages of decision trees:

- Easy to understand and interpret
- Require minimal data preprocessing
- Handle both numerical and categorical features
- Implicitly perform feature selection
- Model non-linear relationships
- No assumptions about data distribution

Limitations:

- Prone to overfitting, especially with deep trees
- Can be unstable (small data changes may result in different trees)
- May create biased trees if classes are imbalanced
- Limited in expressing certain relationships (e.g., XOR problems)

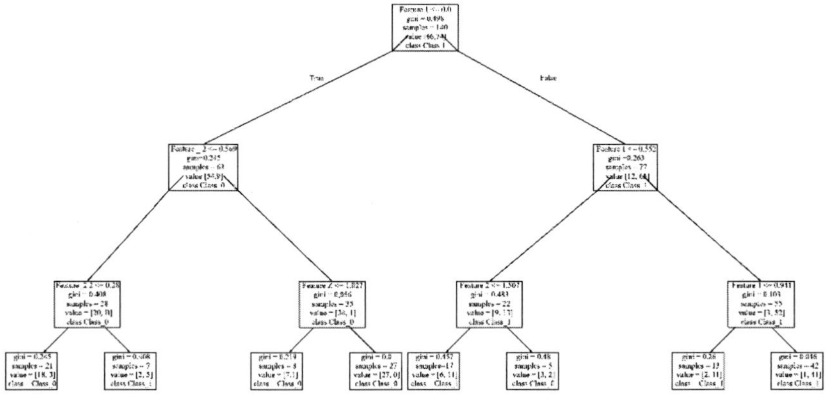

Figure 3.10: Example decision tree for a classification problem

3.7.2 Decision Tree Induction Algorithms

Several algorithms exist for constructing decision trees from data:

CART (Classification and Regression Trees):

- Binary splits at each node
- Gini impurity or MSE as splitting criteria
- Supports both classification and regression

ID3 (Iterative Dichotomiser 3):

- Information gain as splitting criterion
- Handles categorical features naturally
- Only for classification problems

C4.5 (successor to ID3):

- Uses information gain ratio to address bias toward features with many values
- Handles both continuous and discrete attributes
- Pruning to reduce overfitting

Common splitting criteria:

1. **Gini impurity:**

$$Gini\ Impurity = 1 - \sum_{-=1}^{nc} p_i^2) \ldots\ldots\ldots 3.31(a)$$

Where C is the number of classes and p is the proportion of elements belonging to class i

2. **Information gain:**

$$Information\ gain = H(Parent) \sum_{i=1}^{m} \frac{nj}{n} H(Child_j) \ldots\ldots\ldots 3.31(b)$$

- H(parent): Entropy of the parent node.
- H(childj): Entropy of the jjj-th child node.
- n: Total number of samples in the parent node.
- n_j: Number of samples in the jth child node.
- m: Total number of child nodes.

3. **Variance reduction: $var(parent) - sum_{j=1}^{m} frac{n_j}{n} var(child_j)$**

$$Variance\ reduction = var(parent) - \sum_{i=1}^{m} \frac{nj}{n} variance(Child_j) \ldots\ldots\ldots 3.31(c)$$

Where

- var(parent): variance of the parent node.
- var(childj): variance of the jjj-th child node.
- n: Total number of samples in the parent node.
- n_j: Number of samples in the jth child node.
- m: Total number of child nodes.

Pruning techniques:

- **Pre-pruning**: Early stopping during tree construction
- **Post-pruning**: Building the full tree then removing nodes
- **Cost-complexity pruning**: Trading off tree size and accuracy

Pseudocode for basic decision tree induction:

```
function BuildTree(data, features):
  if stopping_condition(data) is True:
    return create_leaf_node(data)
  best_feature = find_best_split(data, features)
  tree = create_node(best_feature)
  for each value v of best_feature:
    subset = data where best_feature = v
    subtree = BuildTree(subset, features - {best_feature})
    add subtree as child of tree with branch v
  return tree
```

Figure 3.10 illustrates how the maximum depth parameter affects decision tree complexity and performance. It shows that as depth increases, trees grow more complex with more nodes and leaves, leading to higher training accuracy but potentially worse test accuracy due to overfitting.

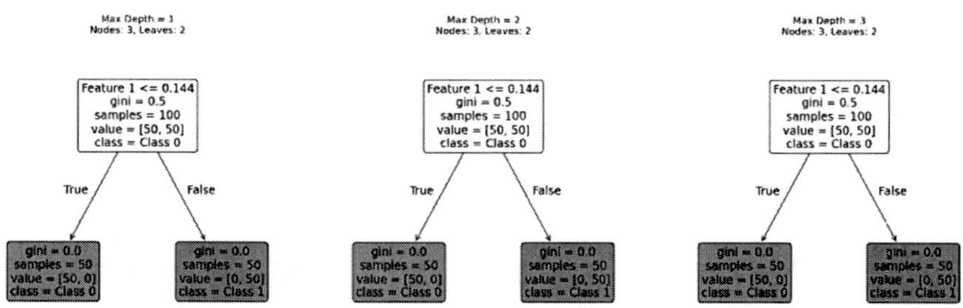

(a)

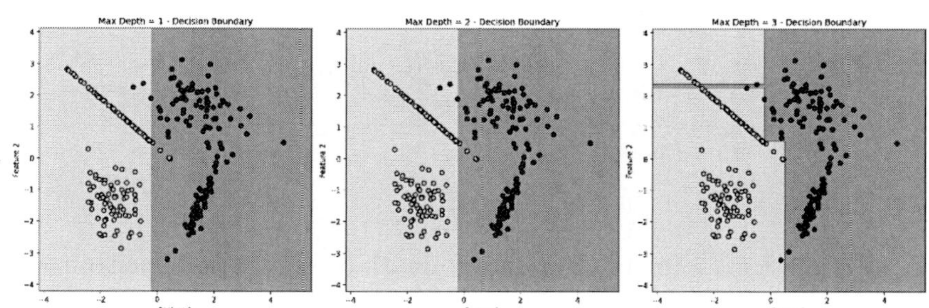

(b)

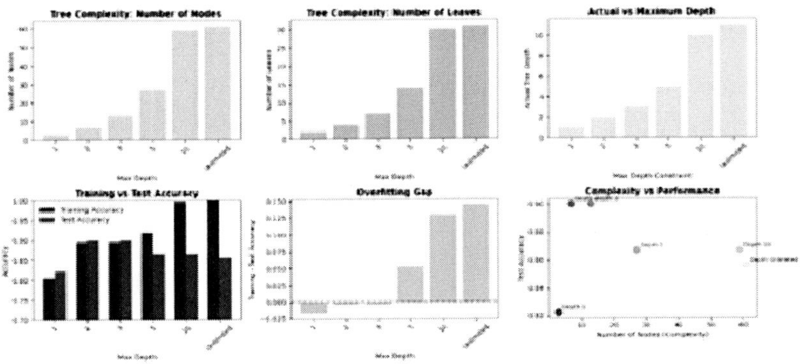

(c)

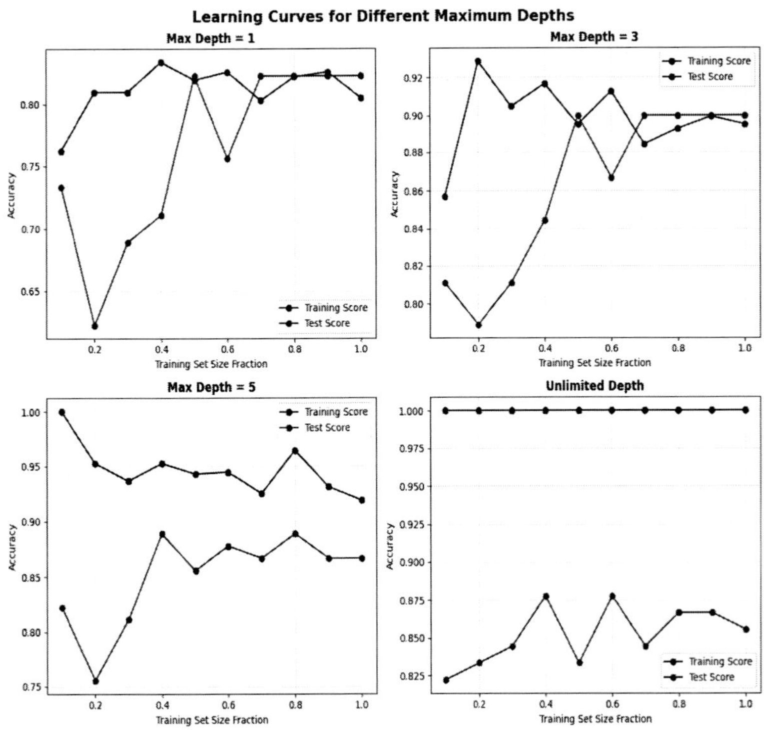

(d)

Figure 3.11: Effect of maximum depth constraint on decision tree complexity

Key Observations from figure 3.10:

Complexity Growth: As maximum depth increases, the number of nodes and leaves increases exponentially, indicating greater model complexity, as shown in the tree structures and decision boundaries, figure 3.10 (a). **Optimal Depth:** The optimal maximum depth balances complexity and generalization, typically around 2–5 for this dataset, where test accuracy is high and overfitting is minimal.

Training Accuracy: Deeper trees provide higher training accuracy, often reaching 100% for unlimited depth, since they fit the training data more precisely, including noise. figure 3.10 (b)

Test accuracy and overfitting: Test accuracy peaks at moderate depths (e.g., 2 or 3, with 0.900 accuracy) and decreases for deeper trees (e.g., 0.856 at unlimited), indicating overfitting, as measured by the growing overfitting gap (e.g., 0.144 at unlimited) figure 3.10 (c).

Learning Curves: The separate learning curves illustration indicates that shallower trees (e.g., depth 1) perform consistently with less data, whereas deeper trees require more data to avoid overfitting, emphasizing the importance of having enough data with complicated models. figure 3.10 (d)

Chapter Summary and Concluding Thoughts:

Summary

Chapter 3 delves into fundamental machine learning approaches such as similarity-based learning, regression analysis, and decision trees. It begins with similarity-based algorithms like k-Nearest Neighbors (k-NN), which categorizes data points based on their proximity to training examples, and its variants like weighted k-NN and nearest centroid, which improve performance and efficiency. The section that follows next delves into locally weighted regression, a method that adapts to local data patterns utilizing kernel functions and bandwidth selection, allowing for greater flexibility in predicting non-linear connections. Regression analysis is fully treated, starting with linear regression and extending to polynomial regression, including major assessment metrics like MSE, RMSE, and R-squared (R^2). Logistic regression is introduced as a classification strategy that uses the logistic function to predict class probabilities and evaluates them using metrics like precision, recall, and F1-score. Finally, decision trees are given as hierarchical models that partition the feature space, using methods such as CART, ID3, and C4.5, as well as pruning strategies to manage complexity and prevent overfitting. These methods work together to offer a powerful toolkit for solving a wide range of machine learning challenges, each with its own set of strengths and limitations.

Concluding thoughts

As we wrap up Chapter 3, it is evident that the techniques presented form the foundation of machine learning, offering a range of approaches from simple, interpretable models to more complex, adaptive ones. Each method offers distinct advantages and challenges: k-NN's simplicity and flexibility are offset by its computational demands; locally weighted regression excels at capturing local patterns but at the cost of increased complexity; linear and polynomial regression are interpretable but can overfit if not regularized; logistic regression provides a probabilistic framework for classification but requires careful metric selection; and decision trees balance interpretability A common feature throughout these strategies is the bias-variance trade-off, in which models must be modified to avoid underfitting or overfitting. The decision between parametric and non-parametric approaches is determined by the data and problem, with parametric methods making strong assumptions about data distribution while non-parametric methods allow the data to create the model. Computational concerns and feature engineering are also important in determining model scalability and performance.

These fundamental ideas not only provide a strong knowledge of basic machine learning techniques, but also serve as a foundation for more sophisticated methods such as ensemble learning and neural networks. Recent improvements demonstrate their long-term significance; for example, k-NN has proven critical in healthcare for forecasting heart attack risks and early cancer detection using genomic sequence analysis, GPU-accelerated nearest neighbor searches, and AI-driven models. Similarly, decision trees continue to be an important component of cutting-edge ensemble approaches such as random forests and gradient boosting, which are used in many applications. As machine learning advances, the principles of similarity-based learning, regression, and decision trees remain critical intuition and tools for practitioners, assuring optimal model selection and improvement. Future chapters will build on these foundations, presenting more sophisticated approaches for dealing with complex data and relationships, highlighting the essential notions'

Conceptual Questions

1. What is similarity-based learning, and how does it mimic human reasoning in classification tasks?
2. Explain the k-Nearest Neighbors (k-NN) algorithm. How do you choose an optimal value for kkk?
3. Compare and contrast standard k-NN with weighted k-NN. Under what circumstances would you prefer weighted k-NN?
4. Define Locally Weighted Regression (LWR). How does it differ from global regression models?
5. Discuss the difference between parametric and non-parametric regression techniques.
6. Explain the key differences between linear regression, polynomial regression, and logistic regression.
7. Describe the structure and working of a decision tree. What are the main splitting criteria used in decision trees?
8. What are the advantages and limitations of using decision trees for classification and regression tasks?

Application-Based Questions

9. Given a dataset with non-linear relationships, outline steps to apply Locally Weighted Regression (LWR) effectively.
10. Propose a preprocessing and feature selection pipeline for optimizing the performance of k-NN on a high-dimensional dataset.
11. For a dataset with overlapping classes, discuss how you would use the Nearest Centroid Classifier and its variants.
12. Create a scenario where decision trees would outperform logistic regression for binary classification.

Critical Thinking Questions

13. How does the choice of distance metric influence the performance of similarity-based learning algorithms?

14. In what scenarios might Locally Weighted Regression (LWR) fail? How can these limitations be mitigated?

15. Discuss the impact of regularization techniques like Lasso and Ridge on regression models with highly correlated features.

Chapter - 4

Probabilistic Models and Neural Networks

- Bayesian Learning
- Probability-Based Learning Fundamentals
- Bayes Theorem and Classification
- Naïve Bayes Algorithm for Continuous Attributes
- Artificial Neural Networks (ANN)
- Biological and Artificial Neurons
- Perceptron and Learning Theory
- Types and Applications of ANNs
- Advantages, Disadvantages, and Challenges of ANNs

Chapter Overview

This chapter examines the synergy between probability theory and machine learning, focusing on Bayesian models and artificial neural networks (ANNs). It begins with Bayesian learning, exploring foundational concepts like Bayes' theorem and its application to classification problems, including the Naïve Bayes algorithm—a simple yet effective probabilistic classifier. The latter half transitions to ANNs, tracing their inspiration from biological neurons and foundational theories. It covers the perceptron model, various neural network architectures, and their practical applications, concluding with an exploration of the challenges and limitations in implementing ANNs.

4.1 Bayesian Learning

4.1.1 Fundamentals of Probability and Bayes' Theorem

Probability theory provides the foundation for managing uncertainty in machine learning by quantifying and modeling randomness. Among its key notions, Bayes' Theorem stands out as a cornerstone, providing a systematic method for updating beliefs in light of new data. The theorem mathematically expresses the relationship between conditional probabilities as follows:

$$P(A|B)=\frac{P(B|A)\cdot P(A)}{P(B)} \quad \text{........4.1}$$

Where,

- **P(A|B)** - the posterior probability (what we want to find after observing evidence B)
- **P(B|A)** - the likelihood (how probable the evidence B is given hypothesis A)
- **P(A)** - the prior probability (our initial belief about A before seeing evidence)
- **P(B)** - the marginal probability (the total probability of observing evidence B)

Incorporating Prior Knowledge

One of Bayes' theorem's primary strengths is its capacity to incorporate prior knowledge into decision-making. For example, in a spam email classifier, the system could begin with a prior probability that reflects the past prevalence of spam emails. When new emails are analyzed, the classifier refines the posterior probability of spam based on the likelihood of observable features (for example, the frequency of specific terms). This iterative updating process is consistent with the concept of learning from data, which is an essential cornerstone of machine learning.

Applications in Machine Learning

Bayesian inference has broad applications in machine learning. Naïve Bayes classifiers use Bayes' theorem's conditional independence to simplify feature classification. Despite its simplicity, this method works exceptionally well in fields such as text classification and sentiment analysis. Furthermore, Bayesian models under pin/serve as the foundation for more complex algorithms such as Bayesian Networks and Gaussian Processes, which deal with uncertainty and anticipate outcomes based on sparse or noisy data.

Beyond Classical Applications

Bayes' theorem is also important in modern advancements such as probabilistic programming and Bayesian deep learning. These paradigms incorporate uncertainty estimates into predictions, allowing models to express confidence in their results/outputs such as medicine and autonomous systems where dependability is critical. Machine learning systems that embrace the ideas of Bayes' theorem can progress beyond deterministic outputs to probabilistic reasoning, providing more nuanced insights and supporting robust decision-making under uncertainty.

Probability Basics:

- **Random Variables**: A **random variable** is a numerical representation of the outcomes of a random phenomenon. It is a key concept in probability theory and can be either **discrete** (taking on countable values) or **continuous** (taking on values from an interval or real numbers). Variables whose possible values represent outcomes of a random phenomenon.

- **Discrete Random Variables**: Examples include the roll of a six-sided die (X) where X can take values {1,2,3,4,5,6}, another example number of family members, no of students in a class and so on

- **Continuous Random Variables**: Examples include the height of individuals (Y) which can take any value within a range (e.g., 150 cm≤Y≤200 cm150. Examples include weights of students in a class,

Random variables provide a way to quantify uncertainty, allowing us to compute probabilities and expectations related to their outcomes.

- **Probability Distribution**: A function that describes the likelihood of a random variable taking certain values. A probability distribution describes how probabilities are assigned to the possible values of a random variable.
- **For Discrete Random Variables**: The probability mass function (PMF), P(X=x), specifies the probability of each value. For example:
- **Joint Probability**: The probability of two events occurring together, denoted as P(A,B) or P(A∩B)
- **Conditional Probability**: The probability of event A occurring given that event B has occurred, written as P(A|B)
- **Marginal Probability**: The probability of an event irrespective of the values of other random variables

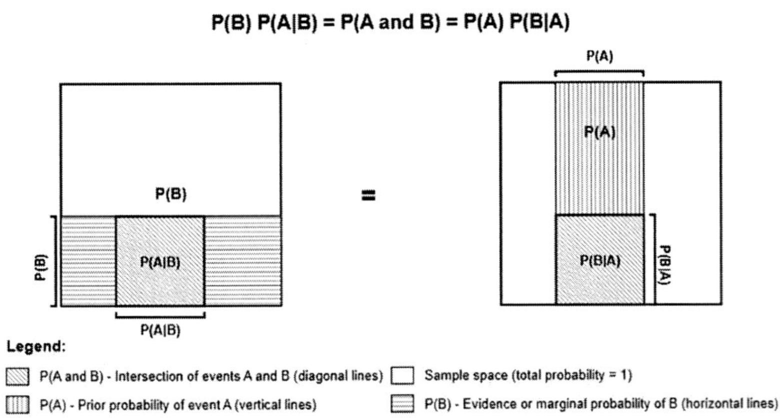

Bayesian Inference Process:

1. Start with prior beliefs about possible hypotheses
2. Observe new data
3. Update beliefs using Bayes' theorem
4. The posterior becomes the new prior for future inferences

Bayesian learning allows for sequential updating of beliefs as new evidence becomes available, making it particularly suitable for online learning scenarios where data arrives incrementally.

4.1.2 Classification Using Bayesian Models

Bayesian classification applies Bayes' theorem to determine the most probable class for a given instance based on its attributes. Bayesian classification is a probabilistic approach to classification that uses **Bayes' theorem** to compute the probability of a data instance belonging to each class and assigns it to the most probable one.

Probabilistic Decision Making

The classifier leverages the **prior probabilities** of the classes, the likelihood of the observed attributes given each class, and the evidence. It is particularly effective when dealing with uncertainty, as it explicitly models probabilistic relationships. Bayesian classification is a basic approach to machine learning that uses Bayes' theorem to make probabilistic predictions about class membership. Unlike deterministic classification methods, that assign definite labels, Bayesian classifiers compute the chance that a given instance belongs to each potential class before selecting the class with the highest posterior probability. This probabilistic framework not only makes predictions but also quantifies the uncertainty associated with them, making it especially useful in applications where understanding confidence levels is crucial.

The Mathematical Foundation

At its core, Bayesian classification strives at finding the class C that maximizes $P(C|X)$, where X is an instance's feature vector. Using Bayes' theorem, the posterior probability is computed as $P(C|X) = P(X|C) \times P(C)/P(X)$. The prior probability $P(C)$ reflects our initial belief about class frequency, whereas the likelihood $P(X|C)$ indicates how likely the features/characteristics observed are for each class. The evidence $P(X)$ serves as a normalizing factor. This mathematical elegance enables the classifier to systematically incorporate both prior knowledge and observed evidence, updating beliefs when new data becomes available.

Process of Bayesian Classification

The process starts by calculating the posterior probabilities for all possible classes. The classifier then assigns the instance to the class with the highest posterior probability. This approach can be represented as:

$$C_{predicted} = argmax P(C| X) \text{......} \mathbf{4.2}$$

For example, in email classification, the goal might be to classify an email as "spam" or "not spam" based on features such as word frequency. Bayesian classifiers use the prior probability of emails being spam (P(Spam)P(\text{Spam})P(Spam)) and the likelihood of observing specific words in spam emails (P(Words|Spam) to determine the posterior probability.

In practice, **Naïve Bayes classifiers** simplify computations by assuming conditional independence between features given the class. This assumption allows the likelihood to be expressed as a product of probabilities for each feature:

$$P(X| C) = \prod_{i=1}^{n} P(X_i| C) \text{...........} \mathbf{4.3}$$

Despite the simplicity of this assumption, Naïve Bayes performs remarkably well in domains like text classification, document filtering, and sentiment analysis.

Practical Implementations and Benefits: The most common implementation is the Naive Bayes classifier, which assumes feature independence to simplify the likelihood calculations; despite this "naive" assumption, it frequently works brilliantly in practice. Advanced variations, such as Gaussian Naive Bayes, handle continuous features, whereas Multinomial Naive Bayes does well with text classification tasks. Bayesian classifiers have several compelling advantages: they require small training datasets, handle missing values, provide probabilistic outputs for risk assessment, and can include domain expertise through informed prior distributions. Furthermore, they are computationally efficient and can handle multi-class problems without modification.

Real-World Applications and Considerations: Bayesian classification has been widely successful in a variety of domains, such as spam email detection, medical diagnosis, sentiment analysis, and recommendation systems. In medical applications, the probabilistic nature is very useful—a doctor must know not just whether a patient has a condition, but also the level of confidence in that prediction. However, practitioners must be aware of limitations: the independence assumption in Naive Bayes can be unduly restrictive for correlated features, and the quality of outputs is strongly reliant on representative training data and proper prior distributions. Despite these limitations, Bayesian approaches remain a cornerstone of machine learning because of their interpretability, theoretical underlying, and strong performance across a wide range of problem domains.

Maximum A Posteriori (MAP) Hypothesis:

The MAP hypothesis is the one with the highest posterior probability:

$$h_{MAP} = \arg\max_{h \in H} P(h \mid D) = \arg\max_{h \in H} \frac{P(D \mid h).P(h)}{P(D)} \quad ...4.4(a)$$

Since P(D) is constant across all hypotheses being considered, this simplifies to

$$h_{MAP} = \arg\max_{h \in H} P(D \mid h) \cdot P(h) \quad ....4.4(b)$$

Bayesian Classification Process:

At its core, Bayesian classification estimates the **posterior probability** of a class C given a set of observed attributes (features) X. Using Bayes' theorem, this is expressed as

$$P(C \mid X) = \frac{P(X \mid C) \cdot P(C)}{P(X)} \quad .....4.4$$

Here:

- P(C|X) is the posterior probability (the probability of class CCC given the data X).
- P(C) is the prior probability of class C,
- P(X|C) is the likelihood of observing X given class C, and
- P(X) is the evidence, which acts as a normalizing constant.

Bayesian Classifier Process

1. For each class ci, calculate $P(c_i|x)$, where x is the instance to be classified.
2. Assign x to the class with the highest $P(c_i|x)$.
3. Using Bayes' theorem: $P(c_i|x) = [P(x|c_i) \times P(c_i)] / P(x)$
4. Since P(x) is constant for all classes, the classification rule becomes classify(x) = argmax[i] $P(x|c_i) \times P(c_i)$.

Advantages of Bayesian Classification:

- Provides probabilistic predictions rather than just class labels
- Naturally incorporates prior knowledge
- Can handle incomplete data and uncertainty
- Offers a theoretical framework for combining evidence

Challenges in Bayesian Classification:

- Computing $P(x|c_i)$ can be difficult for complex attribute relations.
- Prior probabilities might not be readily available.
- Computational complexity. grows with model complexity

Table 4.1: Comparison of Bayesian Classification with Other Classification Methods

Feature	Bayesian Classification	Decision Trees	Support Vector Machines (SVM)	k-Nearest Neighbours (k-NN)
Output Type	Probabilistic predictions	Deterministic class labels	Deterministic class labels	Deterministic class labels
Handling Uncertainty	Excellent (uses probabilities)	Limited	Limited	Limited
Incorporates Prior Knowledge	Yes (through priors)	No	No	No

Scalability	High for simple models (e.g., Naïve Bayes)	Moderate	High	Low for large datasets
Assumptions	Conditional independence (Naïve Bayes)	No assumptions on feature relations	Linear separability of classes	No assumptions
Computational Complexity	Low (for Naïve Bayes) to moderate	Low to moderate	High (depends on kernel)	High for large datasets
Interpretability	High (easy to understand probabilities)	High (visual representation)	Low (hard to interpret)	Low (non-parametric)
Performance on Complex Data	Moderate	Good	Good	Poor without proper distance metric
Ability to Handle Noise	Good (robust due to probabilistic nature)	Moderate	Good	Poor without smoothing

4.2 Naïve Bayes Algorithm

The Naïve Bayes algorithm employs Bayes' theorem to categorize data into predefined categories. It is especially useful for applications like text classification, spam filtering, and sentiment analysis. The "naïve" approach posits that data features are conditionally independent of class label. Despite simplifying assumptions, the Naïve Bayes method performs well in practical situations, particularly when the independence assumption is approximately true.

The algorithm is computationally efficient, scalable, and robust for high-dimensional datasets, making it a popular choice for large-scale problems. Its ability to work with probabilistic models ensures that it not only provides a classification label but also outputs the probabilities associated with each class, which can be useful for decision-making under uncertainty.

4.2.1 Principles and Assumptions

The Naïve Bayes algorithm is a simple probabilistic classifier based on Bayes' theorem with a strong (naïve) independence assumption.

The Independence Assumption:

The core principle of the Naïve Bayes algorithm is to apply Bayes' theorem to compute the posterior probability of a class C_i given the observed features $X = \{x_1, x_2, \ldots, x_n\}$. Using Bayes' theorem, this probability is expressed as equation 4.5.

$$P(C_i \mid X) = \frac{P(X \mid C_i) \cdot P(C_i)}{P(X)} \quad \ldots\ldots\ldots 4.5$$

Naïve Bayes assumes that features are conditionally independent given the class label:

$$P(x_1, x_2 \ldots\ldots x_n \mid c_i) = P(x_1 \mid c_i) \cdot P(x_2 \mid c_i) \cdots\cdots P(x_n \mid c_i) \ldots\ldots 4.6$$

This simplifies the computation of the likelihood $P(x|c_i)$, as we only need to estimate the individual conditional probabilities $P(x_j|c_i)$ for each feature x_j.

Naïve Bayes Classification Rule:

Given an instance with n attributes ($x_1, x_2, \ldots, x_n$), the classification rule becomes:

$$\text{classify}(x_1, x_2 \ldots\ldots x_n) = \text{argimax}\left[P(c_i) \cdot \prod_{j=1}^{n} P(x_j \mid c_i) \right] \ldots\ldots 4.7$$

In practice, it's common to work with logarithms to prevent numerical underflow.

$$\text{classify}(x_1, x_2 \ldots\ldots x_n) = \text{argimax}\left[\log P(c_i) + \sum_{j=1}^{n} \log PP(x_j \mid c_i) \right] \ldots 4.8$$

Learning Process:

1. Estimate class priors $P(c_i)$ from training data.
2. For each class and feature, estimate $P(x_j|c_i)$ from training data.
3. For classification, apply the Naïve Bayes rule to new instances.

Types of Naïve Bayes Models:

- **Bernoulli Naïve Bayes**: For binary features
- **Multinomial Naïve Bayes**: For discrete features (e.g., word counts)
- **Gaussian Naïve Bayes**: For continuous features with normal distribution

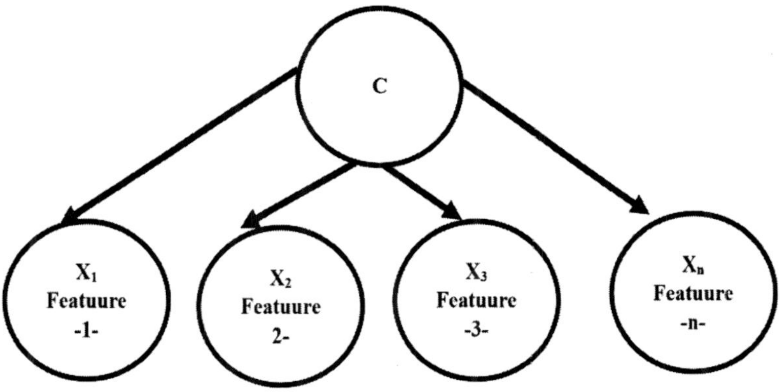

Figure 4.1: Graphical model representation of Naïve Bayes showing conditional independence

4.2.2 Handling Continuous Attributes

When dealing with continuous attributes, the most common approach is to assume that the values follow a Gaussian (normal) distribution within each class.

Gaussian Naïve Bayes:

- For each class ci and continuous attribute xj, estimate the mean μij and variance $\sigma^2 ij$ from training data.
- The conditional probability is then calculated as:

$$\mathbf{P}\left(\mathbf{x} | \mathbf{c}_{j}\right)=\frac{1}{\sqrt{2\pi\sigma_{ij}^{2}}}\exp(-\frac{\left(\mathbf{x}_{i}-\mu_{ij}\right)^{2}}{2\sigma_{ij}^{2}} \quad \ldots.4.9$$

Alternative Approaches:

1. **Discretization**: Convert continuous attributes into discrete intervals.
   - Equal-width binning
   - Equal-frequency binning
   - Entropy-based discretization
2. **Kernel Density Estimation:** A non-parametric way to estimate the probability density function
3. **Hybrid Methods**: Combine different approaches for different attributes.

In table 4.2, Comparison of methods for handling continuous attributes in Naïve Bayes is presented.

Table 4.2: Comparison of methods for handling continuous attributes in Naïve Bayes

Method	Description	Advantages	Disadvantages
Gaussian Naïve Bayes	Assumes features are distributed according to a Gaussian (normal) distribution: [P(xj }	Refer to equation 4.9	Simple to implement; works well when the Gaussian assumption is valid.
Binning (Discretization)	Continuous values are divided into bins, and the algorithm treats them as categorical data.	No assumption about the distribution; straightforward to implement.	Information loss due to discretization; choice of bin size affects performance.

Kernel Density Estimation (KDE)	Estimates the probability density function of the data using kernels (e.g., Gaussian kernels).	Flexible; does not assume a specific distribution for the data.	Computationally expensive; sensitive to kernel and bandwidth parameters.
Non-parametric Naïve Bayes	Uses non-parametric methods (e.g., histograms) to estimate probabilities.	Makes no assumptions about the underlying distribution.	Requires a large amount of data for accurate estimation.
Logistic Regression as an Alternative	Uses logistic regression to approximate continuous feature handling in probabilistic terms.	Handles continuous data directly without binning or distribution assumptions.	Computationally more intensive; not strictly a Naïve Bayes method.

4.2.3 Applications in Text Classification

The Naïve Bayes algorithm performs well for classification of texts because to its ease of use, efficiency, and ability to handle high dimensional datasets. Naïve Bayes' conditional independence assumption simplifies computations for text data with hundreds or millions of unique characteristics, such as vocabulary words. Despite its simplicity, Naïve Bayes is particularly effective for applications such as spam filtering, sentiment analysis, and document categorization.

Naïve Bayes is used in spam filtering for identifying if an email is "spam" or "non-spam" based on its words or phrases. The algorithm uses a training dataset of labeled emails to determine the chance of specific terms appearing in each category. Words such as "free," "offer," and "discount" may appear frequently in spam emails. Naïve Bayes recognizes new emails that come in as spam or non-spam based upon their posterior probabilities.

In sentiment analysis, Naïve Bayes classifies text as positive, negative, or neutral. The algorithm learns patterns that distinguish between distinct sentiments by examining the frequency of specific words or phrases in labeled data (for example, reviews or tweets). This makes it an effective tool for tasks such as analyzing feedback from customers or monitoring social media channels. Naïve Bayes categorizes documents, such as news stories, into predetermined categories like politics, sports, or entertainment. Its capacity to successfully handle sparse and high-dimensional data is critical for these applications, making it one of the most widely used classification of texts algorithms.

Text Classification Process:

1. **Preprocessing**: Tokenization, stemming, removing stop words
2. **Feature Extraction**: Typically using the bag-of-words model
3. **Training**: Learning conditional probabilities for each word given each class
4. **Classification**: Applying the Naïve Bayes rule to new documents

Multinomial Naïve Bayes for Text:

- Models the distribution of word counts
- For each class ci and word wj, calculate

$$P(wj \mid ci) = \frac{count(wk, ci) + \alpha}{\sum_k count(wj, ci) + \alpha |V|} \quad \text{......4.10}$$

where α is the smoothing parameter and |V| is the vocabulary size

Explanation:

- $count(w_j, c_i)$: The number of times word w_j appears in documents of class c.
- $\sum_k count(w_k, c_i)$: The total count of all words across all documents in class cic_ici.
- α: The **smoothing parameter** (e.g., α=1 for Laplace smoothing) to prevent zero probabilities for unseen words.

- |V| The size of the vocabulary (total unique words across all documents).

This equation ensures that even words not observed in the training data for a class c_i are assigned a small probability, preventing the model from assigning zero likelihood to new instances.

Laplace (Add-One) Smoothing: Prevents zero probabilities for unseen words by adding 1 to each word count and adjusting the denominator accordingly. This ensures that every word in the vocabulary |V| has a non-zero probability, making the model robust to handling new or rare words.

To avoid zero probabilities for words not seen in training examples, we add a small constant to all counts: as per the equation 4.11 (substituting α with 1)

$$P(wj|ci) = \frac{count(wk,ci)+1}{\sum_k count(wj,ci)+1|V|} \quad ......4.11$$

Advantages in Text Classification:

- Performs well despite the simplistic independence assumption
- Fast training and classification
- Requires relatively small amounts of training data
- Handles high-dimensional feature spaces efficiently

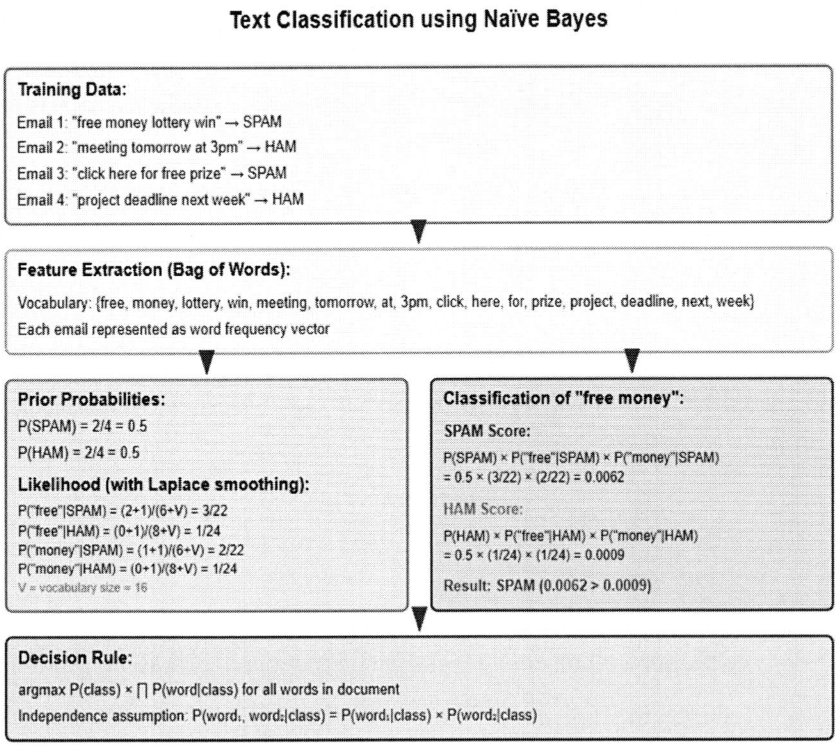

Figure 4.2: Example of text classification using Naïve Bayes

4.3 Introduction to Artificial Neural Networks (ANNs)

Artificial Neural Networks (ANNs) are computational models based on the structure and operation of biological neural networks in the human brain. They comprise up of interconnected nodes known as neurons, which have been organized into layers. Each neuron receives input, processes it with an activation function, and produces an output. These outputs are subsequently passed on to neurons in succeeding layers, resulting in a network capable of learning complicated patterns and correlations in data. The design of ANNs allows them to perform a variety of tasks such as classification, regression, and pattern recognition.

At the core of an ANN is its ability to learn from data through a process called training. During training, the network adjusts the weights associated with the connections between neurons to minimize the difference between predicted and actual results-the outcomes. This optimization is often accomplished by algorithms like gradient descent and backpropagation. The network's architecture, including the number of layers and neurons in each layer, is important to its performance and capabilities.

ANNs are particularly helpful for tasks requiring non-linear relationships or high-dimensional data. They have been effective in a variety of applications, including image and speech recognition, natural language processing, and predictive analytics. A key attribute of ANNs is their ability to generalize, allowing them to generate accurate predictions on unseen data. However, constructing and training ANNs requires careful consideration to avoid issues like overfitting and vanishing gradients.

Recent advances in ANN technology, such as the creation of deep learning architectures, have greatly increased its application. Deep neural networks, a type of artificial neural network (ANN), use numerous hidden layers to learn hierarchical data representations. This has resulted in achievements in fields such as autonomous driving, medical diagnostics, and gaming. As processing power and data availability increase, ANNs will play a more significant role in artificial intelligence and machine learning applications.

4.3.1 Biological vs. Artificial Neurons

Artificial neural networks are inspired by the structure and function of the human brain, but with significant simplifications. In the human brain, billions of neurons communicate with one another via synapses, which transfer electrical signals that enable complicated mental functions. Similarly, ANNs are composed of artificial neurons that analyze and transmit information. These artificial neurons are split into layers, with each layer executing a specific transformation on the data. While the biological brain is incredibly complex and adaptable, ANNs seek to replicate this behaviour in a computationally efficient manner.

Despite its simple nature, ANNs can learn and generalize patterns in data. Each neuron in an ANN is linked to others through weighted links, similar to synapses. These weights determine the significance of input signals and are adjusted during training to enhance the network's performance. In contrast to the brain's complex biochemical processes, ANNs simulate learning and decision-making using mathematical operations like dot products and activation functions.

Parallel processing and distributed representation are two examples of biologically inspired concepts. Just as the brain processes information through interconnected networks of neurons, ANNs leverage their layered structure to capture complicated, hierarchical patterns. However, although biological neurons act asynchronously and are highly flexible, artificial neurons adhere to predetermined mathematical rules and require particular training procedures to function. This distinction emphasizes both the promise and limitations of ANNs as compared to their biological counterparts.

Biological Neurons:

- Consists of dendrites (inputs), cell body (processing), and axon (output)
- Receive electrochemical signals through dendrites
- If combined input exceeds a threshold, the neuron "fires" an action potential
- Signal transmission occurs at synapses between neurons
- Learning involves adjusting the strength of synaptic connections

Artificial Neurons:

- Mathematical models that mimic biological neurons
- Inputs (x1, x2, ..., xn) are combined using weights (w1, w2, ..., wn).
- The weighted sum is passed through an activation function.
- Output is transmitted to other neurons in the network
- Learning involves adjusting the weights based on error feedback.

The Table 4.3 highlights key differences and similarities between biological neurons and their artificial counterparts, providing insight into their respective structures and functions.

Table 4.3: Comparison of Biological and Artificial Neurons

Component/Process	Biological Neurons	Artificial Neurons
Structure	Consists of dendrites (inputs), cell body (processing), and axon (output).	Mathematical models with input layer, processing unit, and output
Input Reception	Receive electrochemical signals through dendrites from multiple synapses.	Receive numerical inputs ($x_1, x_2, ..., x_n$) from previous layer or external sources
Signal Integration	Dendrites collect and integrate incoming signals in the cell body	Inputs are combined using weighted sum: $\mathbf{\Sigma(w_i \times x_i)}$
Activation Mechanism	If combined input exceeds a threshold, the neuron "fires" an action potential	Weighted sum is passed through an activation function $f(\Sigma(w_i \times x_i))$
Threshold Behavior	All-or-nothing response when threshold potential is reached (~-55mV)	Activation function determines output based on input magnitude
Signal Transmission	Action potential travels down axon to axon terminals	Output value is transmitted to connected neurons in next layer
Connection Points	Signal transmission occurs at synapses between neurons	Connections represented by weighted links between nodes

Learning Mechanism	Learning involves adjusting the strength of synaptic connections (synaptic plasticity)	Learning involves adjusting the weights (w_1, w_2, ..., w_n) based on error feedback
Adaptation Process	Hebbian learning: "Cells that fire together, wire together"	Backpropagation: weights updated to minimize prediction error
Signal Type	Electrochemical (ions: **Na^+, K^+, Ca^{2+}, Cl^-**)	Mathematical (real numbers, typically **0-1 or -1 to 1**)
Processing Speed	Milliseconds per firing cycle	Microseconds to nanoseconds per computation
Energy Consumption	~20 watts for entire brain (~10^{11} neurons)	Varies with hardware; can be energy-intensive for large networks
Fault Tolerance	High redundancy; can function with damaged neurons	Depends on network architecture; typically, less fault-tolerant
Memory Storage	Distributed across synaptic strengths and neural patterns	Stored in weight matrices and network parameters
Plasticity	Lifelong synaptic plasticity and neurogenesis	Weights typically fixed after training (though online learning possible)

Key Mathematical Relationships

Biological Neuron Model

Membrane Potential = Σ(Synaptic Inputs) + Resting Potential

If membrane potential > threshold, action potential fires.

Artificial Neuron Model

Net Input = $\Sigma(w_i \times x_i)$ + bias

Output = f(Net Input)

where f() is the activation function (sigmoid, ReLU, tanh, etc.).

The McCulloch-Pitts neuron model, introduced in 1943, is a simplified mathematical representation of a biological neuron. It operates as a binary threshold unit, where the neuron activates (outputs 1) if the weighted sum of its inputs exceeds a specified threshold; otherwise, it remains inactive (outputs 0). This foundational model laid the groundwork for modern artificial neural networks, demonstrating the potential of logical operations in neural computation.

- Binary threshold unit with weighted inputs
- Output y is given by equation 4.12

$$y = \begin{cases} 1 \; if \sum_i w_i x_i \geq otherwise \\ 0 \; otherwise \end{cases} \quad .....4.12$$

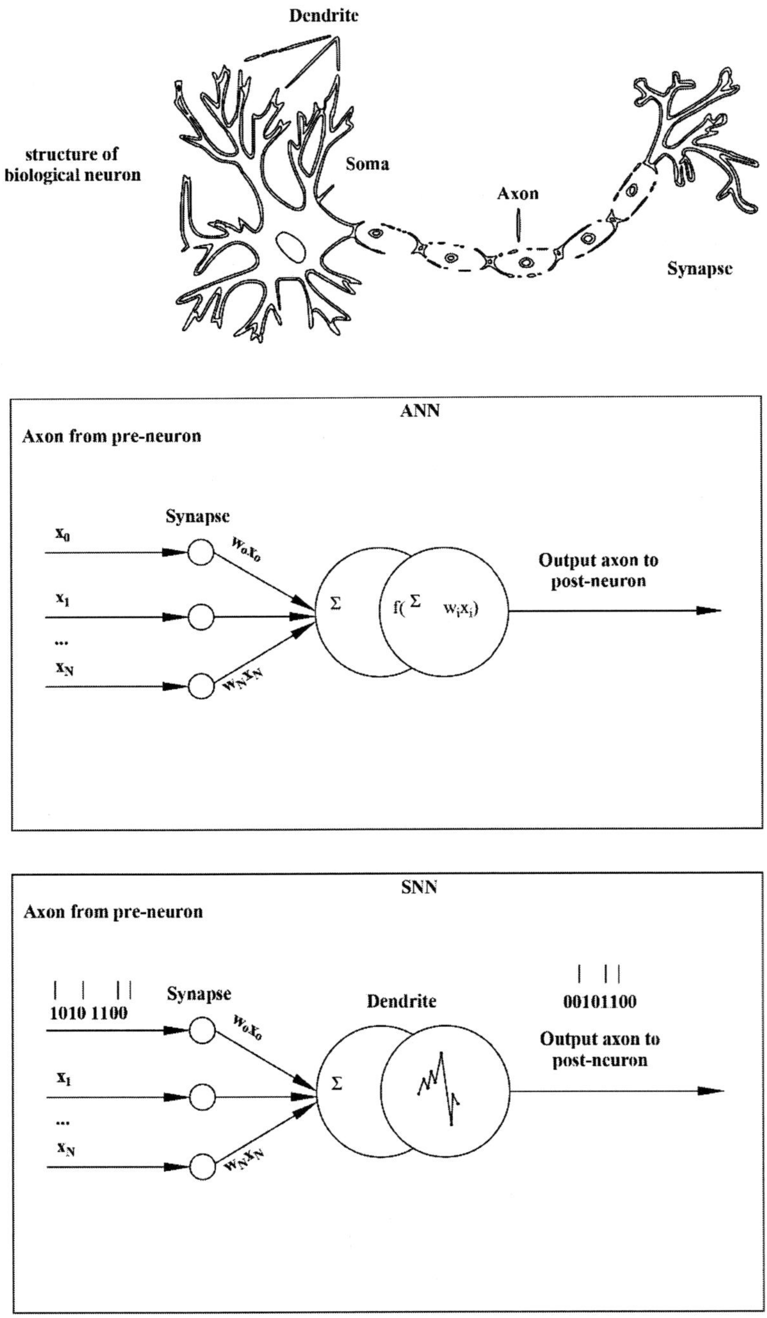

Figure 4.3: Comparison between biological neuron and artificial neuron model

4.3.2 Perceptron and Its Learning Theory

Frank Rosenblatt developed the perceptron in 1958, and it remains a fundamental concept in neural networks and machine learning today. It is the simplest type of feedforward neural network, consisting of a single neuron with adjustable weights and a bias term. The perceptron takes multiple input values, computes their weighted sum, and then proceeds/passes the result by means of a step activation function to get a binary output. This simple approach allows the perceptron to classify linearly separable datasets effectively.

The perceptron system of learning is iterative and supervised. This entails modifying the model's weights and biases in response to observable prediction error. When the perceptron misclassifies an input, its weights are adjusted in a way that minimizes the errors for that particular input. The update rule is straightforward and plausible because for each misclassified sample, weights are increased or lowered appropriately to the input features, scaled by a learning rate. This assures that the perceptron discovers a solution if the dataset is linearly separable.

Despite its simplicity, the perceptron has limitations. The most significant drawback is its inability to solve problems involving non-linearly separable data, as demonstrated by Minsky and Papert in their 1969 critique. Problems like the XOR classification challenge cannot be addressed by a single-layer perceptron due to its linear decision boundary. This limitation eventually led to the development of more advanced models, including multilayer perceptrons and deep learning architectures, which can handle non-linear relationships. However, the perceptron continues to be an important building block for comprehending neural networks. Its design introduces key concepts including weight optimization, learning rates, and decision boundaries. In addition, it served as the foundation for the creation of more sophisticated algorithms such as the Adaline (Adaptive Linear Neuron) and modern methods for deep learning. By studying the perceptron, learners get insight into the evolution of artificial intelligence and the fundamental concepts that underpin/underline modern machine learning.

Perceptron Model:

- Input vector: $x = (x_1, x_2, ..., xn)$
- Weight vector: $w = (w_1, w_2 ..., w_n)$
- **Net Input (Weighted Sum)**:

$$z = w \cdot x + b = \sum_{i=1}^{n} w_i x_i + b \text{......4.13}$$

Where b is the bias term

- Output:

$$y = f(z) \text{.....4.13}(a)$$

- For binary classification, f is typically a step function:

$$f(z) = \begin{cases} 0 \text{ if } z<0 \\ 1 \text{ if } z\geq 0 \end{cases} \text{.......4.13}(b)$$

Perceptron Learning Algorithm:

1. Initialize weights and bias to small random values.
2. For each training example (x, d):
   - Calculate the output.

   $$\mathbf{y} = \mathbf{f}(w_i x_i + b) \text{.....4.14}(\mathbf{a})$$

   - Update weights:

   $$\mathbf{w} = \mathbf{w} + \eta(\mathbf{d} - \mathbf{y})\mathbf{x} \text{.....4.14}(\mathbf{b})$$

   - Update bias:

   $$\mathbf{b} = \mathbf{b} + \eta(\mathbf{d} - \mathbf{y}) \text{....4.14}(\mathbf{c})$$

3. Repeat until convergence or maximum iterations, where η is the learning rate and d is the desired output

Perceptron Learning and Convergence Theorem

The perceptron learning algorithm is a fundamental machine learning technique used for binary categorization. It iteratively adjusts the weights of a perceptron model based on training data. Whenever a misclassification occurs, the perceptron learning rule adjusts the weights, guiding the model to correctly separate the data. The algorithm continues until all training examples have been accurately classified or a stopping requirement is satisfied met.

Perceptron Convergence Theorem: gives a crucial guarantee on the algorithm's behavior. It states that if the training data is linearly separable (that is, there is a hyperplane that can completely partition the classes), the perceptron learning algorithm will discover a solution in a finite number of iterations. The number of iterations necessary is determined by the degree of separation between the two classes as well as the initial weights. This ensures that the perceptron is not only computationally efficient for such applications but also consistently achieves a separating hyperplane when feasible.

However, the theorem demonstrates a shortcoming of the perceptron: it does not guarantee convergence if the data is not linearly separable. In certain circumstances, the algorithm will loop endlessly or oscillate/swing between weight updates without producing a solution. Modern machine learning advances, such as support vector machines (SVMs) and artificial neural networks (ANNs), enable the perceptron concept to handle more complex datasets, including those that are non-linearly separable.

Limitations of the Perceptron:

- Can only learn linearly separable functions
- Cannot solve the XOR problem (as demonstrated by Minsky and Papert)
- Limited expressiveness for complex patterns

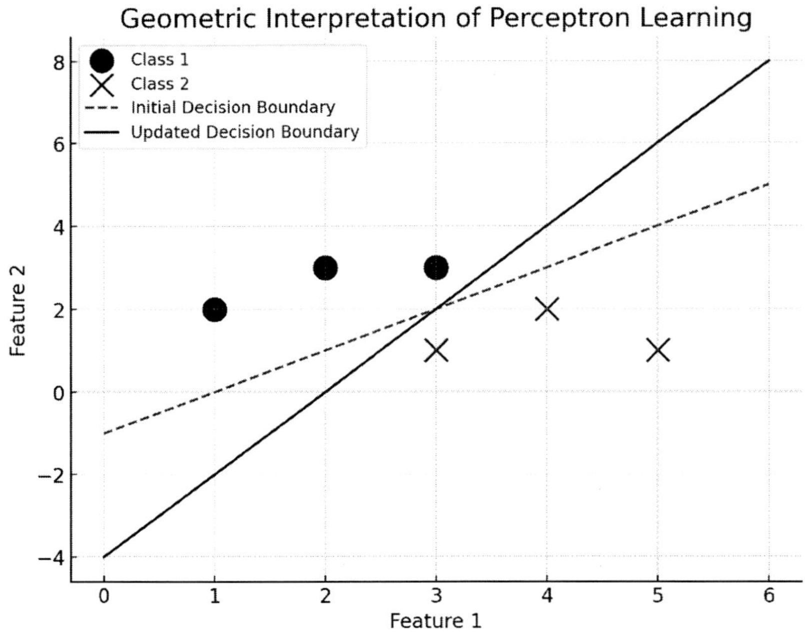

Figure 4.4: Geometric interpretation of perceptron learning showing decision boundary update

4.4 Types and Architectures of Artificial Neural Networks (ANNs)

Artificial Neural Networks (ANNs) are computational models inspired by the human brain's structure and functionality. Over the years, different types and architectures of ANNs have been developed to cater to various tasks such as classification, regression, feature extraction, and prediction. These architectures are distinguished by the number of layers, types of connections between neurons, and specific tasks they are designed to handle.

Types of Neural Networks

1. **Feedforward Neural Networks (FNNs)**: These are the simplest form of ANNs where information flows in one direction from input to output, without any cycles or loops. They are ideal for tasks like image classification and time-series prediction. However, they lack the capability to retain memory or process sequential data effectively.

2. **Recurrent Neural Networks (RNNs)**: RNNs incorporate feedback loops, allowing them to retain information over time. This makes them suitable for tasks like natural language processing (NLP) and speech recognition. Variants such as Long Short-Term Memory (LSTM) and Gated Recurrent Units (GRUs) address the vanishing gradient problem commonly associated with RNNs.

3. **Convolutional Neural Networks (CNNs)**: CNNs are designed for spatial data like images and videos. They employ convolutional layers to extract features such as edges and textures, making them highly effective for object detection and image recognition tasks.

4. **Generative Adversarial Networks (GANs)**: GANs consist of two neural networks—a generator and a discriminator—that compete with each other. They are used for tasks such as image synthesis, style transfer, and data augmentation.

Table 4.4 summarizes the key types of neural networks, their characteristics, and typical applications.

Table 4.4: Types of Neural Networks and Their Applications

Type of Neural Network	**Description**	**Applications**
Feedforward Neural Networks (FNNs)	Simplest form of ANN where information flows in one direction from input to output, without any cycles or loops.	Image classification, time-series prediction
Recurrent Neural Networks (RNNs)	Incorporate feedback loops, allowing them to retain information over time. Variants like LSTM and GRU solve the vanishing gradient problem.	Natural language processing (NLP), speech recognition

Convolutional Neural Networks (CNNs)	Designed for spatial data like images and videos. Use convolutional layers to extract features such as edges and textures.	Object detection, image recognition
Generative Adversarial Networks (GANs)	Comprise two networks (generator and discriminator) competing with each other. Used for generating new data from existing data.	Image synthesis, style transfer, data augmentation

Architectures of Neural Networks

1. **Single-Layer Perceptron: A** single-layer perceptron consists of an input layer connected directly to an output layer. It can solve linearly separable problems but lacks the complexity to handle non-linear data.
2. **Multilayer Perceptron (MLP)**: MLPs include one or more hidden layers between the input and output layers, enabling them to capture non-linear patterns. They utilize activation functions like ReLU, Sigmoid, and Tanh to introduce non-linearity.
3. **Deep Neural Networks (DNNs)**: DNNs are MLPs with multiple hidden layers, designed to model complex functions. They are the backbone of deep learning applications like autonomous driving, voice assistants, and advanced robotics.
4. **Autoencoders:** Autoencoders are unsupervised learning models used for dimensionality reduction and feature learning. They consist of an encoder to compress the input data and a decoder to reconstruct it.

Each type and architecture of ANN has its strengths and limitations, making them suitable for specific applications. Understanding these nuances is essential for selecting the right model for a given problem.

Figure 4.5 presents the architectures of neural networks

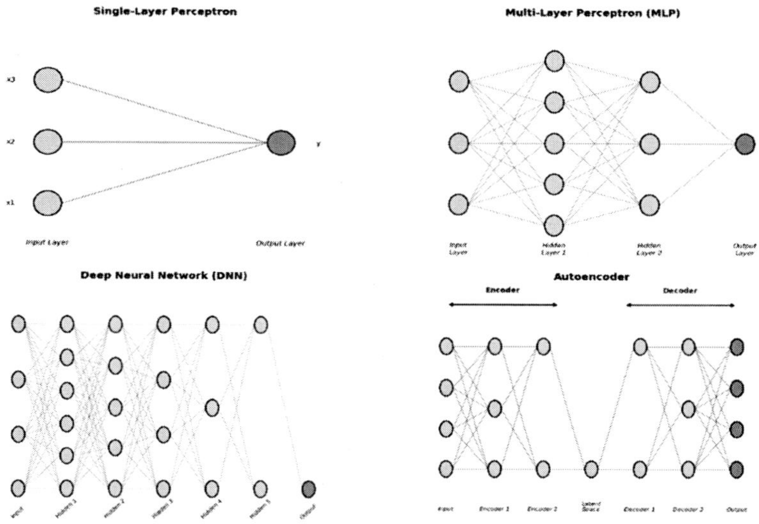

Figure 4.6 (a) the architectures of neural networks

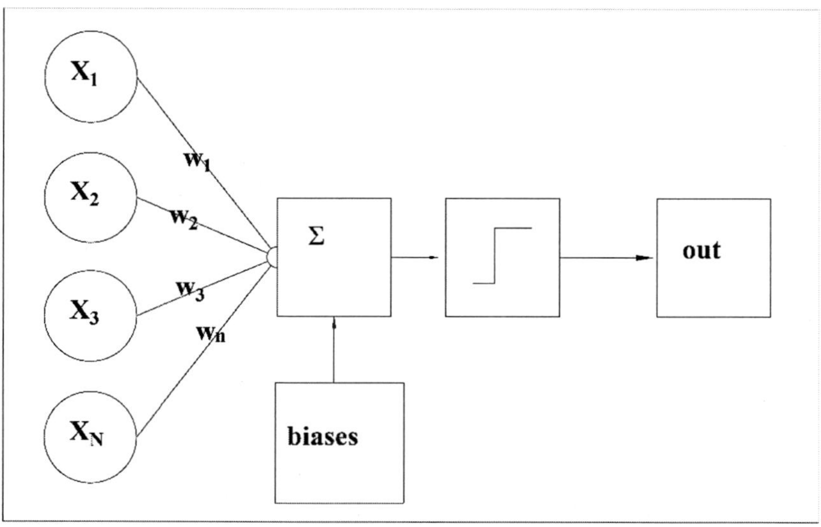

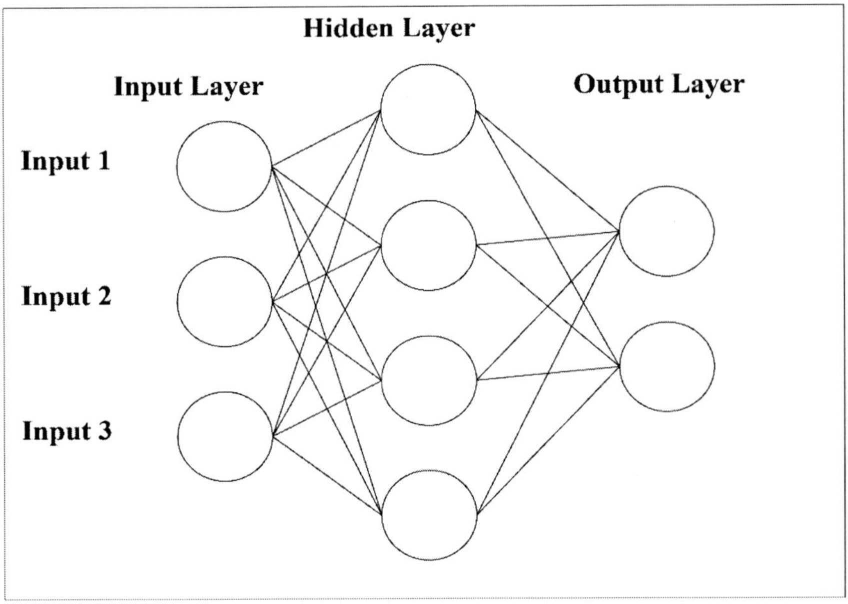
Hidden Layer
Input Layer
Output Layer
Input 1
Input 2
Input 3

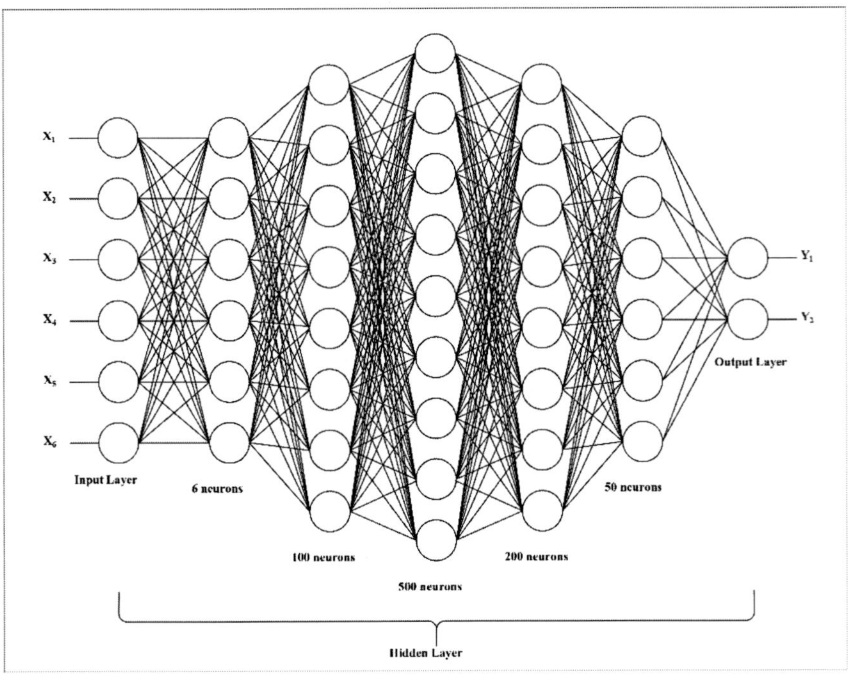
Input Layer
6 neurons
100 neurons
500 neurons
200 neurons
50 neurons
Output Layer
Hidden Layer

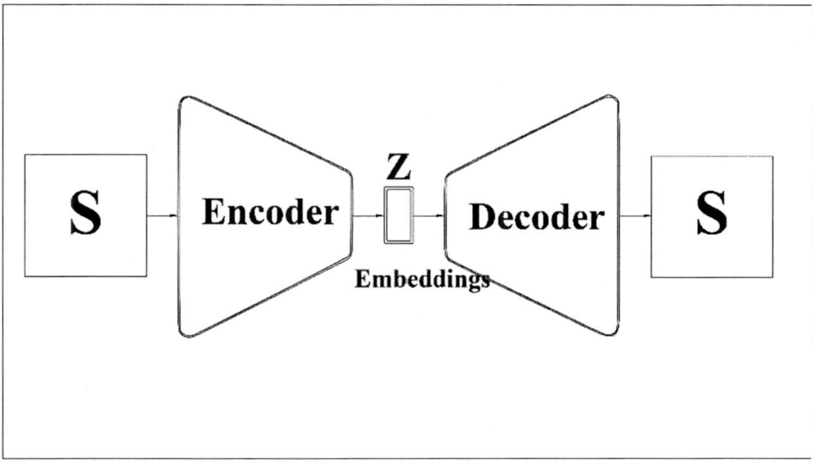

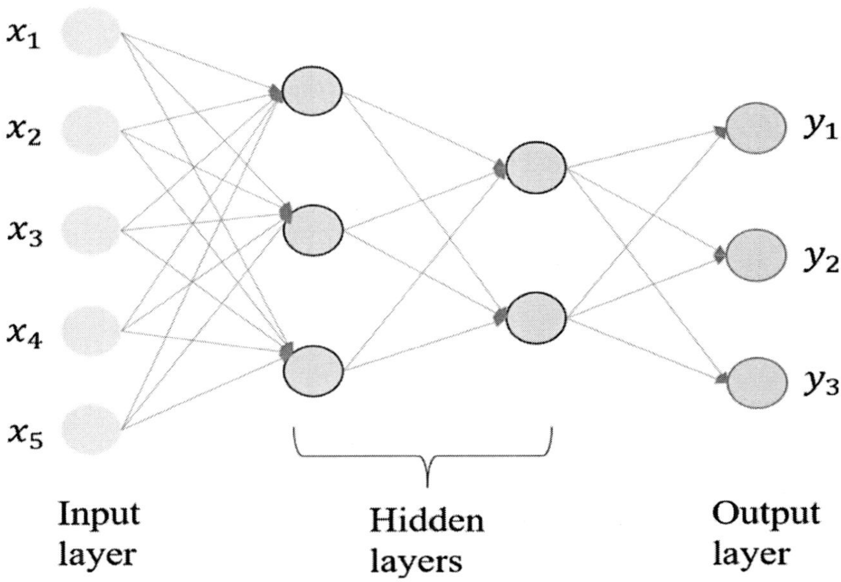

Activation Functions:

Activation functions are mathematical transformations applied to a neuron's input that introduce nonlinearity in neural networks. They play an important role in allowing the network to learn complicated relationships and trends in data. Different activation functions are tailored to specific tasks and architectures. For example, the Sigmoid function transfers input values to the (0, 1) range, which has historical significance but is limited by the vanishing gradient problem. The Hyperbolic Tangent (tanh) function maps to (-1, 1) and frequently outperforms sigmoid due to its centered output. The Rectified Linear Unit (ReLU) is frequently employed due to its simplicity, computing efficiency, and reduced vanishing gradient issues, although it might result in dormant neurons ("dying ReLU"). The Leaky ReLU addresses this issue by allowing modest gradients for negative inputs. The Softmax function, which is generally employed in the output layer for multi-class classification, provides probabilities by normalizing the output values so that they sum up to 1.

The mathematical equations of these activation functions are given in the following equations

- **Sigmoid function**

$$f(z)=\frac{1}{(1+(e^{-z})} \text{......4.15}$$

- **Hyperbolic Tangent (tanh)**:

$$f(z)=\frac{(e^{z}-e^{-z})}{(e^{z}+e^{-z})} \text{......4.16}$$

- **Rectified Linear Unit (ReLu)**

$$\mathbf{f(z)=max(0,z)......4.17}$$

- **Leaky ReLU**

$$\mathbf{f(z)=max(\alpha z,z)......4.18}$$

- **Softmax**

$$\mathbf{f(z_i)=\frac{e^{z_i}}{\sum_{j=1}^{N} e^{z_i}}.......4.19}$$

Table 4.5: Activation Functions

Activation Function	Equation	Range	Key Features
Sigmoid	$f(z)=\frac{1}{(1+(e^{-z}))}$ 4.15	(0, 1)	Historical importance, prone to vanishing gradient
Hyperbolic Tangent (tanh)	$f(z)=\frac{(e^{z}-e^{-z})}{(e^{z}+e^{-z})}$ 4.16	(-1, 1)	Centered output, often better than sigmoid
Rectified Linear Unit (ReLU)	$\mathbf{f(z)=max(0,z)}$ 4.17	[0, ∞)	Reduces vanishing gradient, computationally efficient
Leaky ReLU	$\mathbf{f(z)=max(\alpha z,z)}$ 4.18	(-∞, ∞)	Addresses the "dying ReLU" problem
Softmax	$\mathbf{f(z_i)=\frac{e^{z_i}}{\sum_{j=1}^{N} e^{z_i}}}$ 4.19	(0, 1)	Used in multi-class classification, outputs probabilities

Figure 4.7 Illustrates key activation functions used in neural networks. The first subplot highlights Sigmoid, Tanh, and relu functions, while the second focuses on Leaky ReLU and softmax. These functions play a crucial role in introducing non-linearity, addressing gradient issues, and enabling probability distribution interpretations in neural network models.

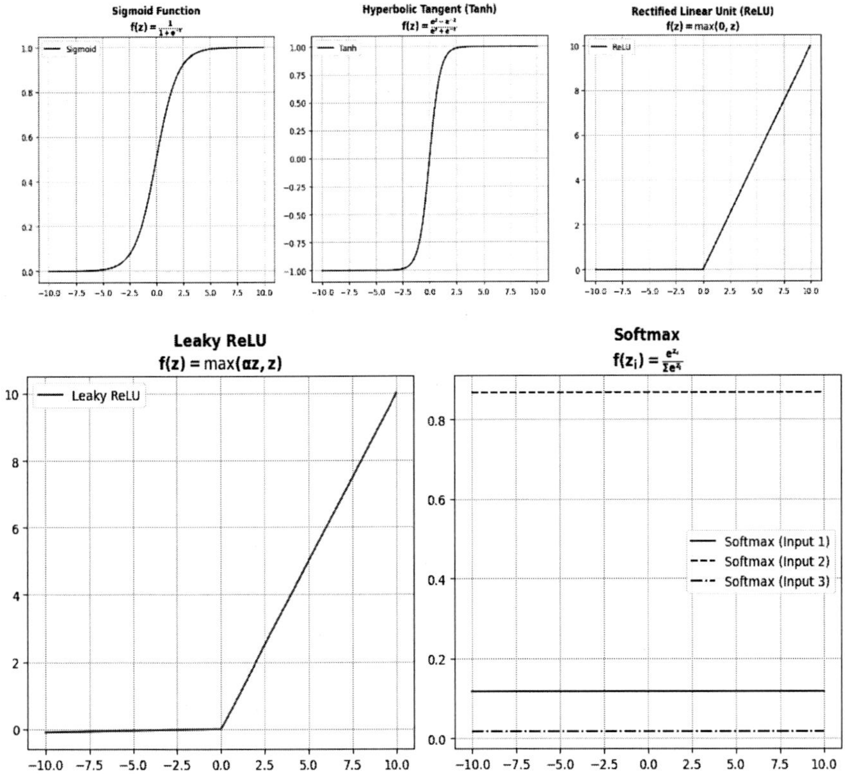

Figure 4.7 Activation Functions

Backpropagation Algorithm:

1. **Forward Pass**: Compute outputs for all neurons
2. **Calculate Error**: Determine the difference between predicted and actual outputs
3. **Backward Pass**: Propagate error backward and compute gradients
4. **Update Weights**: Adjust weights using gradient descent or variants

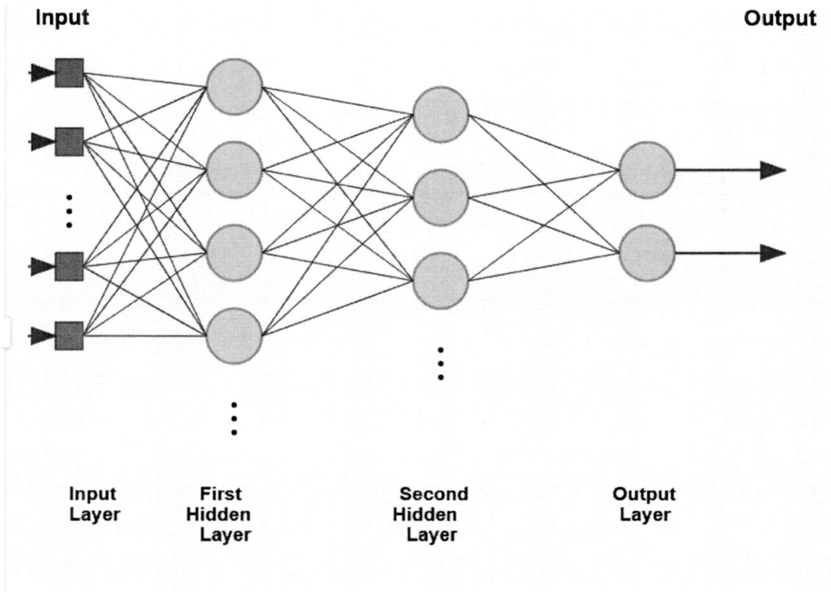

Figure 4.8: Architecture of a multilayer perceptron with hidden layers.

The figure 4.8 represents the architecture of a Multilayer Perceptron (MLP), a foundational type of artificial neural network. The architecture consists of an input layer, multiple hidden layers, and an output layer.

1. **Input Layer**: This layer accepts raw data in the form of numerical values. Each node in the input layer corresponds to a feature in the dataset.

2. **Hidden Layers**: These intermediate layers process the input data by performing weighted summations followed by activation functions. The network learns hierarchical feature representations as the data propagates through these layers. Each node in a hidden layer is fully connected to nodes in adjacent layers.

3. **Output Layer**: This layer provides the final output of the network. Depending on the task, it may use activation functions like Softmax (for classification tasks) or linear functions (for regression tasks).

This figure illustrates the forward pass where input data propagates through the network, as well as the connections between nodes representing the flow of information.

4.4.2 Recurrent and Convolutional Neural Networks:

Recurrent Neural Networks (RNNs) are a type of neural network that has been designed to handle sequential input by including memory mechanisms that allow information to remain across time. Unlike standard feedforward networks, which process inputs separately, RNNs have hidden states that store information from prior inputs in the sequence, allowing them to model temporal relationships and patterns. The primary advancement of RNNs is their recurrent connections, which feed the output of hidden units back as input to the same units in subsequent time steps. This architecture makes RNNs ideal for sequence-based applications such as natural language processing, speech recognition, time series prediction, and machine translation, where the context and order of inputs have an important influence on the desired output.

Despite their theoretical attraction, RNNs have major practical limitations, particularly the vanishing and exploding gradient issues that arise during backpropagation through time. When gradients are carried backward through several time steps, they either diminish exponentially (vanishing gradients) or grow uncontrollably (exploding gradients), making it impossible to understand long-term dependencies effectively. To overcome these issues, more sophisticated variations have been developed, such as Long Short-Term Memory (LSTM) networks and Gated Recurrent Units (GRUs), which use gating mechanisms to better manage information flow and retain relevant information across longer sequences. These advanced architectures have proven extremely successful in applications that require the modeling of complex temporal relationships, but they are increasingly being supplemented or replaced by attention-based models such as Transformers in many domains due to their superior parallelization capabilities and ability to capture long-range dependencies more effectively.

Recurrent Neural Networks (RNNs):

- Process sequential data by maintaining internal state (memory)
- Connections form directed cycles, allowing information persistence
- Well-suited for time series, text, speech, and other sequential data
- Basic RNN units suffer from vanishing/exploding gradient problems

Long Short-Term Memory (LSTM):

- Special RNN architecture designed to address vanishing gradient
- Contains memory cells with input, output, and forget gates
- Can learn long-term dependencies in data
- More complex but more effective than basic RNNs

Gated Recurrent Unit (GRU):

- Simplified version of LSTM with fewer parameters
- Combines forget and input gates into a single "update gate"
- Often comparable performance to LSTM with lower computational cost

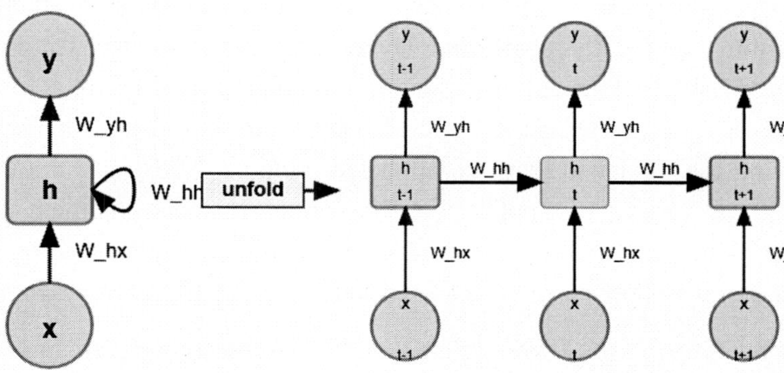

Figure 4.9: Basic RNN architecture unfolded through time.

The figure 4.9 illustrates how an RNN's recurrent structure can be conceptually "unfolded" through time, revealing the network's ability to process sequential inputs by maintaining hidden state information that flows from one time step to the next, where each time step represents the same network parameters applied to different inputs in the sequence.

Convolutional Neural Networks (CNNs):

Convolutional Neural Networks (CNNs) are a subset of deep learning models designed to interpret data with a grid-like architecture, such as images. CNNs, which are inspired by the human visual system, use convolutional layers to uncover hierarchical patterns from input data, making them extremely successful for image identification, object detection, and other similar tasks. CNNs' vital concept is the convolution operation, which employs small, learnable filters to glide over input data and produce feature maps that highlight certain patterns such as edges, textures, or shapes. CNNs, unlike typical fully connected networks, are spatially invariant, which means they can recognize patterns regardless of where they appear in the input.

A typical CNN architecture has three important components: convolutional layers, pooling layers, and fully connected layers. Convolutional layers collect features, pooling layers reduce the spatial dimensions of feature maps to improve computation efficiency and avoid overfitting, and fully connected layers combine extracted features to perform tasks such as classification or regression. In addition, activation functions such as ReLU (Rectified Linear Unit) introduce nonlinearity, allowing the model to learn complicated patterns. CNNs are frequently used in a variety of applications, including medical imaging, facial recognition, autonomous cars, and video analytics, demonstrating their adaptability and power in visual and spatial data handling/processing.

Modern advances in CNN architecture, including as ResNet, Inception, and EfficientNet, have improved their performance and efficiency, allowing them to handle more complex tasks. These architectures incorporate innovations such as skip connections, multi-scale processing, and automated architectural search to enhance training stability, computational efficiency, and generalization capabilities. As a result,

CNNs continue to play an important role in computer vision research and applications.

Key aspects of Convolutional Neural Networks (CNNs):

- Specialized for processing grid-like data (e.g., images)
- Key operations include convolution, pooling, and fully connected layers
- Feature detection through shared weights and local connectivity
- Automatically learns hierarchical feature representations

CNN Components:

1. **Convolutional Layer**: Applies filters to detect local patterns

   Parameters: filter size, stride, padding, number of filters

2. **Pooling Layer**: Downsamples feature maps

   Common types: max pooling, average pooling

   Reduces spatial dimensions and computational load

3. **Fully Connected Layer**: Typically used in final stages for classification

4. **Batch Normalization**: Stabilizes and accelerates training.

Figure 4.10 illustrates CNN Architecture

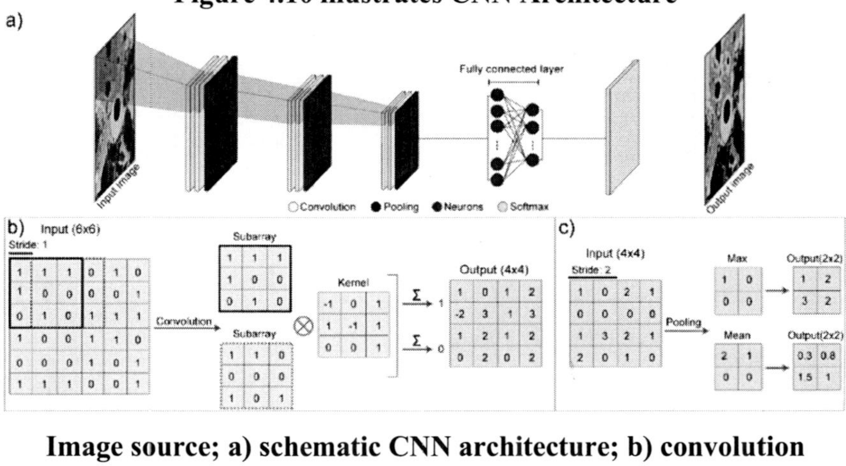

Image source; a) schematic CNN architecture; b) convolution example; c) pooling example. | Download Scientific Diagram

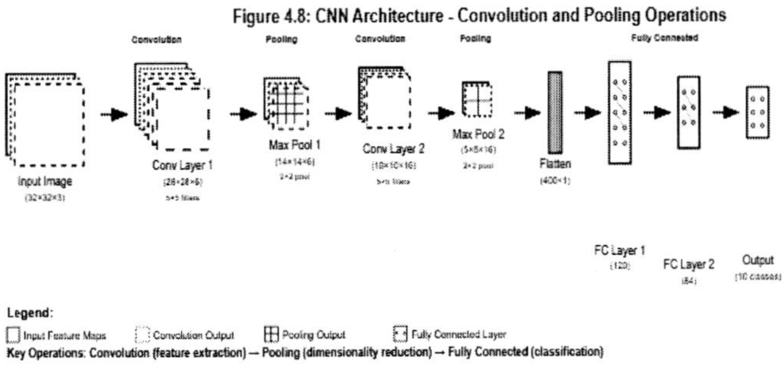

Figure 4.11: CNN architecture showing convolution and pooling operations.

Other Important Architectures:

- **Autoencoders**: Unsupervised learning for dimensionality reduction
- **Generative Adversarial Networks (GANs)**: Two competing networks for generating realistic data
- **Transformer Networks**: Attention-based architecture for sequence processing
- **Deep Belief Networks**: Stack of restricted Boltzmann machines

Table 4.6: Comparison of neural network architectures for different applications

Architecture	Key Characteristics	Primary Applications	Advantages	Limitations
Feedforward Neural Networks (FNN)	Simple layered structure, unidirectional information flow	Classification, regression, function approximation	Simple to implement, fast training, good for tabular data	Cannot handle sequential data, limited feature extraction
Convolutional Neural Networks (CNN)	Convolutional layers, pooling, local connectivity, parameter sharing	Image recognition, computer vision, medical imaging	Translation invariant, hierarchical feature learning,	Computationally intensive, requires large datasets, poor for sequential data

			efficient for spatial data	
Recurrent Neural Networks (RNN)	Recurrent connections, memory through hidden states	Natural language processing, speech recognition, time series	Handles sequential data, memory of previous inputs	Vanishing gradient problem, slow training, limited long-term memory
Long Short-Term Memory (LSTM)	Gating mechanisms, cell state, forget/input/output gates	Language modeling, machine translation, sentiment analysis	Solves vanishing gradient, better long-term dependencies	Complex architecture, computationally expensive, many parameters
Gated Recurrent Unit (GRU)	Simplified gating, reset and update gates	Text generation, speech processing, sequence modeling	Simpler than LSTM, faster training, fewer parameters	Less expressive than LSTM for complex tasks
Transformer	Self-attention mechanism, encoder-decoder architecture	Machine translation, language understanding, text generation	Parallelizable, captures long-range dependencies, state-of-the-art performance	Requires large amounts of data, computationally intensive, high memory usage
Autoencoder	Encoder-decoder structure, bottleneck layer	Dimensionality reduction, feature learning, anomaly detection	Unsupervised learning, data compression, noise reduction	May lose important information, requires careful architecture design
Generative Adversarial Networks (GAN)	Two competing networks (generator and discriminator)	Image generation, data augmentation, style transfer	High-quality synthetic data generation, creative applications	Training instability, mode collapse, difficult to evaluate

Residual Networks (ResNet)	Skip connections, residual blocks	Deep image classification, computer vision tasks	Enables very deep networks, addresses vanishing gradient	Increased computational complexity, memory requirements
Graph Neural Networks (GNN)	Operates on graph-structured data, message passing	Social network analysis, molecular property prediction, recommendation systems	Handles irregular data structures, captures relational information	Limited to graph data, scalability challenges for large graphs

4.5 Applications and Challenges of ANNs

The applications gamut of ANNs spans almost every field of current technology and scientific research, displaying amazing adaptability and effectiveness in solving complex problems. CNNs have revolutionized recognition of images, medical imaging, and autonomous vehicle navigation in computer vision, whilst RNNs and Transformers have transformed natural language processing through applications in machine translation, chatbots, and text generation systems such as GPT models. ANNs are widely utilized in healthcare for drug development, disease diagnosis, and individualized therapy recommendations, and in finance for automated trading, fraud detection, and credit risk assessment. Other notable uses include e-commerce and streaming platform recommendation systems, speech recognition and synthesis, robotics and control systems, weather forecasting, and scientific research from protein folding prediction to materials science discovery.

Despite their outstanding capabilities, artificial neural networks face significant challenges that limit their broad adoption and reliability. The "black box" aspect of deep neural networks presents interpretability concerns, making it difficult to understand how choices are made. This is particularly challenging in essential applications such as healthcare and criminal justice. ANNs often require huge quantities of labeled training data and substantial computer resources, making them costly to build and implement. They are vulnerable to adversarial attacks in which slight, unnoticeable input changes can produce large misclassifications, and they frequently exhibit bias inherited from training data, resulting in inconsistent results across demographic groups. Furthermore, ANNs suffer from catastrophic forgetting when learning new tasks, have limited ability to generalize beyond their training distribution, and face difficulties in handling uncertainty quantification and out-of-distribution detection, making them potentially unreliable in safety-critical applications where robust performance is essential.

4.5.1 Use Cases in Image and Speech Recognition

Image Recognition Applications:

- **Object Detection**: Identifying and localizing objects in images
- **Image Classification**: Assigning categories to images
- **Facial Recognition**: Identifying individuals from facial features
- **Medical Image Analysis**: Detecting anomalies in X-rays, MRIs, etc.
- **Autonomous Vehicles** : Perceiving and interpreting the environment

Key CNN Architectures for Vision:

- **AlexNet**: Pioneering architecture that popularized CNNs
- **VGG**: Deep network with small filters and simple architecture
- **ResNet**: Introduced residual connections to train very deep networks
- **Inception/GoogLeNet**: Used inception modules with parallel convolutions
- **EfficientNet**: Optimized architecture scaling for efficiency

Figure 4.9 shows the evolution of CNN architectures on ImageNet from 2010 to 2015, demonstrating how deeper networks (from 8 layers in AlexNet to 152 layers in ResNet) achieved dramatically lower error rates, with ResNet-152 reaching just 3.57% error compared to 28.2% for the shallow networks of 2010.

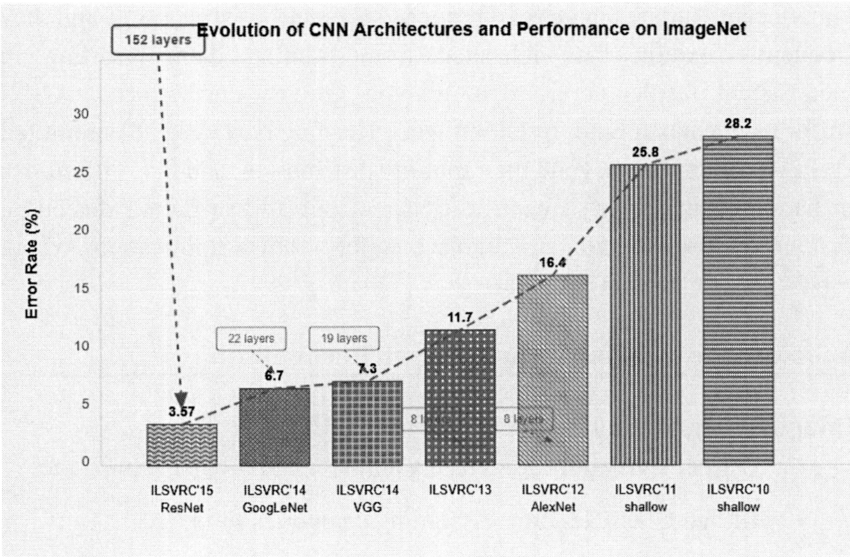

Figure 4.12: Evolution of CNN architectures and their performance on ImageNet.

Speech Recognition Applications:

- **Automated Speech Recognition (ASR)**: Converting spoken language to text
- **Speaker Identification**: Recognizing individuals by voice
- **Voice Command Systems**: Voice assistants like Siri, Alexa
- **Speech-to-Speech Translation**: Real-time translation between languages
- **Medical Applications**: Diagnosing conditions from voice patterns

Neural Network Approaches for Speech:

- **Traditional**: Combination of RNNs/LSTMs with Hidden Markov Models
- **End-to-End**: Direct speech-to-text using deep networks
- **Transformer-Based**: Using attention mechanisms for improved performance

- **Wav2Vec/Wav2Letter**: Self-supervised approaches for speech representation

Table 4.7 Performance Comparison of Neural Network Architectures for Speech Recognition Tasks

Architecture	Key Features	Strengths	Challenges	Example Use Case
Convolutional Neural Networks (CNNs)	Extracts local features, spatial invariance	Robust to variations in input signals	Limited ability to capture temporal dependencies	Acoustic feature extraction
Recurrent Neural Networks (RNNs)	Sequence modeling, temporal dependencies	Effective for sequential data	Difficulty handling long-term dependencies	Phoneme recognition
Long Short-Term Memory (LSTM)	Memory cells for long-term dependencies	Solves vanishing gradient issues	Computationally intensive	Word-level recognition
Transformer Models	Attention mechanism, parallel processing	Handles long-range dependencies efficiently	Requires large datasets and resources	End-to-end speech-to-text systems
Deep Speech (RNN-based)	End-to-end learning, large-scale RNN	Simplifies feature engineering	Requires extensive labeled data	Large vocabulary continuous speech
Connectionist Temporal Classification (CTC)	Sequence-to-sequence alignment	Does not require pre-segmented data	Performance depends on quality of training data	Speech-to-text transcription
WaveNet	Autoregressive model for raw audio data	Generates high-quality audio representations	Computationally expensive	Text-to-speech synthesis

This table 4.4 provides an overview of various architectures, their features, strengths, challenges, and specific applications.

4.5.2 Overfitting, Vanishing Gradients, and Computational Demands:

Overfitting: Overfitting is an important challenge in neural network training, especially when models are excessively complex in relation to the number and diversity of training data. Overfitting happens when a model learns not just the underlying patterns but also noise and random fluctuations in training data, resulting in poor generalization to new/unseen data. Dropout, regularization, and early halting are common techniques for combating overfitting. Dropout randomly disables neurons during training, forcing the network to learn redundant representations, whereas regularization methods like as L1 and L2 penalize excessively complex models. Additional ways for improving generalization include increasing the size and diversity of the training dataset and using data augmentation.

- Occurs when model performs well on training data but poorly on new data
- Indicators: large gap between training and validation error
- **Causes**:
    - Insufficient training data
    - Model complexity exceeding data complexity
    - Noisy data

Solutions to Overfitting:

1. **Regularization Techniques**:
    - L1 regularization (Lasso): Encourages sparse weights
    - L2 regularization (Ridge): Penalizes large weights
    - Elastic Net: Combination of L1 and L2
2. **Dropout**: Randomly deactivating neurons during training

3. **Early Stopping**: Halting training when validation error begins to increase
4. **Data Augmentation**: Artificially expanding the training set
5. **Batch Normalization**: Normalizing activations within mini-batches the figure 4.10 illustrates overfitting in training vs validation performance.

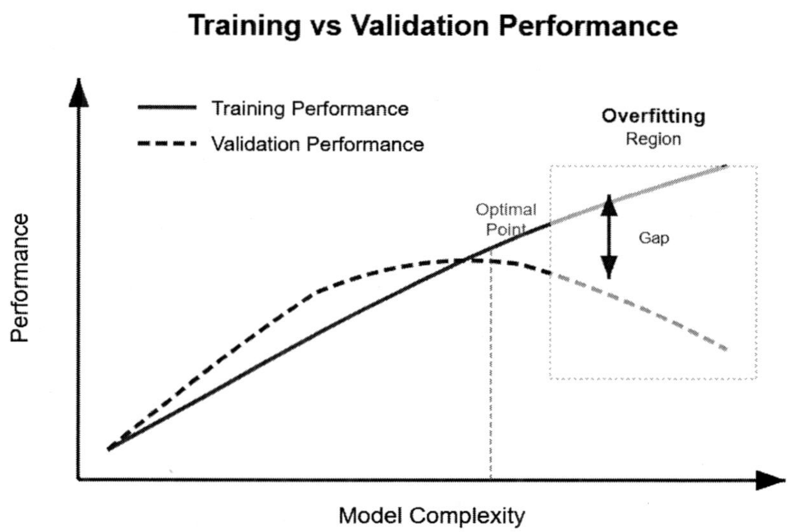

Figure 4.13: Illustration of overfitting showing training vs. validation error curves

Vanishing and Exploding Gradients:

Another significant challenge is the vanishing gradient problem, which occurs in deep networks with several layers. As gradients are backpropagated through the network, they can diminish exponentially, making it difficult to update weights in earlier layers effectively. This causes training to stagnate since the network is unable to acquire relevant features in deeper layers. The problem is especially prominent in networks with sigmoid or hyperbolic tangent (tanh) activation functions. This problem can be resolved by using activation functions such as ReLU (Rectified Linear Unit), which avoids gradient shrinkage by maintaining positive gradients for non-negative inputs, and architectures such as

LSTMs and residual networks (ResNets), which mitigate gradient decay by introducing memory cells or skipping connections.

- **Vanishing Gradient Problem**:
    - Gradients become extremely small as they propagate backward
    - Earlier layers learn very slowly or not at all
    - Common in deep networks with sigmoid/tanh activations
- **Exploding Gradient Problem**:
    - Gradients become extremely large during backpropagation
    - Can cause unstable training and parameter updates

Solutions to Gradient Problems:

1. **Alternative Activation Functions**: ReLU and variants
2. **Weight Initialization Strategies**: Xavier/Glorot, He initialization
3. **Gradient Clipping**: Limiting gradient magnitude
4. **Specialized Architectures**: LSTM, GRU, ResNet
5. **Batch Normalization**: Stabilizing internal activations

Computational Challenges:

Computational needs are another important factor when developing and training neural networks, particularly large-scale models. Deep network training necessitates significant processing power, memory, and time, making it difficult for researchers and practitioners with limited finances to enter the field. The choice of hardware, such as GPUs or TPUs, is critical for accelerating calculations, as is improving model architectures to eliminate redundancy yet preserve performance. Model pruning, quantization, and knowledge distillation are all techniques aimed at increasing network efficiency and enabling deployment on resource-constrained devices such as smartphones and IoT sensors. Balancing model complexity, accuracy, and computational efficiency is critical for overcoming these challenges in real-world applications.

- **Time Complexity**: Training deep networks requires significant computation
- **Memory Requirements**: Storing parameters, activations, and gradients
- **Energy Consumption**: Environmental and cost implications
- **Hardware Limitations**: Need for specialized hardware (GPUs, TPUs)

Addressing Computational Challenges:

1. **Model Compression:**
    - Pruning: Removing insignificant connections
    - Quantization: Reducing precision of weights
    - Knowledge Distillation: Training smaller models to mimic larger ones
2. **Efficient Architectures**:
    - MobileNet, EfficientNet: Designed for resource-constrained environments
3. **Distributed Training**:
    - Data parallelism: Same model across multiple devices
    - Model parallelism: Different parts of model on different devices
4. **Transfer Learning**:
    - Reusing pre-trained models to reduce training time

Table 4.8: Computational Requirements for Training Various Neural Network Architectures

Architecture	Memory Requirements	Computational Complexity	Training Time	Suitable Hardware
Fully Connected Networks	Low to moderate	$O(n^2)$ for weight updates	Short to moderate	CPUs, entry-level GPUs
Convolutional Neural Networks (CNNs)	Moderate to high	$O(k^2 .n^2)$ for convolution	Moderate to long	GPUs, TPUs
Recurrent Neural Networks (RNNs)	High for long sequences	$O(t^2 \cdot n^2)$due to time steps	Long	High-memory GPUs
Long Short-Term Memory (LSTM)	Very high	$OO(t.n^2)$with additional gates	Very long	High-memory GPUs
Transformer Models	Extremely high	$O(n^2 \cdot d))$ for attention	Very long	GPUs, TPUs with large VRAM
Generative Adversarial Networks (GANs)	High	O(n2) for both generator and discriminator	Long	High-performance GPUs
WaveNet	Extremely high	$O(t \cdot n)$ for autoregression	Extremely long	High-performance GPUs, TPUs

Legend:

- n: Number of neurons or parameters
- t: Sequence length

- k: Kernel size in convolution
- d: Embedding dimensions in transformers

Table 4.5, summarizes the computational requirements for training various neural network architectures, including their memory demands, complexity, training duration, and ideal hardware for training.

Chapter Summary and Concluding Thoughts

This chapter provided a comprehensive exploration of two fundamental approaches to machine learning: Bayesian learning and artificial neural networks. Bayesian models leverage probability theory for reasoning under uncertainty, with Bayes' theorem forming the backbone of probabilistic classification, as demonstrated by the Naïve Bayes algorithm's effectiveness in handling both discrete and continuous attributes.

Artificial neural networks, inspired by biological systems, offer highly flexible models capable of learning intricate patterns in data. The chapter traced their evolution from perceptrons to advanced architectures, highlighting their use in image and speech recognition while addressing the practical challenges they face, such as overfitting and high computational demands.

The interplay between Bayesian models and neural networks underscores their complementary strengths. Bayesian methods provide interpretability and robust uncertainty quantification, while neural networks excel at complex pattern recognition. Together, they offer diverse tools for solving a wide range of machine learning problems, providing a solid foundation for further exploration of advanced topics and real-world applications.

Conceptual Questions

1. Define Bayes' theorem and its role in probabilistic reasoning.
2. Explain the Naïve Bayes algorithm. What are its key assumptions?
3. Compare and contrast discrete and continuous random variables in the context of Bayesian learning.
4. Describe the architecture of an artificial neural network (ANN). How is it inspired by biological neurons?

5. What are activation functions in ANNs, and why are they important? Compare ReLU, Sigmoid, and Softmax functions.

6. How do CNNs and RNNs differ in terms of structure and applications?

7. Discuss the significance of the perceptron in the history of neural networks.

Application-Based Questions

8. Design a classification pipeline using Naïve Bayes for email spam detection. Highlight preprocessing steps.

9. Explain how recurrent neural networks (RNNs) are applied to time-series prediction problems.

10. Propose a convolutional neural network (CNN) architecture for a medical image analysis task.

Critical Thinking Questions

11. Discuss the challenges and limitations of using Bayesian models in high-dimensional datasets.

12. Evaluate the impact of vanishing gradients on deep networks. How do architectures like LSTMs address this issue?

13. Explore the trade-offs between overfitting and underfitting in the context of ANN training.

Chapter - 5

Clustering Algorithms and Reinforcement Learning

- Introduction to Clustering and Proximity Measures
- Hierarchical and Partitional Clustering Techniques
- Density-Based and Grid-Based Clustering Methods
- Reinforcement Learning Overview, Scope, and Components of Reinforcement Learning
- Problem Types: Markov Decision Process and Multi-Arm Bandit Problem
- Learning Methods: Model-Based, Model-Free, Q-Learning, and SARSA.

Chapter Overview

This chapter explores two fundamental paradigms in machine learning: unsupervised learning through clustering algorithms and reinforcement learning. The first part comprehensively covers clustering approaches, examining various methodologies for discovering hidden patterns and structures in unlabelled data. We begin with proximity measures that form the foundation of clustering, then progress through hierarchical methods that build dendrograms, partitional algorithms that divide data into distinct groups, density-based approaches that identify clusters of varying shapes, and grid-based methods that partition feature space.

The second part introduces reinforcement learning, a powerful paradigm where agents learn optimal behaviour through interaction with their environment. We explore the theoretical foundations including Markov Decision Processes, examine different problem formulations like multi-arm bandits, and delve into both model-based and model-free learning approaches. Special attention is given to Q-learning and SARSA, two cornerstone algorithms that have revolutionized sequential decision-making in artificial intelligence.

This chapter bridges the gap between unsupervised pattern discovery and goal-oriented learning, providing essential knowledge for understanding how machines can both find structure in data and learn to make optimal decisions.

5.1 Clustering Algorithms

5.1.1 Introduction to Clustering Approaches

Clustering is one of the most significant approaches in unsupervised learning, as it reveals hidden patterns and structures in data. Clustering helps to understand the underlying relationships in datasets by grouping data points that are similar together. Clustering, unlike supervised learning, does not depend on predefined labels or outcomes; rather, it is exclusively concerned with the inherent characteristics of the data itself. This makes it an essential tool for exploratory data analysis, consumer segmentation, anomaly detection, and data preprocessing. The efficacy of Clustering depends on its ability to reduce data complexity while also highlighting key patterns that might not be immediately apparent.

The versatility of clustering algorithms allows them to handle diverse data types and structures. For example, hierarchical clustering builds nested clusters through a series of agglomerative or divisive steps, creating a tree-like representation of data relationships. K-means clustering, on the other hand, assigns data points to a fixed number of clusters based on their proximity to cluster centroids, offering simplicity and computational efficiency. Density-based approaches like DBSCAN focus on the density of data points, enabling the identification of irregularly shaped clusters and the exclusion of noise. Each method has its strengths and limitations, making the choice of algorithm context-dependent.

Clustering's current applications go beyond conventional fields like marketing and social science to advanced domains like bioinformatics, image processing, and natural language processing. Clustering helps with tasks such as gene expression analysis, image segmentation, and topic modeling. As datasets grow in size and complexity, clustering approaches evolve to include improvements in scalability, interpretability, and interaction with other machine learning methods. Using these approaches, researchers and practitioners may gain deeper insights and make more accurate data-driven decisions.

Key Characteristics of Clustering:

- **Unsupervised Nature**: No prior knowledge of group labels
- **Similarity-Based**: Groups objects based on feature similarity
- **Exploratory**: Reveals hidden patterns and structures
- **Flexible**: Applicable across diverse domains and data types

Types of Clustering Problems:

- **Hard Clustering**: Each object belongs to exactly one cluster
- **Soft Clustering**: Objects can belong to multiple clusters with varying degrees
- **Hierarchical**: Creates nested cluster structures
- **Partitional**: Divides data into non-overlapping partitions

Applications:

- Customer segmentation in marketing
- Gene expression analysis in bioinformatics
- Image segmentation in computer vision
- Social network community detection
- Market basket analysis in retail

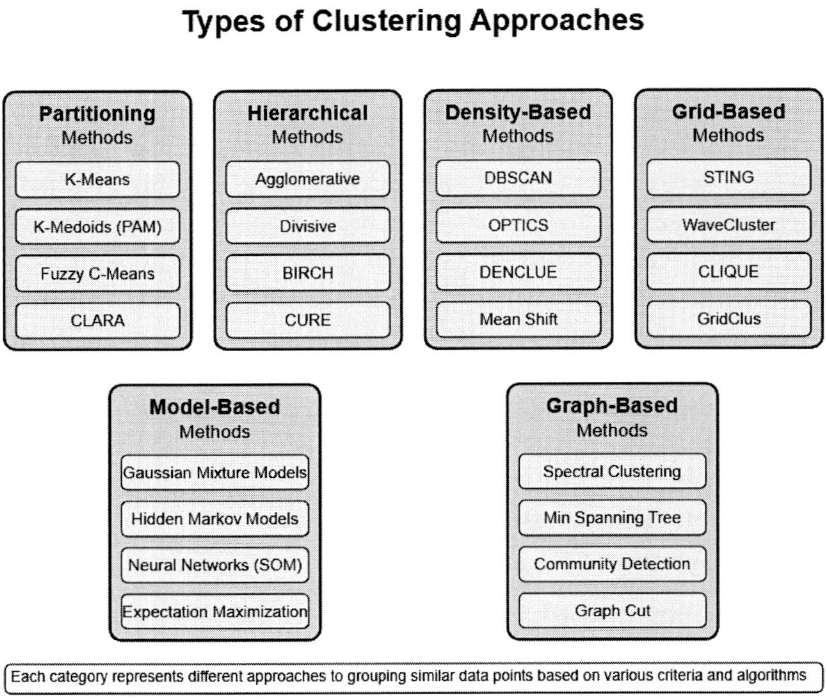

Figure 5.1 Types of Clustering Approaches

5.1.2 Proximity Measures

Proximity measures quantify the similarity or dissimilarity between data points, forming the foundation of all clustering algorithms. The choice of proximity measure significantly impacts clustering results.

5.1.2.1 Distance Measures

Euclidean Distance: The most common distance measure for continuous attributes.

$$d(x,y)=\sqrt{\sum_{i=1}^{n}(x_i-y_i)^2} \quad \text{........}\mathbf{5.1}$$

Manhattan Distance (L1 Norm): Sum of absolute differences, robust to outliers.

$$d(x,y)=\sum_{i=1}^{n}|x_i-y_i| \quad \text{..........}\mathbf{5.2}$$

Minkowski Distance: Generalization of Euclidean and Manhattan distances.

$$d(x,y)=\left(\sum_{i=1}^{n}|x_i-y_i|^{p}x\right)^{\frac{1}{P}} \text{.......5.3}$$

Cosine Distance: Measures angle between vectors, useful for high-dimensional data.

$$d(x,y)=1-\frac{x\cdot y}{\|x\|\|y\|} \text{......5.4}$$

5.1.2.2 Similarity Measures

Jaccard Similarity: For binary attributes and sets.

$$J(A,B)=\frac{|A\cap B|}{|A\cup B|} \text{.......5.5}$$

Pearson Correlation: Measures linear correlation between variables.

$$\mathrm{r}=\frac{\sum_{i=1}^{n}(x_i-\overline{\mathrm{x}}),(y_i-\overline{\mathrm{y}})}{\sqrt{\sum_{i=1}^{n}(x_i-\overline{\mathrm{x}})^2.\sum_{i=1}^{n}(y_i-\overline{\mathrm{y}})^2}} \text{....5.6}$$

Table 5.1 – elaborates a comparison of Proximity Measures.

Table 5.1: Comparison of Proximity Measures

Measure	**Eqn**	**Data Type**	**Advantages**	**Disadvantages**	**Best Use Cases**	**Computational Complexity**
Euclidean Distance	5.1	Continuous numerical	• Most intuitive geometric distance • Works well with spherical clusters • Mathematically well-	• Sensitive to outliers • Affected by curse of dimensionality • Assumes equal importance of all	• Low to moderate dimensional continuous data • Spherical cluster shapes 	O(d) per pair

			defined • Supports many clustering algorithms	dimensions • Poor performance with correlated features	• K-means clustering • Computer vision applications	
Manhattan Distance (L1 Norm)	5.2	Continuous numerical	• Robust to outliers • Less affected by high dimensions • Computationally simpler • Works well with grid-like structures	• Less intuitive than Euclidean • May not capture true geometric relationships • Can produce ties in distance calculations	• High-dimensional data • Data with outliers • Grid-based or city-block layouts • Robust clustering requirements	O(d) per pair
Minkowski Distance	5.3	Continuous numerical	• Generalizes Euclidean and Manhattan • Flexible parameter p • Can be tuned for specific data characteristics • Mathematically elegant	• Parameter p needs tuning • Computational overhead for non-integer p • No clear guidelines for p selection • Still sensitive to dimensionality	• When flexibility in distance measure is needed • Experimental comparison of distance metrics • Domain-specific applications	O(d) per pair

Cosine Distance	5.4	x\	\	y\	)	Continuous numerical (typically positive)
Jaccard Similarity	5.5 |	Binary/ Set data	• Perfect for binary and categorical data • Intuitive interpretation • Handles sparse binary vectors well • Scale-invariant	• Only applicable to binary/set data • Doesn't handle continuous values • Sensitive to data sparsity • No magnitude information	• Market basket analysis • Binary feature clustering • Social network analysis • Categorical data clustering	O(min(|A|,|B|))
Pearson Correlation	5.6	Continuous numerical	• Measures linear relationships • Scale-invariant • Handles different units well • Good for time series data	• Only captures linear relationships • Sensitive to outliers • Requires sufficient data points • May miss non-linear patterns	• Time series clustering • Gene expression analysis • Financial data analysis • Pattern-based clustering	O(d) per pair

5.1.3 Hierarchical Clustering Algorithms

Hierarchical clustering creates a tree-like structure of clusters, offering insights into data organization at multiple granularity levels. Hierarchical clustering is a versatile technique that uses a tree-like structure, often known as a dendrogram, to depict the hierarchical relationships among data points. This method provides a detailed perspective (granular view) of how data points cluster/groups) at various levels of similarity, making it ideal for exploratory data analysis. Unlike partition-based approaches, hierarchical clustering does not require a pre-determined number of clusters. Instead, clusters form dynamically, allowing researchers to determine the appropriate number of clusters through analyzing the dendrogram.

What is the intuition behind a Dendrogram?

A dendrogram pulls together data points into groups that are closest to each other. The distance can be measured using Euclidean or Manhattan distance etc. or any other distance formula as required by the use case and then the dendrogram treats every new group as one unit and then measures the distance of this group from a new data point to make another group at a higher level of the hierarchy.

There are two primary methods to hierarchical clustering: agglomerative (bottom-up) and divisive (top-down). Agglomerative clustering begins by treating each data point as a separate cluster and gradually merging the nearest clusters until all points belong to the same cluster. Divisive clustering, on the other hand, begins with all data points in a single large cluster and then recursively breaks it into smaller ones. Both methods use a distance metric, such as Euclidean or Manhattan distance, and a linkage criterion, such as single, complete, or average linkage, to identify cluster proximity and structure.

The tree-like structure created by hierarchical clustering has various advantages. It provides a comprehensive overview of the natural grouping of data at various sizes, making it appropriate for datasets with an uncertain or not known number of clusters. In addition, the dendrogram allows for flexible grouping decisions, as the process can be stopped at any granularity level. Hierarchical clustering can be computationally demanding for big datasets, with a time complexity of $O(n2)$ or greater, depending on the implementation. Despite this, its ability to show multi-level data links makes it useful in sectors/fields like biology, text mining, and social network analysis.

5.1.3.1 Agglomerative Hierarchical Clustering

Algorithm Steps:

1. Start with each point as individual cluster
2. Repeatedly merge closest cluster pairs
3. Continue until single cluster remains
4. Create dendrogram showing merge history

Linkage Criteria:

Single Linkage (Minimum):

- Distance = minimum distance between cluster points
- Tends to create elongated clusters
- Sensitive to noise and outliers

Complete Linkage (Maximum):

- Distance = maximum distance between cluster points
- Creates compact, spherical clusters
- More robust to outliers

Average Linkage:

- Distance = average of all pairwise distances
- Balances single and complete linkage properties
- Generally, produces balanced clusters

Ward's Method:

- Minimizes within-cluster sum of squares
- Creates compact, similarly sized clusters
- Requires Euclidean distance

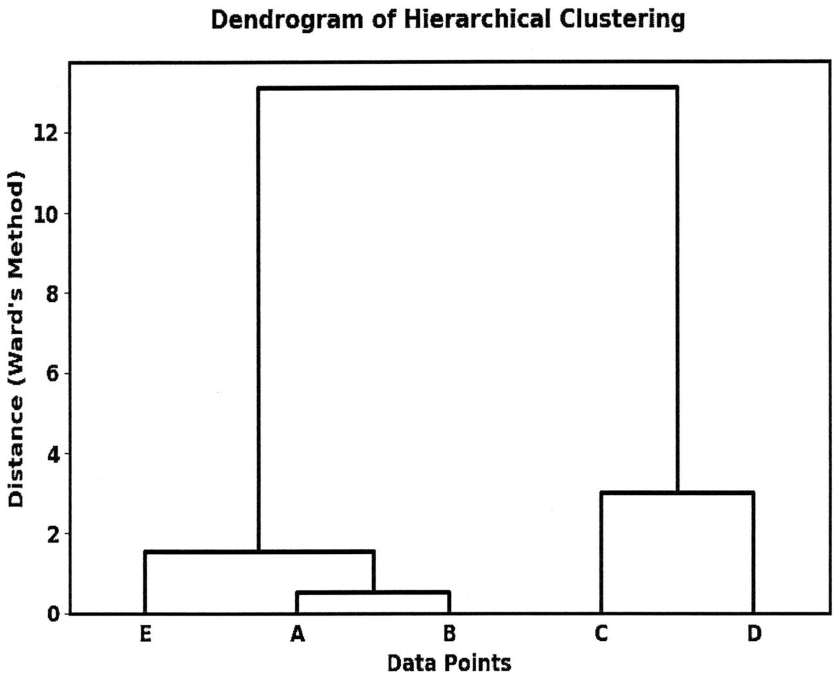

Figure 5.2 Dendrogram Example

5.1.3.2 Divisive Hierarchical Clustering

Characteristics:

- Top-down approach starting with all data in one cluster
- Recursively splits clusters until individual points remain
- Computationally more expensive than agglomerative
- Less commonly used in practice

Advantages of Hierarchical Clustering:

- No need to specify number of clusters beforehand
- Provides clustering at multiple resolutions
- Deterministic results
- Useful for understanding data structure

Disadvantages:

- High computational complexity **$O(n^3)$**
- Sensitive to noise and outliers
- Difficult to handle large datasets
- No global optimization objective

Table 5.2 Comparison of Hierarchical Methods

Method/Criterion	Approach	Distance Metric	Cluster Characteristics	Advantages	Disadvantages
Agglomerative	Bottom-up: Start with individual points, merge closest pairs	Euclidean, Manhattan, or custom	Depends on linkage criterion	• No need to specify cluster count • Shows hierarchical relationships • Flexible granularity	• High computational complexity $O(n^2)$ • Sensitive to distance metric choice
Divisive	Top-down: Start with all points, recursively split	Euclidean, Manhattan, or custom	Depends on splitting criterion	• Natural top-down decomposition • Good for identifying major groups first	• More complex implementation • Computationally expensive • Less commonly used

5.1.4 Partitional Clustering Algorithms

Partitional clustering divides data into non-overlapping subsets, typically optimizing a specific criterion function. Partitional clustering is a method fordividing a dataset into discrete, non-overlapping subsets or clusters, with each data point assigned to just one cluster. Unlike hierarchical clustering, partitional algorithms optimize a single criterion, such as minimizing within-cluster variance or maximizing inter-cluster separation. This method is especially useful in situations when the desired number of clusters is known in advance, as most partitional algorithms, such as K-means, require the number of clusters to be supplied. The clusters are produced iteratively with the goal of optimizing the grouping depending on the chosen optimization criterion.

K-means, one of the most popular partitional algorithms, works by initializing cluster centroids and assigning data points to the nearest centroid. The centroids are then recalculated using the assigned coordinates, and the process continues until convergence. Partitional clustering is computationally efficient for large data sets, particularly when paired with centroid initialization algorithms. However, it has disadvantages, such as sensitivity to the original positioning of centroids and difficulty finding non-spherical clusters. Despite these problems, partitional clustering remains an important part of unsupervised learning, with applications ranging from market segmentation to image compression.

5.1.4.1 K-Means Clustering

K-Means clustering is a popular approach for splitting datasets into k clusters, where k is a user-defined value. It works by minimizing the within-cluster sum of squares (WCSS), making it a useful strategy for grouping data points into compact and well-separated clusters. The procedure begins by randomly initializing k centroids. Each data point is then assigned to the nearest centroid using a distance measure, usually Euclidean distance. After the assignments are completed, the centroids are recalculated as the average position of all points within a cluster. This method repeats until the centroids stabilize or the change in assignment falls below a predetermined threshold.

One of the K-Means' main merits is its simplicity and computational efficiency, making it ideal for large datasets. However, the approach has some drawbacks, including sensitivity to the initial placement of centroids, which might result in inferior solutions. This problem can be solved by employing improved initialization methods such as K-Means++, which ensure better beginning positions. K-Means also struggles with non-spherical clusters and datasets with outliers because it calculates centroids using the mean. Despite these disadvantages, it is still a popular choice because of its interpretability and applicability to a range of use cases.

K-Means clustering has a wide range of applications, including image segmentation, market segmentation, and document clustering. In image processing, it is frequently used to compress images via restricting the color palette. In marketing, it aids in customer segmentation based on purchase behavior, allowing for more focused advertising and personalized experiences. K-Means' flexibility and ease of implementation have made it a cornerstone of unsupervised learning, setting the groundwork for more advanced clustering approaches and acting as a benchmark for evaluating other algorithms.

Algorithm:

1. Initialize k cluster centroids randomly.
2. Assign each point to the nearest centroid.
3. Update centroids as cluster means
4. Repeat steps 2-3 until convergence

Objective Function: Minimize within-cluster sum of squares (WCSS):

$$J = \sum_{j=1}^{k} \sum_{i \in Cj} \lVert xi - \mu j \rVert^2 \quad .....5.7$$

Explanation:

- J: The objective function to minimize (within-cluster sum of squares, or WCSS).
- k: The total number of clusters.
- Cjj: The set of data points assigned to cluster j.
- x_i: A data point in cluster j.
- μ_j : The centroid of cluster j.

- $\|x_i - \mu_j\|^2$: The squared Euclidean distance between the data point x and its cluster centroid μ_j .

This equation quantifies the sum of squared distances between all points and their respective cluster centroids, which K-Means aims to minimize.

Advantages:

- The time complexity of the K-Means algorithm is indeed related to the number of iterations, clusters, and data points. However, the correct notation and explanation for its complexity are:
- O(t.k.n.d)
- t: The number of iterations (typically small and bounded).
- k: The number of clusters.
- n: The number of data points.
- d: The dimensionality of the data.

Explanation:

The complexity $O(t \cdot k \cdot n \cdot d)$ reflects:

1. Assigning each of the n points to the nearest cluster centroid, which takes $O(k \cdot n \cdot d)$ per iteration.
2. Updating the k centroids, which involves computing the mean of the points in each cluster and requires $O(n \cdot d)$.

Thus, over ttt iterations, the overall complexity is $O(t \cdot k \cdot n \cdot d)$ t k If d is small (e.g., low-dimensional data), it simplifies to $O(t \cdot k \cdot n)$, which might be the original intent of the statement.

- Works well with spherical clusters
- Scales well to large datasets
- Guaranteed convergence

Disadvantages:

- Requires pre-specifying k
- Sensitive to initialization

- Assumes spherical clusters
- Affected by outliers

5.1.4.2 K-Means Variations

K-Means++:

- Improved initialization strategy
- Selects initial centroids probabilistically
- Reduces likelihood of poor clustering

K-Medoids (PAM—Partitioning Around Medoids):

- Uses actual data points as cluster centers
- More robust to outliers
- Works with any distance measure
- Higher computational cost

Fuzzy C-Means:

- Soft clustering approach
- Points belong to multiple clusters with membership degrees
- Useful when cluster boundaries are unclear

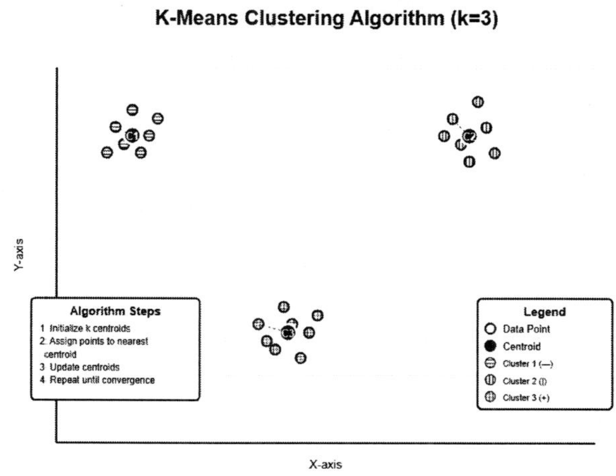

Figure 5.3 K-Means Algorithm Illustration

5.1.4.3. Determining Optimal Number of Clusters

Elbow Method:

- Plot WCSS vs. number of clusters
- Look for "elbow" point where improvement diminishes
- Subjective interpretation required

Silhouette Analysis:

The Silhouette Score measures the variation within and between clusters. It evaluates the clustering quality by comparing the average distance (a) between a data point and all other points in the same cluster with the average distance (b) between the data point and all points in the nearest neighboring cluster. The Silhouette Score is calculated for each data point, and the overall score is determined by averaging these values.

- Measures cluster cohesion and separation
- Values range from -1 to 1
- Higher average silhouette indicates better clustering

$$s = \frac{1}{N}\sum_{i=1}^{N}\frac{b_i - a_i}{max(a_i, b_i)} \text{..........5.8}$$

- N: Total number of data points in the dataset.
- a_i : Average distance between data point iii and other points in the same cluster (within-cluster distance).
- b_i: Average distance between data point iii and points in the nearest neighbouring cluster (between-cluster distance).
- max (a_i, b_i): The larger of a_i, and b_i
- $\frac{b_i - a_i}{max(a_i, b_i)}$ Silhouette Score for a single data point iii.
- s: The overall average Silhouette Score across all NNN data points in the dataset.

Gap Statistic:

- Compares clustering quality to random data
- More principled approach than elbow method
- Computationally intensive

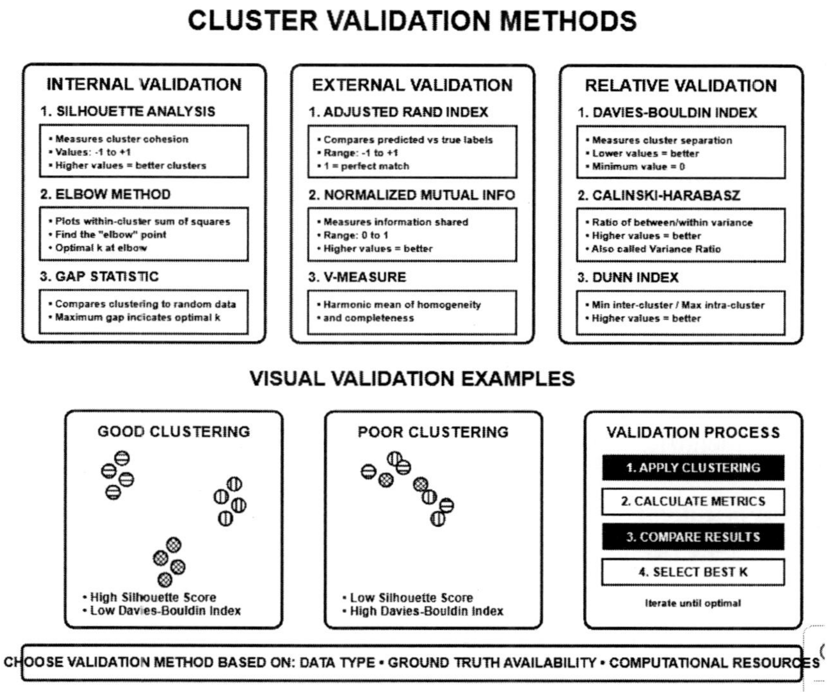

Figure 5.4 Cluster Validation Methods

5.1.5 Density-Based Methods

Density-based clustering identifies clusters as regions of high data density separated by regions of low density.

5.1.5.1 DBSCAN (Density-Based Spatial Clustering)

Core Concepts:

- **Core Point**: Has at least MinPts neighbors within ε distance
- **Border Point**: Within ε distance of core point but not core itself
- **Noise Point**: Neither core nor border point

Algorithm:

1. For each unvisited point, check if it's a core point
2. If core, start new cluster and add all density-reachable points
3. If border, assign to existing cluster
4. If noise, mark as outlier

Parameters:

- **ε (epsilon)**: Neighbourhood radius
- **MinPts**: Minimum points to form dense region

Advantages:

- Discovers clusters of arbitrary shape
- Robust to outliers
- No need to specify number of clusters
- Identifies noise points

Disadvantages:

- Sensitive to parameter selection
- Struggles with varying densities
- High-dimensional data challenges
- Memory intensive for large datasets

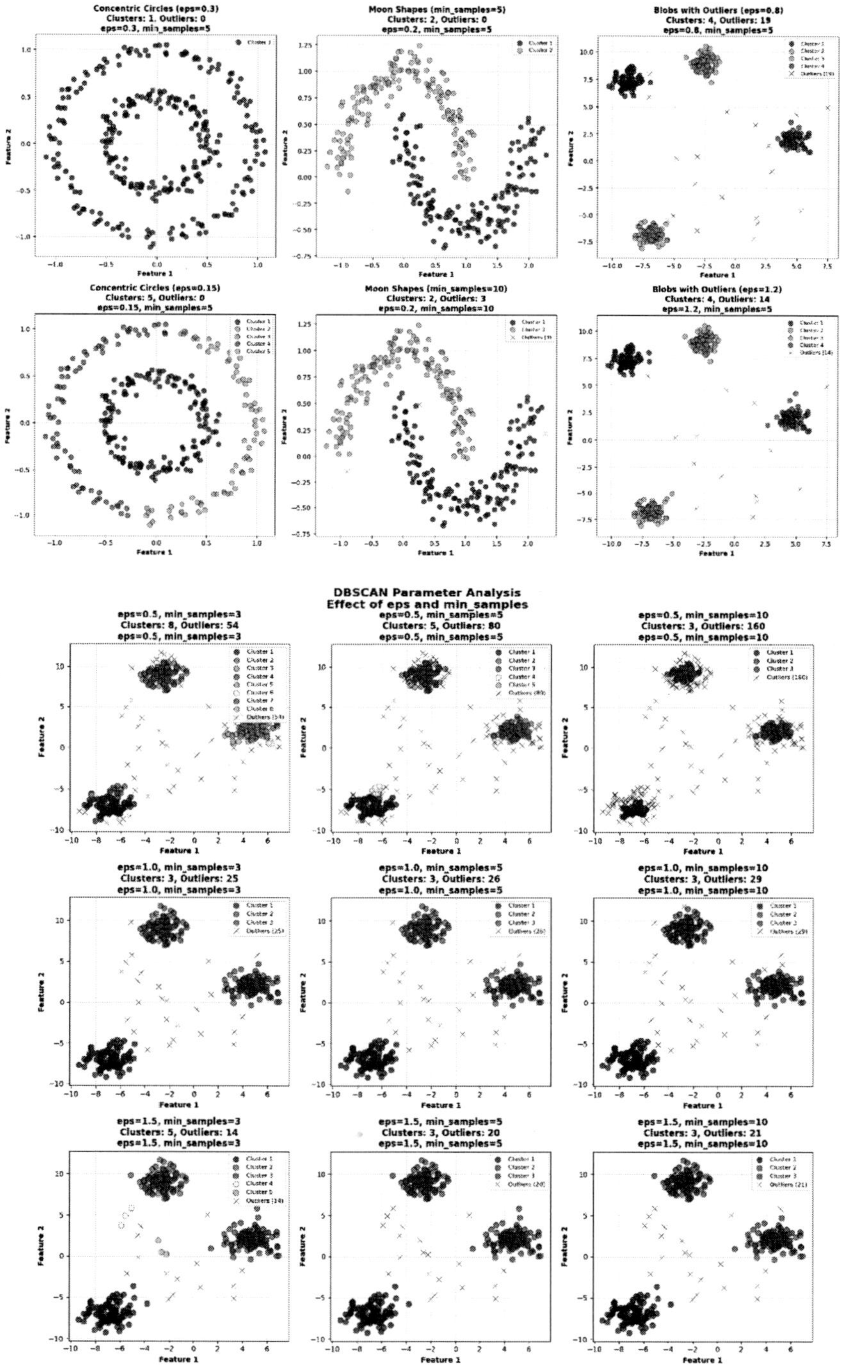

Figure 5.5 DBSCAN Clustering Example

5.1.5.2 OPTICS (Ordering Points to Identify Clustering Structure)

The **OPTICS (Ordering Points To Identify the Clustering Structure)** reachability plot is a visualization tool used in the OPTICS clustering algorithm. It is a graphical representation that helps to identify the clustering structure in the data by showing how "reachable" each point is from its neighbors, based on a specified distance measure.

Key Concepts in the Reachability Plot:

1. **Reachability Distance:**
   - This measures how far a point is from its nearest neighbors within a given neighborhood radius (ϵ\epsilonϵ).
   - Points that are part of dense clusters have smaller reachability distances, while points in sparse regions or noise have larger distances.
2. **Ordering of Points:**
   - The OPTICS algorithm orders data points based on their density connectivity. The reachability plot displays these points along the x-axis in the order determined by the algorithm.
3. **Vertical Axis (y-axis):**
   - This represents the reachability distance of each point.
4. **Clusters:**
   - Clusters appear as valleys (low reachability distances) in the plot.
   - Noise or outliers appear as peaks or regions with high reachability distances.

How to Interpret the Reachability Plot:

- **Low Reachability Distance:** Indicates points that are part of dense clusters.
- **High Reachability Distance:** Indicates points in sparse regions or noise.

- **Cluster Boundaries:** The transitions between low and high regions mark the boundaries of clusters.

In Figure 5.6 - OPTICS Reachability Plots are presented

Advantages of the Reachability Plot:

- Unlike methods like K-Means, OPTICS and its reachability plot do not require the number of clusters to be specified beforehand.
- It provides a visual understanding of the density and structure of clusters at multiple scales.
- It is particularly useful for identifying clusters of varying densities and arbitrary shapes.

The reachability plot is a fundamental part of the OPTICS algorithm, making it a robust tool for exploring clustering structures in complex datasets.

Advantages over DBSCAN:

- Less sensitive to parameter selection
- Handles varying densities better
- Provides richer cluster information

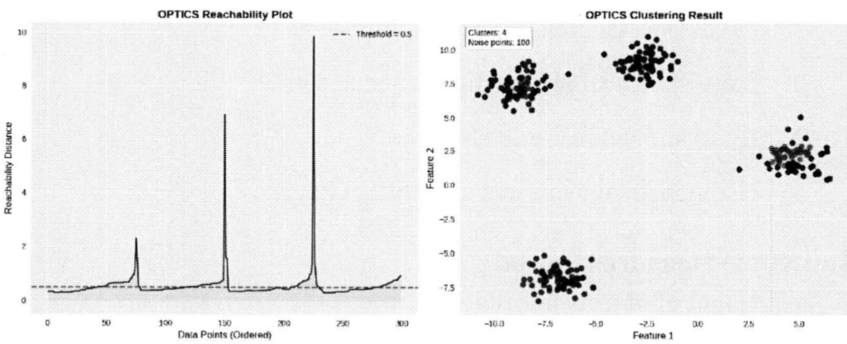

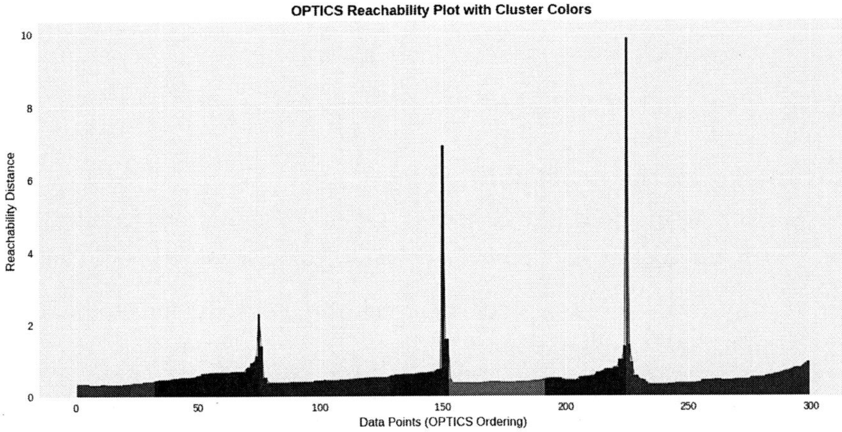

Figure 5.6 OPTICS Reachability Plot

5.1.6 Grid-Based Approaches

Grid-based clustering partitions feature space into finite number of cells, performing clustering on the grid structure rather than individual data points.

5.1.6.1 STING (Statistical Information Grid)

Methodology:

1. Divide spatial area into rectangular cells
2. Store statistical information for each cell
3. Build hierarchical grid structure
4. Use statistical measures to identify clusters

Statistical Measures Stored:

- Count of objects in cell
- Mean, standard deviation, min, max values
- Distribution type information

Advantages:

- Fast processing due to grid structure
- Suitable for large datasets

- Supports different clustering criteria
- Parallel processing friendly

Disadvantages:

- Quality depends on grid size
- May not capture irregular cluster shapes
- Boundary effects between cells

5.1.6.2 CLIQUE (Clustering in Quest)

Approach:

- Density-based clustering in subspaces
- Identifies dense regions in high-dimensional data
- Uses grid-based approach for efficiency

Key Features:

- Automatic subspace selection
- Insensitive to attribute ordering
- Scales linearly with data size
- Handles high-dimensional data

Grid-based clustering methods quantize the data space into a finite number of cells (grids) and perform clustering operations on the grid structure rather than on individual data points. This approach offers fast processing times and efficient handling of large datasets.

Table 5.3 - compares major grid-based clustering algorithms across key dimensions including computational complexity, scalability, parameter sensitivity, and suitability for different da

Table 5.3 Comparison of Grid-Based Methods

Method	Full Name	Year	Key Principle	Advantages	Disadvantages	Time Complexity	Best Use Cases
STING	STatistical INformation Grid	1997	Hierarchical grid structure with statistical information at each level	• Fast query processing • Multi-resolution analysis • Statistical summaries at each grid level • Good for range queries	• Grid structure may not align with natural clusters • Fixed grid boundaries • May lose cluster boundary information	O(K) where K is number of grid cells	• Large spatial databases • Geographic information systems • Range queries
CLIQUE	CLustering In QUEst	1998	Density-based subspace clustering using grids	• Handles high-dimensional data • Finds clusters in subspaces • Automatic dimensionality reduction •	• Grid resolution affects results • Difficulty in determining optimal parameters • May miss clusters spanning	O(ck) where c is number of cells, k is dimensionality	• High-dimensional data • Subspace clustering • Data with irrelevant dimensions

				Insensitive to outliers	multiple grids		
WaveCluster	Wavelet-based Clustering	1998	Uses wavelet transforms to find dense regions in grid	• Handles arbitrary cluster shapes • Multi-resolution analysis • Automatic noise filtering • Good boundary detection	• Wavelet choice affects performance • Complex parameter tuning • High memory requirements	O(N) where N is number of objects	• Image processing • Spatial data with complex shapes • Large datasets with noise
OptiGrid	Optimal Grid	2002	Uses cutting planes to create optimal grid partitions	• Automatic grid determination • Handles clusters of different densities • No predefined grid structure • Good for high-dimensional data	• Computationally expensive • Complex algorithm • Parameter sensitive	$O(N^2d)$ where N is objects, d is dimensions	• High-dimensional clustering • Datasets with varying densities • Intrusion detection
GRIDCLUS	Grid-based	2004	Density-based	• Simple and efficient<b	• Fixed grid size •	O(N + M) where	• Large spatial datasets<br

	Clustering		grid clustering with connected components	r>• Handles arbitrary shapes • Parameter independent • Linear time complexity	Sensitive to grid positioning • May split natural clusters	M is number of grid cells	>• Real-time applications • Stream data clustering
MAFIA	Merging of Adaptive Finite Intervals	1999	Adaptive grid intervals in subspaces	• Adaptive interval selection • Handles varying densities • Good for subspace clustering	• Complex parameter setting • High computational overhead • Memory intensive	$O(k^{2d})$ exponential in dimensions	• Market basket analysis • Bioinformatics • Text mining
BANG	BAlaNCed IteratIve reductiON and Clustering using Hierarchies	2000	Hierarchical grid structure with balanced partitioning	• Balanced tree structure • Efficient for range queries • Multi-level clustering • Good indexing capability	• Tree balancing overhead • Complex data structure • Memory requirements	O(N log N)	• Hierarchical data • Multi-level analysis • Database indexing

5.2 Reinforcement Learning

5.2.1 Overview of Reinforcement Learning

Reinforcement learning (RL) addresses the fundamental question of how an autonomous agent, capable of sensing and acting in its environment, can learn to choose optimal actions to achieve its goals. This general problem encompasses tasks such as training a mobile robot to navigate its surroundings, optimizing operations in factories, or mastering the strategies required to excel at board games. Each time the agent performs an action, feedback is provided in the form of rewards or penalties, indicating the desirability of the resulting state. For example, in the context of training an agent to play a game, the trainer might assign a positive reward for winning, a negative reward for losing, and a neutral (zero) reward for all intermediate states. The agent's task is to learn from this indirect and often delayed feedback to develop strategies that maximize cumulative rewards over time.

This learning process parallels how humans learn from infancy through adulthood, continually refining their behaviour to become effective and adaptive agents in their environments. From a young age, humans learn through experiences shaped by rewards and consequences. A child might receive praise or treats for completing a chore (positive reinforcement), or face a timeout for misbehavior (negative reinforcement). As adults, rewards become more nuanced, such as promotions, awards, or social recognition for achievements, while punishments could include missed opportunities, professional setbacks, or the lessons learned from mistakes.

Through this lifelong process of interacting with their environment, receiving feedback, and adapting their actions, humans develop the ability to navigate complex situations and pursue goals effectively. Similarly, reinforcement learning algorithms mimic this iterative learning process, enabling agents to handle a wide range of tasks by drawing on cumulative experiences to refine their decisions and optimize outcomes.

The Term "Reinforcement in Reinforcement Learning"

In Reinforcement Learning (RL), the term "reinforcement" primarily emphasizes the role of **rewards** as the guiding mechanism through which an agent learns to improve its behavior. Each action taken by the agent in the environment leads to a reward or penalty, which reflects the desirability of the resulting state. Positive rewards reinforce beneficial actions, encouraging the agent to repeat them, while negative rewards (penalties) discourage actions that lead to undesirable outcomes. For example, an agent navigating a maze might receive a reward upon reaching the goal or a penalty for hitting an obstacle. These rewards serve as the foundation for the agent to evaluate the effectiveness of its actions and adjust its strategy to maximize cumulative rewards over time.

Beyond individual rewards, reinforcement in RL incorporates a broader learning framework driven by trial and error. The agent initially explores various actions, receiving feedback and refining its decision-making process through the interplay of exploration and exploitation. Exploration allows the agent to discover new actions and their effects, while exploitation leverages known information to optimize outcomes. This iterative cycle of learning, informed by rewards, enables the agent to develop an optimal policy for achieving its objectives. Ultimately, reinforcement in RL is a reward-driven process where feedback not only evaluates actions but also shapes the agent's ability to make better decisions over repeated interactions with its environment.

Key Characteristics:

- **Trial-and-Error Learning**: Agent explores environment through actions
- **Delayed Rewards**: Consequences of actions may not be immediate
- **Sequential Decision Making**: Actions affect future states and opportunities
- **Goal-Oriented**: Maximizes cumulative reward over time

Distinction from Other Learning Paradigms:

- **Supervised Learning**: Learns from labelled examples
- **Unsupervised Learning**: Finds patterns in unlabelled data
- **Reinforcement Learning**: Learns from interaction and feedback

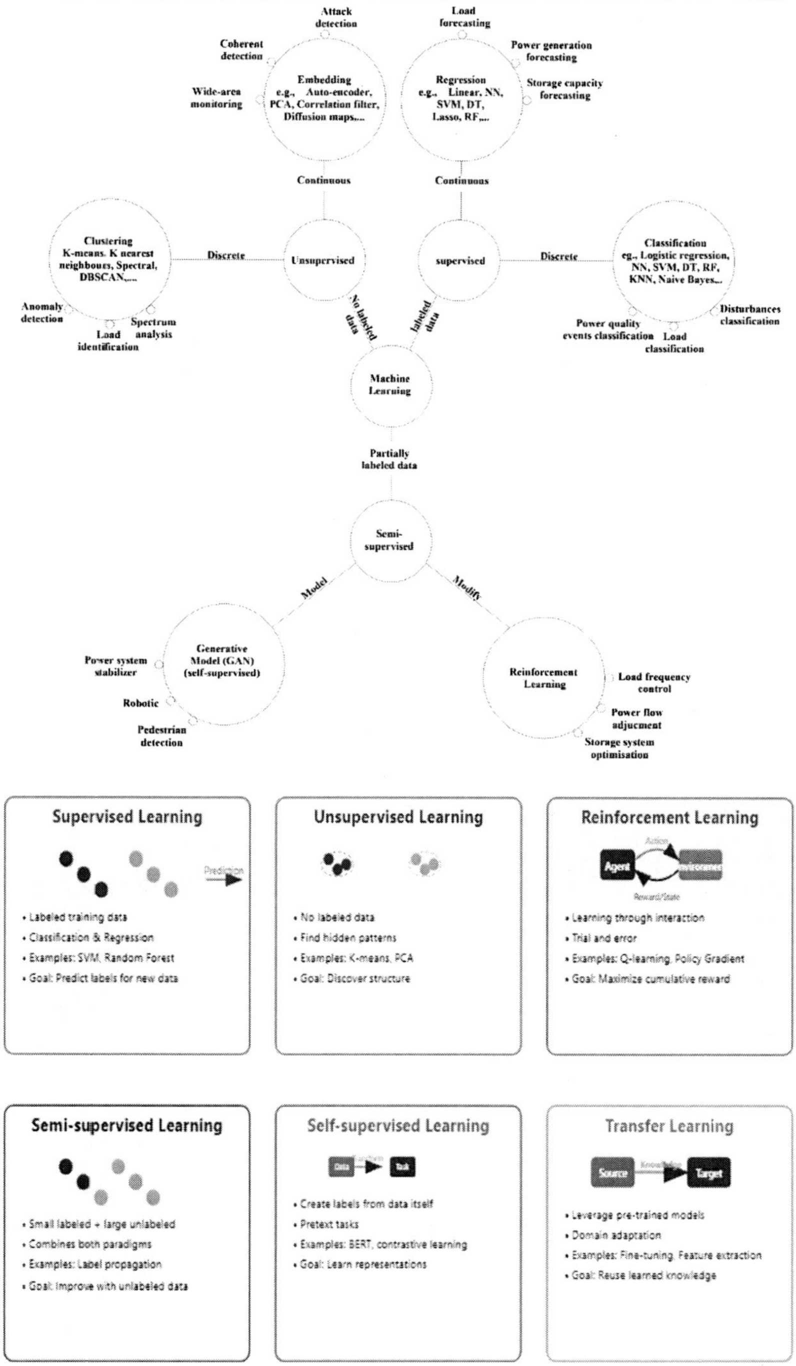

Figure 5.7 Machine Learning Paradigms Comparison.

5.2.2 Scope of Reinforcement Learning

Reinforcement Learning (RL) has a broad and diverse application, encompassing fields where decision-making and flexibility are essential. RL's fundamental idea of learning optimal methods through interaction with an environment makes it suitable to a wide range of problems, from basic tasks to highly complex systems. RL is widely used in robotics to provide autonomous control, allowing robots to navigate, manipulate items, and adapt to dynamic situations. It is critical in game AI, where agents learn strategies to outperform human players in games such as chess, Go, and video games. Furthermore, RL is being used in a variety of industries to optimize resource allocation, including manufacturing scheduling, supply chain management, and energy distribution.

Beyond traditional applications, RL is making inroads into emerging sectors, demonstrating its broad applicability. In healthcare, RL is used for personalized treatment planning, drug discovery, and resource optimization in hospitals. Autonomous systems, including self-driving cars and unmanned aerial aircraft, use RL to make real-time judgments in uncertain situations. In addition, RL has a substantial impact on financial systems, helping in the development of adaptive trading algorithms and the optimization of investment portfolios. With breakthroughs in deep learning, RL is scaling to address more complicated, high-dimensional problems, paving the way for innovation in fields such as climate modeling, smart city development, and even creative jobs like procedural content generation.

5.2.2.1 Applications

Game Playing:

- Chess, Go, poker playing agents
- Video game AI characters
- Strategic decision making

Robotics:

- Robot navigation and path planning
- Manipulation and grasping tasks

- Autonomous vehicle control

Finance:

- Algorithmic trading strategies
- Portfolio optimization
- Risk management

Healthcare:

- Treatment planning and optimization
- Drug discovery processes
- Personalized medicine

Recommendation Systems:

- Dynamic content recommendation
- Personalized advertising
- User experience optimization

5.2.2.2 Problem Types Suitable for RL

Sequential Decision Problems:

- Actions affect future states
- Long-term consequences matter
- Multiple interacting decisions

Optimization Under Uncertainty:

- Stochastic environments
- Incomplete information
- Adaptive strategies needed

Learning Through Interaction:

- Expensive or impossible to obtain labelled data
- Environment provides natural feedback
- Exploration vs. exploitation trade-offs

The table 5.4 summarizes key application domains of reinforcement learning, showcasing its versatility in addressing problems across robotics, healthcare, finance, and beyond.

Table 5.4: RL Application Domains

Domain	Description	Examples
Robotics	Enables robots to learn tasks through trial and error in dynamic environments.	Path planning, object manipulation.
Game Playing	AI agents learn to master games by optimizing strategies.	Chess, Go, Atari games.
Healthcare	Optimizes treatment strategies and resource allocation.	Personalized medicine, drug discovery.
Finance	Improves decision-making in trading and portfolio management.	Algorithmic trading, risk management.
Autonomous Vehicles	Trains vehicles to navigate and make decisions in real-world traffic scenarios.	Self-driving cars, UAVs.
Energy Optimization	Reduces energy consumption and enhances efficiency in systems.	Smart grid management, HVAC control.
Manufacturing	Optimizes processes and operations to improve efficiency.	Inventory management, scheduling.
Natural Language Processing	Enhances language-based interactions by optimizing policies.	Chatbots, conversational agents.

The table summarizes key application domains of reinforcement learning, showcasing its versatility in addressing problems across robotics, healthcare, finance, and beyond.

5.2.3 Reinforcement Learning as Machine Learning

Reinforcement Learning (RL) is a unique paradigm within the broader field of machine learning that focuses on teaching agents to make sequential decisions through interaction with their (surrounding) environment. Unlike supervised learning, where models learn from labeled datasets, RL employs no explicit labels. Instead, the agent learns by trial and error, led by a reward mechanism that determines the value of its actions. The agent's goal is to create a policy that maximizes the cumulative rewards over time. RL uses this feedback mechanism to allow agents to adapt to changing environments and make decisions that balance immediate rewards with long-term outcomes.

As a subfield of machine learning, RL intersects with other fields such as deep learning and optimization. When integrated with neural networks, RL forms the cornerstone of Deep Reinforcement Learning (DRL), allowing agents to tackle high-dimensional and complicated tasks such as game play, robot control, and resource management in real-world systems. RL's main strength is its capacity to solve issues where the environment is partially observable, ambiguous/uncertain, or involves sequential planning. This makes RL not only a distinct subtopic/subfield in machine learning, but also an important tool for solving complex issues in fields such as robotics, healthcare, finance, and autonomous systems.

5.2.3.1 Learning Paradigm Integration

Supervised Learning Elements:

- Function approximation for value estimation
- Pattern recognition in state representation
- Generalization across similar states

Unsupervised Learning Elements:

- State representation learning
- Feature extraction from raw observations
- Clustering of similar states or actions

Unique RL Characteristics:

- Active learning through environment interaction
- Credit assignment across temporal sequences
- Exploration strategy development
- Policy optimization

5.2.3.2 Computational Aspects

Sample Efficiency:

- RL often requires many interactions
- Data efficiency crucial for real-world applications
- Transfer learning and meta-learning approaches

Scalability:

- High-dimensional state and action spaces
- Continuous control problems
- Distributed and parallel learning

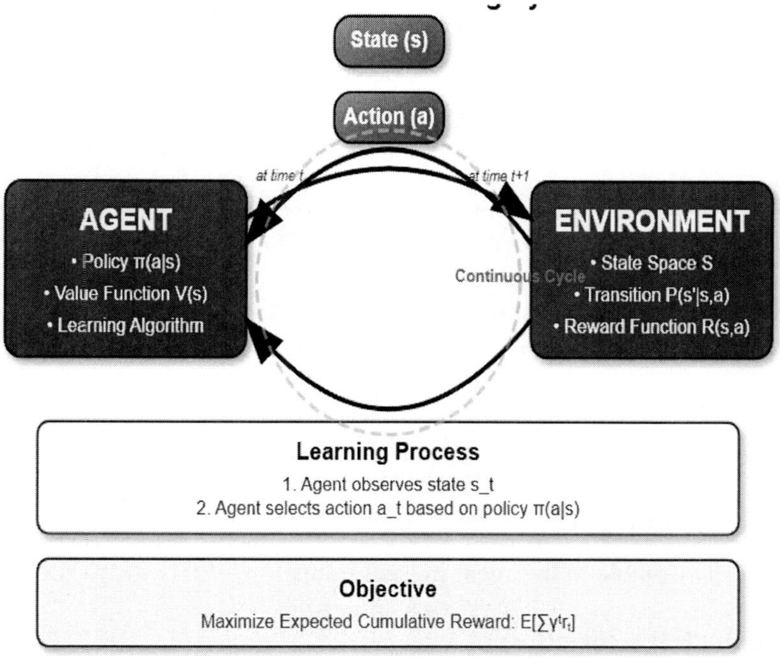

Figure 5.8 RL Learning Cycle

5.2.4 Components of Reinforcement Learning

5.2.4.1 Agent

The learner and decision maker that interacts with the environment.

Agent Characteristics:

- Maintains internal state representation
- Implements decision-making policy
- Updates knowledge based on experience
- Balances exploration and exploitation

5.2.4.2 Environment

The external system the agent interacts with.

Environment Properties:

- **Observable**: Full vs. partial state visibility

- **Deterministic**: Predictable vs. stochastic transitions
- **Episodic**: Finite episodes vs. continuing tasks
- **Static**: Fixed vs. changing dynamics

5.2.4.3 State (S)

Complete description of the environment at a given time.

State Representation:

- **Markov Property**: Current state contains all relevant information
- **State Space**: Set of all possible states
- **Observation**: Partial information about true state

5.2.4.4 Action (A)

Choices available to the agent in each state.

Action Characteristics:

- **Discrete**: Finite set of choices
- **Continuous**: Real-valued action parameters
- **Action Space**: Set of all possible actions

5.2.4.5 Reward (R)

Immediate feedback signal from environment.

Reward Properties:

- **Scalar Value**: Single numerical feedback
- **Immediate**: Received after each action
- **Subjective**: Designed to reflect goals
- **Sparse vs. Dense**: Frequency of non-zero rewards

5.2.4.6 Policy (π)

Strategy or behaviour function mapping states to actions.

Policy Types:

- **Deterministic**: $\pi(s) = a$

- **Stochastic**: **π(a|s)** = probability of action a in state s
- **Stationary**: Policy doesn't change over time
- **Non-stationary**: Policy evolves with learning

5.2.4.7 Value Function

Expected cumulative reward from a given state or state-action pair.

State Value Function:

$$V^{\pi}(s) = \mathrm{E}\left[RR_{t+1} + \gamma R_{t+2} + \gamma^2 R_{t+2} + \gamma 3 R_{t+3} \ldots \middle| St = s \middle| \right] \ldots\ldots \mathbf{5.9}$$

Explanation of terms

$V^{\pi}(s)$:

- This is the **state-value function** for a given policy π.
- It represents the expected cumulative reward when starting in state sss and following policy π

E[·]:

- The **expectation operator**, representing the average reward over all possible outcomes, given the stochastic nature of the environment.

R_{t+1}, Rt_{+2}, Rt_{+3},:

- The rewards received at time steps t+1, t+2, t+3, …

γ:

- The **discount factor** (0≤γ≤1):
  - Determines how future rewards are weighted relative to immediate rewards.
  - A smaller γ places more emphasis on immediate rewards, while a larger γ (closer to 1) values long-term rewards more.

S_t=s:

- The condition that the agent is in states at time t.

At=a:

- The condition that the agent takes action a at time t.

Purpose of the Equation:

This equation defines the **value of a state** under a specific policy π\piπ as the expected sum of discounted rewards that the agent will accumulate over time, starting from state sss. This is a foundational concept in Reinforcement Learning, used to evaluate and improve policies.

Action Value Function (Q-function):

$$Q^{\pi}(s,a) = \mathrm{E}\left[\left[R_{t+1} + \gamma R_{t+1} + \gamma 2 R_{t+1} + \ldots\ldots \middle| S_t = s, A_t = a\right|\right] \ldots.5.10$$

Explanation of the Components

1. **$V^{\pi}(s)$:**

E[·]:

2. The **expectation operator**, representing the average reward over all possible outcomes, given the stochastic nature of the environment.
    - This is the **action-value function** (or Q-value) for a given policy π\piπ.
    - It represents the expected cumulative reward when starting in state sss, taking action aaa, and subsequently following policy π\piπ.
3. **E[·]:**
    - The **expectation operator**, which calculates the average reward over all possible stochastic outcomes in the environment.

R_{t+1}, Rt_{+2}, Rt_{+3},:

- The rewards received at time steps t+1, t+2, t+3, …

S_t=s:

- The condition that the agent is in state s at time t.

At=a:

- The condition that the agent takes action aaa at time ttt.

Purpose of the Equation (5.10)

The action-value function $Q^{\pi}(s,a)$ is central to Reinforcement Learning as it quantifies the expected return of taking a specific action aaa in state sss and then following policy π\piπ. It is used in:

- **Policy Evaluation**: Assessing how good a given policy π is.
- **Policy Improvement**: Finding better policies by identifying actions with higher Q-values.

This equation is the basis for algorithms like **Q-Learning**, which iteratively estimates the optimal Q-values to discover the best policy.

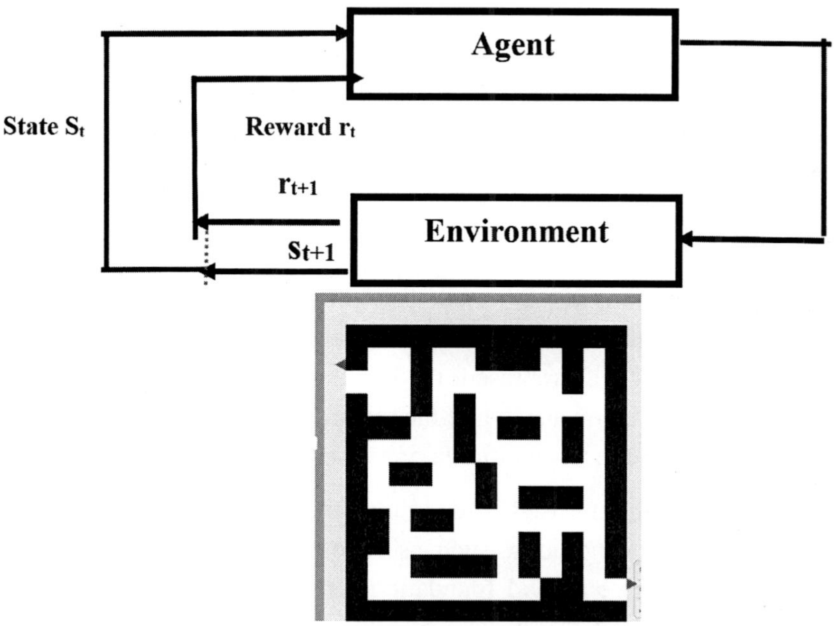

Figure 5.9 RL Components Interaction Diagram
(a maze as an example of Agent's environment)

In figure 5.9 presented is the components of interaction diagram in reincorcement learning

5.2.5 Markov Decision Process (MDP)

5.2.5.1 MDP Framework

Mathematical framework for modelling decision-making in stochastic environments. A Markov Decision Process (MDP) is a mathematical framework for modeling decision-making situations in which the outcomes are both random and partly under the decision-maker's control. MDPs are a fundamental idea in Reinforcement Learning, providing a formal structure for modeling an agent's interaction with its environment. An MDP is comprised of four major components: states (S), actions (A), transition probabilities (P), and rewards (R). A discount factor (γ) can be added to account for future rewards' importance. This structure allows the agent to make sequential judgments that maximize its cumulative reward over time whilst taking into account the probabilistic nature of the environment.

The defining property of an MDP is the **Markov Property**, which states that the future state of the system depends only on the current state and action, not on the sequence of past states. Mathematically, this is expressed as:

$$P\left(S_{t+1} \mid S_t, A_t\right) = P\left(S_{t+1} \mid S_1, A_1, \ldots S_t, A_t\right) \ldots\ldots\mathbf{5.11}$$

This property simplifies the modelling of dynamic systems and allows efficient computation of policies and value functions. The transition probabilities, **P(s′|s,a),** represent the likelihood of moving from state sss to state **s′** given action aaa, while the reward function R(s,a) specifies the immediate reward received after taking action **a** in state **s**.

MDPs are commonly used in domains where decisions must be made under uncertain conditions, such as robotics, finance, healthcare, and logistics. They give a solid foundation for modelling activities such as guiding a robot through a maze, managing inventory in a warehouse, and optimizing treatment plans in medicine. Solving an MDP is determining the optimal policy—a mapping from states to actions—that maximizes the expected cumulative reward. MDPs are solved using techniques like as dynamic programming, Monte Carlo methods, and reinforcement learning algorithms, which vary based on the size and complexity of the state and action spaces.

MDP Tuple: (S, A, P, R, γ)

- **S**: State space
- **A**: Action space
- **P**: Transition probability function P(s'|s,a)
- **R**: Reward function R(s,a,s')
- γ: Discount factor ($0 \leq \gamma \leq 1$)

5.2.5.2 Markov Property

Definition: Future state depends only on current state and action, not on history.

Mathematical Expression:

$$P\left[S_{t+1}=s' \mid S_t=s, A_t=a, S_{t-1}, A_{t-1}, ..\right]=P\left[S_{t+1}=s' \mid S_t=s, A_t=a\right] ...5.12$$

Explanation of the Equation

This equation captures the **Markov Property**, which is central to the concept of a Markov Decision Process (MDP).

- $S_{t+1}=s'$
- This represents the **probability** of transitioning to state s′ at time t+1, given the current and all previous states (S_t,S_{t-1},… and actions (A_t,A_{t-1},…).

1. Simplification via the Markov Property:
    - The equation asserts that the probability of transitioning to the next state s′s's′ depends only on the current state sss and the action aaa taken at that state.
    - The history of past states and actions (S_t,S_{t-1},… and actions (A_t,A_{t-1},…) does not influence the next state directly.

2. Implication for MDPs:
   - This simplification allows the system to be modeled using a compact representation of states and actions, without tracking entire histories.

This property is fundamental for the efficient computation of policies and transition dynamics in MDPs and is why the Markov model is used in reinforcement learning and stochastic processes.

Implications:

- State contains all relevant information
- Enables dynamic programming solutions
- Simplifies learning algorithms

5.2.5.3 Bellman Equations

State Value Function:

$$V^{\pi}(s) = \sum_{a} \pi(a \mid s) s' \Sigma P(s' \mid s, a) \left[R(s, a, s') + \gamma V^{\pi}(s') \right] \ldots .5.13(a)$$

Explanation of the Components

1. **V^π(s):**
   - The value function under policy **π for state s.**
   - Represents the expected cumulative reward starting from state sss and following policy π.
2. **π(a|s):**
   - The policy, which gives the probability of taking action aaa in state sss.
3. **P(s′|s,a)**:
   - The transition probability, representing the likelihood of transitioning to state s′s's′ after taking action a in state s.

4. **R(s,a,s′):**
    - The reward function, representing the immediate reward received for transitioning from state s to state s″ via action a.
5. **γ:**
    - The discount factor (0≤γ≤10 :
        - Determines the weight of future rewards relative to immediate rewards.
6. **Summations (∑a,∑s′):**
    - ∑a: Over all possible actions a in state s.
    - ∑s′ : Over all possible successor states s′

Purpose of the Equation

This equation is the B**ellman** Expectation Equation for the state-value function. It expresses the value of a state s under policy π as:

- The expected value of the immediate reward R(s,a,s′) plus the discounted value of the subsequent state **V^π(s)**s'), weighted by:
    - The probability of taking action a in state s according to **π(a|s)** and
    - The probability of transitioning to s′ from s using **P(s′|s,a)**

This recursive relationship is central to solving MDPs and evaluating policies in reinforcement learning.

Action Value Function:

$$Q^{\pi}(s,a)=\sum_{s'}P(s'\mid s,a)\left[R(s,a,s')+\gamma\sum_{a'}\pi(a'\mid s')Q^{\pi}(s',a')\right]....5.13(b)$$

Explanation of the Components

- **Q^π(s,a):**
    - The **action-value function** for policy π\piπ, which represents the expected cumulative reward of taking action a in state s, and then following policy π

- **P(s′|s,a):**
    - The **transition probability**, representing the likelihood of moving to state s′ after taking action a in state **s**.
- **R(s,a,s′):**
    - The **reward function**, giving the immediate reward received for transitioning from state s to state s′via action a.
- **γ:**
    - The **discount factor** (0≤γ≤10 \leq \gamma \leq 10≤γ≤1):
        - Balances the importance of future rewards relative to immediate rewards.
- **Summations ($\sum_{s'}$ and $\sum_{a'}$):**
    - $\sum_{s'}$ Summing over all possible next states s′.
    - $\sum_{a'}$Summing over all possible actions a′a'a′ that can be taken in the next state s′s's′.
- **π(a′|s′):**
    - The **policy**, specifying the probability of taking action a′ in state s′.

Purpose of the Equation

This is the **Bellman Expectation Equation** for the action-value function **Q^π(s,a)** It expresses the expected value of **Q^π(s,a) as:**

1. The immediate reward **R(s,a,s′)** plus
2. The discounted expected value of the subsequent state-action pairs, **Q^π(s,a)**

averaged over:

- All possible next states s′ **P(s′|s,a)** and
- Actions All actions a′ the agent might take in s″ (weighted by **π(a′|s′):**

This equation helps evaluate a given policy π, forming the foundation for policy evaluation and improvement in reinforcement learning algorithms.

Optimal Value Functions:

$$V^*(s) = max_a \sum_{s'} P(s' \mid s,a)\left[R(s,a,s') + \gamma V^*(s')\right] \text{....5.13}(c)$$

Explanation of the Equations

Optimal State-Value Function (V*(s)

- **(V*(s)**: The maximum cumulative reward achievable starting from state **s**, assuming the agent follows the optimal policy thereafter.
- **max$_a$:** The agent selects the action a that yields the highest expected value.
- $\sum_{s'}P(s'|s,a)$: Transition probabilities, summing over all possible next states s′.
- $R(s,a,s')+\gamma V^*(s')$: The immediate reward plus the discounted value of the next state **s′**.

$$Q^*(s,a) = \sum_{s'} P(s' \mid s,a)\left[R(s,a,s') + \gamma max_{a'} Q*(s',a')\right] \text{....5.13}(d)$$

Optimal Action-Value Function (Q*(s,a)

- **Q*(s,a)**: The maximum cumulative reward achievable by taking action aaa in state sss and following the optimal policy thereafter.
- $\sum_{s'}P(s'|s,a)$: Transition probabilities, summing over all possible next states s′.
- **$R(s,a,s')+\gamma max_a{}'Q^*(s',a')$:** The immediate reward plus the discounted maximum value of the next state-action pair.

Significance

- Both equations define the **Bellman Optimality Equations**, which are central to reinforcement learning.

- Solving these equations allows the agent to compute the optimal policy by identifying the best actions to take in each state to maximize rewards.

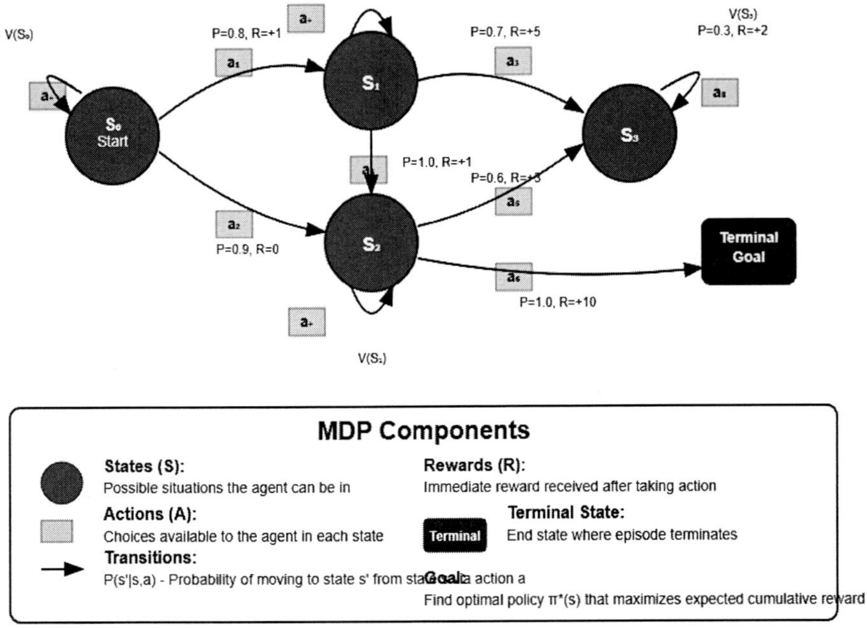

Figure 5.10 MDP State Transition Diagram

Key Components:

- **States**: 4 regular states (S_0, S_1, S_2, S_3) plus 1 terminal state
- **Actions**: 8 different actions (a_1 through a_8) showing various transition possibilities
- **Transitions**: Curved arrows showing state-to-state movements with probabilities
- **Rewards**: Each transition shows both probability (P) and reward (R) values
- **Self-loops**: Some states have actions that keep the agent in the same state

Visual Features:

- **Gray color scheme**: Professional appearance with clear contrast
- **Large, clear fonts**: Easy to read state names and action labels
- **Probability and reward annotations**: Each transition shows P(s'|s,a) and R values
- **Terminal state**: Distinguished by rectangular shape
- **Value function annotations**: V(S) labels for each state
- **Comprehensive legend**: Explains all MDP components

MDP Elements Demonstrated:

- **State space**: {S_0, S_1, S_2, S_3, Terminal}
- **Action space**: {a_1, a_2, a_3, a_4, a_5, a_6, a_7, a_8}
- **Transition probabilities**: Various P values (0.3 to 1.0)
- **Reward function**: Mix of positive and negative rewards
- **Policy representation**: Shows decision points at each state

This diagram effectively illustrates how an MDP works, showing the decision-making process where an agent must choose actions in different states to maximize expected cumulative reward. The visual layout makes it easy to trace possible paths from the start state to the terminal goal state.

5.2.6 Multi-Arm Bandit Problem

The Multi-Armed Bandit (MAB) problem is a fundamental problem in reinforcement learning and decision theory. It is frequently used to represent/model instances in which an agent must choose between multiple options, each with uncertain rewards. The name is derived from a row of slot machines (or "bandits"), each of which has a unique payout probability distribution. The agent's objective is to determine which "arm" to pull at each time step in order to maximize cumulative rewards over time. The problem stems from the exploration-exploitation tradeoff: the agent must strike a balance between testing out multiple arms to learn about their reward distributions (exploration) and using known information to select the arm with the highest expected reward.

MAB problems are used in a variety of domains, including online marketing, where algorithms determine which ads to display to consumers in order to maximize clicks, and clinical trials, where researchers select therapies to determine the most effective while minimizing patient risks. Several strategies have been developed to solve the MAB problem, including: ε-greedy algorithms, which alternate between exploration and exploitation with a fixed probability; Upper Confidence Bound (UCB) methods, which prioritize arms with high uncertainty; and Thompson Sampling, which uses Bayesian inference to guide decision-making. Despite its simplicity, the MAB problem provides the basis for more complicated reinforcement learning scenarios, such as contextual bandits and full Markov Decision Processes.

5.2.6.1 Problem Formulation

Simplified RL problem focusing on exploration-exploitation trade-off without state transitions.

Setup:

- K slot machines (arms) with unknown reward distributions
- Agent selects one arm at each time step
- Goal: maximize cumulative reward over time
- No state information, only reward feedback

5.2.6.2 Exploration vs. Exploitation

Exploitation: Choose arm with highest estimated reward **Exploration**: Try arms with uncertain rewards to improve estimates

Algorithms:

ε-Greedy:

- Select best arm with probability **(1-ε)**
- Select random arm with probability **ε**
- Simple but doesn't adapt exploration

Upper Confidence Bound (UCB):

$$A_t = argamax\left[\hat{Q}_t(a) + c\sqrt{\frac{\ln t}{N_t a}}\right] \quad ....5.14$$

- Balances estimated value and uncertainty
- Automatically reduces exploration over time

Thompson Sampling:

- Bayesian approach using posterior distributions
- Samples from belief about each arm's value
- Naturally balances exploration and exploitation

Table 5.5 Multi-Arm Bandit Algorithms Comparison

Algorithm	**Exploration Strategy**	**Advantages**	**Limitations**
ε-Greedy	Explores randomly with probability ε\varepsilonε.	Simple to implement, balances exploration.	Fixed ε\varepsilonε may not adapt well.
Upper Confidence Bound (UCB)	Uses confidence intervals to prioritize uncertain actions.	Efficient exploration with theoretical guarantees.	Requires careful tuning of exploration constant.
Thompson Sampling	Samples actions based on posterior probability.	Bayesian approach, handles non-stationary problems.	Computationally expensive for complex priors.
Softmax	Selects actions probabilistically using softmax function.	Smooth balance of exploration and exploitation.	Sensitive to temperature parameter.

Greedy (Baseline)	Always chooses the action with the highest estimated reward.	Simple and computationally efficient.	Poor exploration, easily stuck in local optima.

Table 5.5 compares Multi-Arm Bandit algorithms, highlighting their exploration strategies, advantages, and limitations to aid in selecting the right approach for specific scenarios.

5.2.7 Reinforcement Learning Problem Types

5.2.7.1 Episodic vs. Continuing Tasks

Episodic Tasks:

- Natural ending points (terminal states)
- Examples: Games, simulation episodes
- Finite horizon optimization

Continuing Tasks:

- No natural termination
- Infinite horizon problems
- Examples: Process control, recommendation systems

5.2.7.2 Finite vs. Infinite Horizon

Finite Horizon:

- Fixed time limit T
- Optimization over finite time steps
- Time-dependent optimal policies

Infinite Horizon:

- Unbounded time duration
- Discounting ensures finite cumulative rewards
- Stationary optimal policies

5.2.7.3 Deterministic vs. Stochastic

Deterministic Environments:

- State transitions are predictable
- Same action in same state always produces same result
- Simpler planning and learning

Stochastic Environments:

- Probabilistic state transitions
- Uncertainty in action outcomes
- Requires handling of probabilistic effects

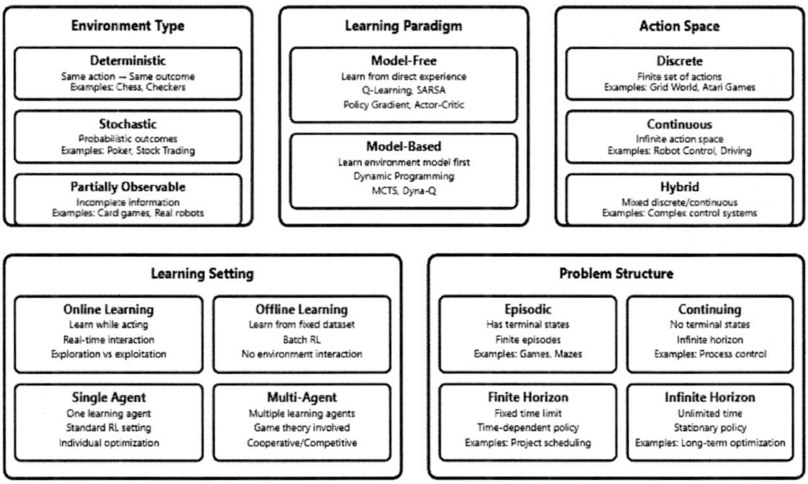

Figure 5.11 RL Problem Classification

5.2.8 Model-Based Learning

Model-Based Learning is an example of reinforcement learning in which the agent creates or uses a model of the environment around it to predict its behaviour. Model-Based Learning incorporates a representation of the environment's dynamics, typically defined by the transition probabilities $P (s ' | s , a)$ P(s ′ |s,a) and the reward function $R (s , a)$ R(s,a), unlike Model-Free methods that rely solely on experience to make decisions. Utilizing this approach, the agent may simulate interactions with the environment in order to plan its behaviors and predict their long-term consequences without requiring substantial real-world exploration. This ability makes Model-Based Learning substantially more sample efficient than Model-Free techniques.

Model-Based Learning applications include robotics, healthcare, and autonomous systems, all of which involve costly or risky real-world interaction. For example, in robotics, a learnt model can simulate movements, reducing wear and tear on physical components. Popular algorithms include Dynamic Programming (where the model is known), Dyna-Q (which combines model-based and model-free methods), and Model Predictive Control (MPC), which is used for short-term planning. However, Model-Based Learning requires accurate models; mistakes/errors in the model might result in suboptimal or unstable policies. As a result, recent advances in deep learning have focused on developing more robust and expressive models capable of handling complex, high-dimensional environments.

5.2.8.1 Approach Overview

Learn explicit model of environment dynamics, then use model for planning.

Model Components:

- **Transition Model**: P(s'|s,a) - probability of next state
- **Reward Model**: R(s,a) - expected immediate reward

5.2.8.2 Dynamic Programming Methods

Policy Iteration:

1. Policy Evaluation: Compute V^π using Bellman equation
2. Policy Improvement: Update policy greedily with respect to V^π
3. Repeat until convergence

Value Iteration:

1. Initialize value function arbitrarily
2. Update values using Bellman optimality equation

3. Extract optimal policy from converged values

Policy Iteration Algorithm:

1. Initialize π arbitrarily

2. Repeat:

a. Policy Evaluation: Solve $V^{\pi}(s)$ for all s

b. Policy Improvement:

$$\pi'(s) = arg\frac{max}{a}s'\sum P(s' \mid s,a)\left[R(s,a,s') + \gamma V^{\pi}(s')\right] \text{......}\mathbf{5.15}$$

c. If π' = π, then stop; else π = π'

5.2.8.3 Advantages and Disadvantages

Advantages:

- Efficient use of experience through planning
- Can perform "mental simulation"
- Theoretical guarantees for convergence
- Sample efficient when model is accurate

Disadvantages:

- Model learning can be challenging
- Model errors compound in planning
- Computational overhead of planning
- May not scale to complex environments

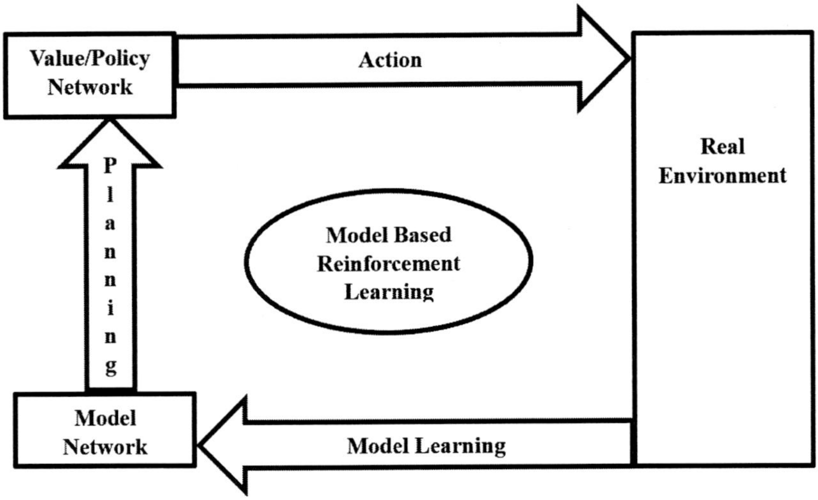

Figure 5.12—Model-Based RL Architecture

5.2.9 Model-Free Methods

Model-free reinforcement learning involves the agent learning to make decisions without explicitly modelling the environment's dynamics, such as transition probabilities ($P(s'|s,a)$ or the reward functionR(s,a). Instead, the agent uses direct interactions with the environment to estimate optimal policy or value functions. These techniques are especially effective when the environment's dynamics are unknown or too complex to model. Model-Free approaches, which rely on learning directly from experience, may handle a wide range of problems, including those with stochastic or partially observable settings.

Model-free methods are divided into two categories: value-based methods and policy-based methods. Value-based techniques, including Q-Learning and Deep Q-Networks (DQN), estimate the action-value function ($Q(s,a)$ and select actions that maximize the estimated value to determine the best policy indirectly. Policy-based approaches, such as Policy Gradient methods, train a parameterized policy by maximizing the predicted cumulative reward. Model-free approaches are extensively utilized because of their simplicity and generality, making them useful in a variety of applications, including game-playing AI and robotic control. However, they frequently require substantial interaction with the environment to converge and may struggle in situations with sparse rewards or high-dimensional state-action spaces.

5.2.9.1 Approach Overview

Learn optimal policy or value function directly from experience without explicit environment model.

Key Characteristics:

- No environment model required
- Learn directly from interaction
- Robust to model misspecification
- Often simpler to implement

5.2.9.2 Monte Carlo Methods

Learn from complete episodes by averaging returns.

Basic Monte Carlo:

1. Generate episode using current policy
2. For each state St in the episode:

$$G_t = R_{t+1} + \gamma R_{t+2} + \cdots + \gamma^{T-t-1} R_T \text{.......} 5.16(a)$$

$$V(S_t) \leftarrow V(S_t) + \alpha\left[G_t - V(S_t)\right] \text{.......} 5.16(b)$$

Explanation of the Components

1. **G_t:**
    - The **return** at time step ttt, representing the cumulative discounted reward from time t+1 to the end of the episode T.
2. **γ:**
    - The **discount factor** (0≤γ≤10 which determines the weight of future rewards relative to immediate rewards.

3. **$V(S_t)$:**
   - The **value function** for state S_t , estimating the expected return starting from state S_t .

4. **α:**
   - The **learning rate**, which controls how much the new information $[G_t - V(S_t)]$ influences the update of $V(S_t)$.

Characteristics:

- Unbiased value estimates
- High variance due to episode sampling
- Requires episodic tasks
- No bootstrap (doesn't use estimates of other states)

5.2.9.3 Temporal Difference Learning

Combines ideas from Monte Carlo and Dynamic Programming.

Basic TD(0):

$$V(S_t) \leftarrow V(S_t) + \alpha\left[R_{t+1} + \gamma V(S_t+1) - V(S_t)\right] \ldots\ldots 5.17(a)$$

TD Error:

$$\delta_t = R_{t+1} + \gamma V(S_t+1) - V(S_t) \ldots\ldots 5.17(b)$$

Advantages:

- Learn online from incomplete episodes
- Lower variance than Monte Carlo
- Can handle continuing tasks
- Bootstrap from current estimates

Table 5.6 Comparison of Model-Free Methods.

Aspect	Value-Based Methods	Policy-Based Methods
Approach	Learns value functions (V or Q).	Learns the policy directly.
Action Selection	Derives policy indirectly from value function.	Selects actions based on learned policy.
Continuous Actions	Struggles to handle; discretization needed.	Handles continuous actions effectively.
Convergence	May face instability or divergence.	Stable convergence with appropriate methods.
Exploration	Relies on exploration strategies (e.g., ε-greedy).	Exploration is built into the policy.
Examples	Q-Learning, Deep Q-Networks (DQN).	Policy Gradient, PPO, REINFORCE.

Table 5.6 compares Model-Free methods, highlighting their differences in approach, action handling, convergence, exploration, and example algorithms to aid in selecting the appropriate method for specific tasks.

5.2.10 Q-Learning

Q-Learning is a fundamental reinforcement learning al that enables an agent to learn the optimal policy for maximizing cumulative rewards without the need for an environmental model. Q-Learning is a model-free, value-based approach that learns the optimal action-value function Q∗ (s,a). This function reflects the highest expected return from a given state s and action a, follows the optimal policy. The algorithm iteratively updates estimates of Q(s,a) based on the agent's interactions with the environment, using the Bellman Optimality Equation to improve its predictions.

At its core, Q-Learning uses the following update rule:

$$Q(s,a) \leftarrow Q(s,a) + \alpha \left[R + \gamma \frac{max}{a'} Q(s',a') - Q(s,a) \right] \text{....} \mathbf{5.18}(a)$$

Here, α is the learning rate, Ris the reward received for taking action **a** in state **s**, γ is the discount factor for future rewards, and $\mathbf{max}_{a'}Q(s',a')$ represents the highest estimated value of the next state-action pair. This equation updates Q(s,a) by incorporating the immediate reward and the estimated value of the best future action. Over time, as the agent explores the environment and updates its Q-values, the function converges to **Q***(s,a), allowing the agent to derive the optimal policy by selecting actions that maximize **Q(s,a).**

Q-Learning has been effectively used in a variety of fields, including robotics, gaming, and optimizing resources. For example, it helped train AI systems to play games like Atari, where agents learned to surpass human players in complicated decision-making scenarios/situations. Although Q-Learning is simple and effective, it has limitations when dealing with high-dimensional state-action spaces due to the exponential expansion of the Q-table. Deep Q-Learning (DQN) uses neural networks to approximate the Q-function, making it more suitable for complex scenarios/environments.

5.2.10.1 Algorithm Description

Off-policy temporal difference method for learning optimal action-value function.

Q-Learning Update Rule:

$$Q(S_t, A_t) \leftarrow Q(S_t, A_t) + \alpha \left[R_{t+1} + \gamma \frac{\max}{a} Q(S_{t+1}, a) - Q(S_t, A_t) \right] \text{....} \mathbf{5.18(b)}$$

Algorithm Steps:

1. Initialize Q(s,a) arbitrarily for all s,a
2. For each episode:
    a. Initialize state S
    b. For each step of the episode:

- Choose action A from S using policy derived from Q (e.g., ε-greedy)

- Take action A, observe reward R and next state S'

- Update: $$Q(S_t, A_t) \leftarrow Q(S_t, A_t) + \alpha\left[R_{t+1} + \gamma \max_a Q(S_{t+1}, a) - Q(S_t, A_t)\right]$$

- S ← S'

c. Until S is terminal

5.2.10.2 Key Properties

Off-Policy Learning:

- Learns optimal policy while following different behavior policy
- Can learn from exploratory or sub-optimal experience
- Separates learning from action selection

Convergence Guarantees:

- Converges to optimal Q-function under certain conditions
- Requires sufficient exploration of state-action pairs
- Learning rate must satisfy specific conditions

Exploration Strategies:

- **ε-greedy**: Random action with probability ε
- **Boltzmann**: Probabilistic selection based on Q-values
- **Optimistic Initialization**: Initialize Q-values optimistically.

5.2.10.3 Advantages and Limitations

Advantages:

- Model-free: No environment model required
- Off-policy: Flexible exploration strategies
- Simple implementation
- Convergence guarantees

Limitations:

- Requires tabular representation (finite state-action space)
- Slow convergence in large state spaces
- No function approximation in basic form
- Overestimation bias in stochastic environments

Figure 5.13 presents the Q-Learning algorithm with an epsilon-greedy strategy, illustrating how it balances exploration and exploitation to learn optimal actions in a reinforcement learning framework.

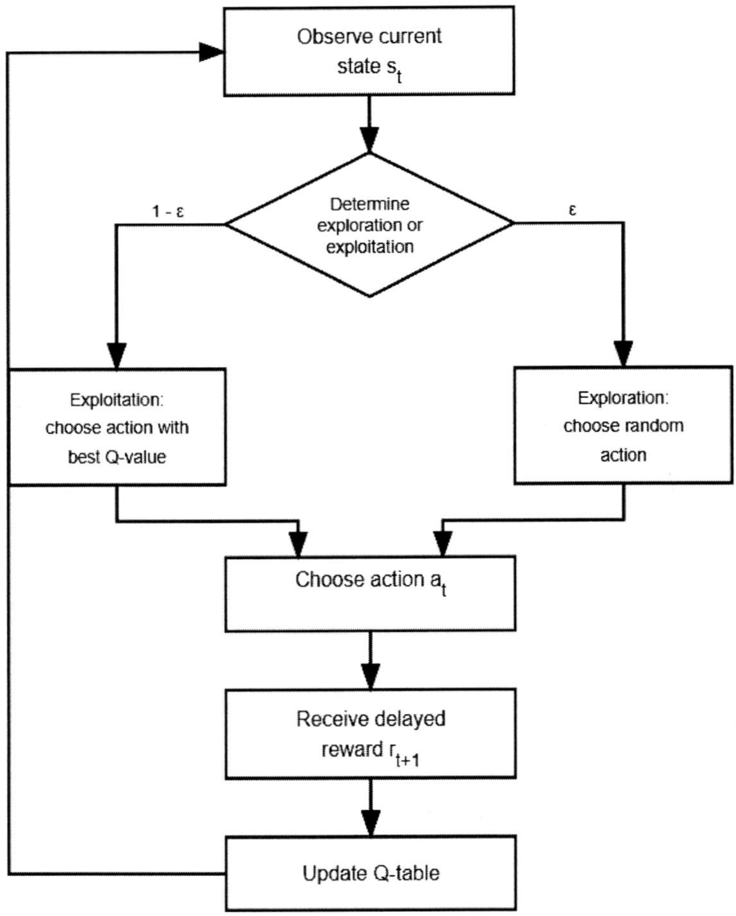

Figure 5.13—Q-Learning Algorithm Flowchart

5.2.11 SARSA Learning

SARSA (State-Action-Reward-State-Action) is an on-policy reinforcement learning system that learns a policy by interacting with its surroundings and updating its knowledge depending on the experience gathered. Unlike Q-Learning, which is an off-policy algorithm, SARSA adheres to the agent's policy while learning, updating depending on the actions it actually does rather than the optimal actions possible. This strategy highlights the agent's current policy, which can result in smoother learning in certain stochastic environments.

The approach uses bootstrapping to update the Q-values (state-action values). SARSA, in particular, adjusts the Q-value for a state-action pair based on the reward received from the environment as well as the Q-value of the next state-action pair selected in accordance with the agent's policy. The update rule is expressed as follows:

$$\mathbf{Q}(S_t,a_t) \leftarrow \mathbf{Q}(S_t,a_t) + \alpha\left[r_{t+1} + \gamma\mathbf{Q}(S_{t+1},a_{t+1}) - \mathbf{Q}(S_t,a_t)\right] \quad \text{...5.19}$$

Here, α is the learning rate, γ is the discount factor, and r_{t+1} is the reward, and $Q(s_{t+1},a_{t+1})$ corresponds to the value of the next state-action pair.

SARSA's policy-driven nature enables it to respond swiftly to changes in the environment or the agent's approach. It is especially useful in situations when adhering to an exploratory policy is critical, such as surroundings that have significant randomness or acts with highly unpredictable outcomes. However, because SARSA updates are dependent on the agent's existing/current policy, its convergence rate may be slower than that of off-policy methods such as Q-Learning when optimal policies are known.

5.2.11.1 Algorithm Description

On-policy temporal difference method for learning action-value function.

SARSA Update Rule:

$$\mathbf{Q}(S_t,A_t) \leftarrow \mathbf{Q}(S_t,A_t) + \alpha\left[R_{t+1} + \gamma\mathbf{Q}(S_{t+1},A_{t+1}) - \mathbf{Q}(S_t,A_t)\right]$$

Algorithm Steps:

1. Initialize Q(s,a) arbitrarily for all s,a
2. For each episode:

   a. Initialize state S

   b. Choose action A from S using policy derived from Q

   c. For each step of episode:

   - Take action A, observe reward R and next state S'
   - Choose action A' from S' using policy derived from Q
   - Update: $\mathbf{Q}(S,A) \leftarrow \mathbf{Q}(S,A) + \alpha\left[R + \gamma\mathbf{Q}(S',A') - \mathbf{Q}(S,A)\right]$
   - S ← S', A ← A'

   d. Until S is terminal

5.2.11.2 On-Policy vs. Off-Policy

SARSA (On-Policy):

- Updates Q-values based on actions actually taken
- Learns value of policy being followed
- More conservative in risky environments
- Policy improvement affects learning directly

Q-Learning (Off-Policy):

- Updates based on optimal action in next state
- Learns optimal policy regardless of behavior policy
- More aggressive exploration possible
- Separates learning target from behavior

5.2.11.3 Comparison with Q-Learning

Convergence:

- Both converge under appropriate conditions
- SARSA converges to policy being followed

- Q-Learning converges to optimal policy

Safety:

- SARSA considers actual policy in updates
- Better for safety-critical applications
- Q-Learning may learn risky optimal actions

Exploration:

- SARSA exploration affects value estimates
- Q-Learning can use any exploration strategy
- Trade-off between safety and optimality

Table 5.7 – SARSA vs Q-Learning Comparison

Aspect	SARSA	Q-Learning
Learning Approach	On-policy	Off-policy
Policy Followed	Follows the agent's current policy	Learns optimal policy regardless of current policy
Update Rule	Based on actual action taken (Q(s, a) to Q(s', a'))	Based on the best possible action (Q(s, a) to max_a Q(s', a))
Equation	Equation 5.19	Equation 5.18
Exploration Behavior	Learns from actions actually taken (explores)	Evaluates the optimal future action (exploits)
Performance in Stochastic Environments	More stable due to learning from actual transitions	Can perform poorly in highly stochastic environments
Speed of Convergence	Slower, as it adheres to exploratory actions	Faster, as it seeks the optimal policy directly

Applicability	Useful when exploratory policies are important	Useful when exploitation of optimal policies is prioritized
Policy Learned	Tends to learn a safer, exploratory policy	Tends to learn an aggressive, optimal policy

5.2.11.4 SARSA Variations

SARSA has evolved into several variations to address specific challenges in reinforcement learning, such as handling large state-action spaces, improving convergence speed, and enhancing exploration strategies. One common variation is **Expected SARSA**, which replaces the Q-value update based on the next action's reward with an expectation over all possible actions weighted by their probabilities under the current policy. This approach reduces variance compared to standard SARSA, leading to smoother and potentially faster learning. Additionally, **Deep SARSA** integrates deep neural networks to approximate Q-values in environments with high-dimensional state spaces, enabling SARSA to be applied effectively to complex problems like continuous control tasks and video game playing.

Another notable variation is **n-step SARSA**, which generalizes the update mechanism by incorporating rewards from multiple future steps instead of just the immediate next step. This method balances between short-term and long-term rewards, improving the agent's ability to plan ahead and learn from extended trajectories. Similarly, **Backward SARSA** integrates eligibility traces, allowing the algorithm to update not only the current state-action pair but also those encountered earlier in the trajectory, weighted by their eligibility. These enhancements aim to improve SARSA's efficiency and adaptability, making it suitable for a broader range of applications.

Expected SARSA:

$$Q(S_t, A_t) \leftarrow Q(S_t, A_t) + \alpha\left[R_{t+1} + \gamma \sum_a \pi(a \mid S_{t+1}) Q(S_{t+1}, a) - Q(S_t A_t)\right] \quad \text{....5.20}$$

- Uses expected value over next actions

- Reduces variance compared to SARSA
- Can be used in both on-policy and off-policy settings

n-step SARSA:

- Updates using n-step returns
- Bridges gap between TD and Monte Carlo
- Faster learning through multi-step updates

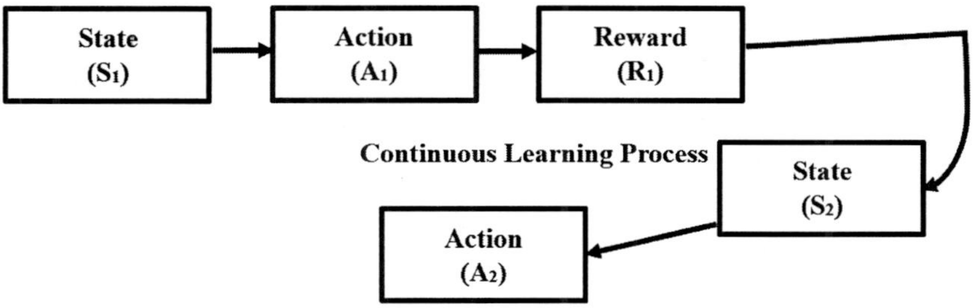

Figure 5.14 – SARSA Learning Process

Chapter Summary

This chapter is a comprehensive exploration of two major machine learning paradigms: clustering algorithms for unsupervised learning and reinforcement learning for sequential decision-making.

The clustering section began with fundamental concepts and proximity measures that form the foundation of all clustering approaches. We examined hierarchical clustering methods, including agglomerative and divisive approaches, which create tree-like structures revealing data organization at multiple levels. Partitional clustering algorithms, particularly K-means and its variations, were explored for their efficiency in dividing data into non-overlapping groups. Density-based methods like DBSCAN demonstrated the capability to discover clusters of arbitrary shapes while identifying outliers. Grid-based approaches showed how spatial partitioning can enable efficient clustering of large datasets.

The reinforcement learning section established the fundamental framework where agents learn optimal behavior through environmental interaction. We explored the key components including agents, environments, states, actions, rewards, policies, and value functions. The

Markov Decision Process provided the mathematical foundation for modeling sequential decision problems. Multi-arm bandit problems illustrated the fundamental exploration-exploitation trade-off. We distinguished between model-based approaches that learn environment dynamics and model-free methods that learn directly from experience. Finally, Q-learning and SARSA algorithms were presented as cornerstone techniques for learning optimal action-value functions, with Q-learning taking an off-policy approach and SARSA following an on-policy strategy.

Both paradigms share the common goal of extracting meaningful patterns and behaviors from data, though through fundamentally different approaches. Clustering reveals hidden structure in static data, while reinforcement learning discovers optimal behavior through dynamic interaction. Understanding these complementary approaches provides a solid foundation for tackling diverse machine learning challenges across numerous application domains.

Concluding Thoughts

The exploration of clustering algorithms and reinforcement learning in this chapter highlights the remarkable diversity and sophistication of modern machine learning approaches. These paradigms demonstrate how computational systems can automatically discover patterns in data and learn optimal behaviors without explicit programming.

Clustering algorithms showcase the power of unsupervised learning, revealing that meaningful structure often exists in data even without labelled examples. The variety of approaches—from hierarchical methods that build cluster trees to density-based algorithms that identify arbitrary shapes—illustrates how different algorithmic perspectives can uncover different aspects of data structure. The choice of clustering method depends critically on data characteristics, domain requirements, and computational constraints, emphasizing the importance of understanding multiple approaches.

Reinforcement learning represents a paradigm shift toward agents that learn through experience, mimicking aspects of biological learning. The framework's elegance lies in its generality—the same mathematical foundations apply whether teaching a robot to walk, optimizing financial portfolios, or playing strategic games. The distinction between model-based and model-free approaches reflects a fundamental trade-off in learning: whether to invest effort in understanding the environment explicitly or to learn optimal behavior directly through trial and error.

The progression from simple multi-arm bandits to full Markov Decision Processes illustrates how reinforcement learning scales from basic exploration-exploitation problems to complex sequential decision-making scenarios. The comparison between Q-learning and SARSA algorithms demonstrates how subtle algorithmic differences can lead to significantly different learning behaviors, particularly regarding safety and exploration strategies.

Looking forward, both clustering and reinforcement learning continue to evolve rapidly. Deep learning integration has revolutionized both fields, enabling clustering of high-dimensional data like images and text, while deep reinforcement learning has achieved remarkable successes in complex domains like game playing and robotics. The fundamental principles explored in this chapter provide the essential foundation for understanding these advanced developments.

The synergy between these paradigms also presents exciting opportunities. Clustering can inform state representation in reinforcement learning, while reinforcement learning can guide dynamic clustering strategies. As machine learning systems become more sophisticated, the integration of unsupervised pattern discovery with goal-oriented learning will likely play an increasingly important role in creating truly intelligent systems.

Understanding both clustering and reinforcement learning equips practitioners with complementary tools for extracting value from data: one reveals what patterns exist, while the other learns how to act optimally within those patterns. This dual capability represents a significant step toward more complete and capable machine learning systems.

Conceptual Questions

1. Define clustering in the context of unsupervised learning. How does it differ from supervised learning?
2. Explain the hierarchical clustering technique. What are the differences between agglomerative and divisive methods?

3. What is the role of proximity measures in clustering? Compare Euclidean and Cosine distances in their application.

4. Describe the DBSCAN algorithm. How does it handle noise and clusters of varying densities?

5. What is the significance of reinforcement learning in machine learning? How does it differ from supervised and unsupervised learning?

6. Explain the Markov Decision Process (MDP) and its components.

7. What is the exploration-exploitation tradeoff in reinforcement learning? Why is it important?

8. Compare Q-Learning and SARSA in terms of their policy learning approach.

Application-Based Questions

9. Design a clustering pipeline for customer segmentation in a marketing dataset. Specify steps and algorithms.

10. Propose a reinforcement learning strategy for training a robot to navigate a dynamic environment.

11. How would you determine the optimal number of clusters in a dataset using the elbow method and silhouette analysis?

12. Illustrate the use of the Bellman equation in evaluating state value functions in reinforcement learning.

Critical Thinking Questions

13. Discuss the challenges and limitations of applying reinforcement learning in high-dimensional state-action spaces.

14. Compare the practical applicability of density-based and grid-based clustering methods.

15. Evaluate the implications of using an on-policy algorithm like SARSA versus an off-policy algorithm like Q-Learning in a real-world setting.

Machine Learning Numerical Questions

Chapter 1: Introduction to Machine Learning

Statistical Analysis Problems

Q1. IQR Calculation

- **Dataset:** {12, 14, 19, 22, 24, 26, 28, 31, 34}
- **Task:** Find the Interquartile Range (IQR)

Q2. Five-Point Summary & Boxplot

- **Dataset:** {13, 11, 2, 4, 8, 9}
- **Task:** Find the 5-point summary (Min, Q1, Median, Q3, Max) and plot the boxplot

Q3. Variance and Standard Deviation

- **Dataset:** [12, 15, 18, 20, 25, 28, 30]
- **Task:** Calculate the variance and standard deviation

Q4. Percentile Calculation

- **Dataset:** [10, 15, 20, 25, 30, 35, 40, 45, 50]
- **Task:** Find the 25th, 50th, and 75th percentiles

Q5. Outlier Detection (IQR Method)

- **Dataset:** [12, 14, 16, 18, 20, 22, 24, 26, 45, 50]
- **Task:** Identify outliers using the IQR method

Regression Problems

Q6. Simple Linear Regression

- **Data:** X: [1, 2, 3, 4, 5], Y: [2, 4, 6, 8, 10]
- **Task:** Find the equation of the regression line y = mx + b

Q7. Mean Squared Error Calculation

- **Actual:** [3, 5, 7, 9, 11]
- **Predicted:** [2.8, 5.2, 6.9, 8.8, 11.3]
- **Task:** Calculate MSE and RMSE

Q8. Logistic Regression Probability

- **Equation:** $p = 1/(1 + e\^(-(-2.5 + 0.8x_1 + 1.2x_2)))$
- **Task:** Find the probability of class 1 when $x_1 = 3$ and $x_2 = 2$

Chapter 2: Data Analysis and Feature Engineering

Q9. Principal Component Analysis (PCA)

- **Data Points:** [2,6] and [1,7]
- **Task:** Apply PCA and find the transformed data

Q10. Singular Value Decomposition (SVD)

$$A = \begin{bmatrix} 1 & 2 \\ 4 & 9 \end{bmatrix}$$

Q11. Candidate Elimination Algorithm

- **Dataset:**

CGPA	Instructiveness	Practical Knowledge	Communication	Logical thinking	Job offer
≥9	Yes	Excellent	Good	Fast	YES
≥9	Yes	Good	Good	Fast	YES
≥8	No	Good	Good	Fast	NO
≥9	Yes	Good	Good	Slow	YES

- **Task:** Apply candidate elimination algorithm to obtain the complete version space

Q12. Find-S Algorithm

- **Dataset:**

Sky	Air temp	Humidity	Wind	Water	Forecast	Enjoy Sport
Sunny	Warm	Normal	Strong	Warm	Same	YES
Sunny	Warm	High	Strong	Warm	Same	YES
Rainy	Cold	High	Strong	Warm	Change	NO
Sunny	Warm	High	Strong	Cool	Change	YES

- **Task:** Apply the Find-S algorithm to obtain the hypothesis

Q13. Feature Scaling

- **Dataset:** [5, 10, 15, 20, 25]
- **Task:** Apply Min-Max normalization and Z-score normalization and compare results

Chapter 3: Similarity Based Learning and Regression

Q14. K-Nearest Neighbour Algorithm

- **Test instance:** (6.1, 40, 5)
- **Training Dataset:**

CGPA	Assessment	Project submitted	Result
9.2	85	8	PASS
8	80	7	PASS
8.5	81	8	PASS
6	45	5	FAIL
6.5	50	4	FAIL
5.8	38	5	FAIL

- **Task:** Apply K-NN with k=3 to classify the test instance

Q15. Nearest-Centroid Classifier

- **Test instance:** (6, 5)
- **Training Dataset:**

X	Y	Class
3	1	A
5	2	A
4	3	A
7	6	B
6	7	B
8	5	B

- **Task:** Apply nearest-centroid classifier to predict the class

Chapter 4: Probabilistic Models and Neural Networks

Bayesian Learning Problems

Q16. Naïve Bayes Classifier

- **New data:** (Red, SUV, Domestic)
- **Training Dataset:**

COLOR	Type	Origin	Stolen
Red	Sports	Domestic	YES
Red	Sports	Domestic	NO
Red	Sports	Domestic	YES
Yellow	Sports	Domestic	NO
Yellow	Sports	Imported	YES
Yellow	Sun	Imported	NO
Yellow	Sun	Imported	YES

- **Task:** Classify using Naïve Bayes classifier

Q17. Bayes' Theorem Application

- **Given:**
    - P(Disease) = 0.01
    - P(Positive Test | Disease) = 0.99
    - P(Positive Test | No Disease) = 0.05
- **Task:** Calculate P(Disease | Positive Test)

Q18. Gaussian Naive Bayes

- **Class A:** [1, 2, 3, 4, 5]
- **Class B:** [6, 7, 8, 9, 10]
- **Task:** Calculate mean and variance for each class, then classify test point x = 4.5

Q19. Maximum Likelihood Estimation

- **Dataset:** [2, 4, 6, 8, 10]
- **Task:** Find the MLE estimate of the mean (μ) assuming normal distribution

Neural Network Problems

Q20. Perceptron Learning

- **Parameters:** $w_1 = 0.5$, $w_2 = -0.3$, bias = 0.1, learning rate $\eta = 0.1$
- **Training example:** input = [1, 2], desired output = 1
- **Task:** Calculate updated weights after one iteration

Q21. Activation Function Calculations

- **Input:** x = 2
- **Task:** Calculate output for:
    - a) Sigmoid: f(z) = $$f(z) = \frac{1}{\left(1+\left(e^{-z}\right)\right.} \quad \text{......4.15}$$

- b) Tanh: f(z) = $f(z)=\frac{(e^{z}-e^{-z})}{(e^{z}+e^{-z})}$ **4.16**
- c) ReLU: f(z) = $\mathbf{f(z)=max(0,z)}$......**4.17**

Q22. Backpropagation Error Calculation

- **Target output:** [0.8, 0.2]
- **Actual output:** [0.7, 0.3]
- **Task:** Calculate error at output layer using mean squared error

Chapter 5: Clustering Algorithms and Reinforcement Learning

Clustering Problems

Q23. K-Means Clustering

- **Dataset:**

Objects	X-Coordinate	Y-Coordinate
1	2	4
2	4	6
3	6	8
4	10	4
5	12	4

- **Initial centroids:** Object 2 (4,6) and Object 5 (12,4)
- **Task:** Perform K-means clustering

Q24. Distance Measures

- **Points:** (0,3) and (5,8)
- **Task:** Find Manhattan and Chebyshev distance

Q25. Hierarchical Clustering

	A	B	C	D
A	0	2	6	10
B	2	0	5	9
C	6	5	0	4
D	10	9	4	0

Task: Perform agglomerative hierarchical clustering using single linkage method

Q26. DBSCAN Parameters

- **Dataset:** (1,1), (1.5,2), (3,4), (5,7), (3.5,5), (4.5,5), (3.5,4.5)
- **Parameters:** eps=2, minPts=3
- **Task:** Determine clusters using DBSCAN

Reinforcement Learning Problems

Q27. Q-Learning Update

- **Parameters:**
  - Current state: S_1, Action taken: A_1, Reward: R = 10, Next state: S_2
  - Learning rate: $\alpha = 0.1$, Discount factor: $\gamma = 0.9$
- **Q-table**

State \ Action	A_1	A_2
S_1	5	3
S_2	8	6

- **Task:** Calculate updated Q-value for $Q(S_1, A_1)$

Q28. Multi-Armed Bandit

- **Reward history:**
    - Arm 1: [1, 0, 1, 1, 0] (5 pulls)
    - Arm 2: [0, 1, 1, 0] (4 pulls)
    - Arm 3: [1, 1, 0] (3 pulls)
- **Strategy:** ε-greedy with $\varepsilon = 0.1$
- **Task:** Which arm should be selected next?

Advanced Problems (Multiple Chapters)

Decision Tree Problems

Q29. Information Gain Calculation

- **Dataset:** Total: 8 positive, 6 negative examples
- **After splitting on attribute A:**
    - A = True: 6 positive, 2 negative
    - A = False: 2 positive, 4 negative
- **Task:** Calculate information gain

Q30. Gini Impurity

- **Class distribution:**
    - Class 1: 40 samples
    - Class 2: 30 samples
    - Class 3: 30 samples
- **Task:** Calculate Gini impurity for the node

Evaluation Metrics

Q31. Confusion Matrix Calculations

- **Confusion Matrix**

Actual \ Predicted	P (Positive)	N (Negative)
P (Positive)	85	15
N (Negative)	10	90

- **Task:** Calculate Accuracy, Precision, Recall, F1-Score, and Specificity

Q32. Cross-Validation

- **Dataset:** 1000 samples, k=5
- **Task:** Determine training set and test set sizes for each fold

Q33. Learning Curve Analysis

- **Training accuracies:** [0.65, 0.78, 0.85, 0.89, 0.91]
- **Validation accuracies:** [0.62, 0.75, 0.80, 0.78, 0.76]
- **Task:** Identify if model is overfitting and at which epoch

Index

D

E

F

G

H

I

J

K

O

P

Q

R

S

T

U

V

W

X

Glossary

A

Accuracy: The proportion of correct predictions out of total predictions made by a model. Formula: (TP + TN) / (TP + TN + FP + FN).

Activation Functions: Mathematical transformations applied to a neuron's input that introduce nonlinearity in neural networks, enabling the network to learn complex relationships and patterns in data.

Action (A): The choices available to an agent in each state of the environment. Actions can be discrete (finite set of choices) or continuous (real-valued parameters).

Action Space: The set of all possible actions that an agent can take in a given environment.

Action Value Function (Q-function): A function Q^π(s,a) that represents the expected cumulative reward when starting in states, taking action a, and subsequently following policy π.

AdaBoost: Adaptive Boosting algorithm that sequentially trains weak learners, focusing on previously misclassified examples to improve overall performance.

Adaptability: Design principle for learning systems that enables them to evolve with changing data patterns and incorporate new knowledge efficiently.

Agent: The learner and decision maker in reinforcement learning that interacts with the environment, maintains internal state representation, and implements decision-making policies.

Agglomerative Hierarchical Clustering: A bottom-up clustering approach that starts with each data point as an individual cluster and progressively merges the closest clusters until all points belong to a single cluster.

Algorithm complexity: The computational cost of an algorithm in terms of time and space requirements, typically expressed using Big O notation.

Algorithm Selection: The process of choosing appropriate machine learning algorithms based on problem characteristics, data properties, and performance requirements.

Algorithmic Trading: The use of machine learning algorithms to make automated stock trading decisions based on real-time data analysis and pattern recognition.

AlexNet: A pioneering CNN architecture that popularized the use of convolutional neural networks for image classification tasks, achieving breakthrough performance on ImageNet.

Artificial Intelligence (AI): A broad field encompassing reasoning, planning, decision-making, and other cognitive functions, with machine learning as one of its key components.

Artificial Neural Networks (ANNs) : Computational models inspired by the human brain's structure and functionality, consisting of interconnected nodes (neurons) that process information through weighted connections.

Autoencoders: Unsupervised learning neural network models used for dimensionality reduction and feature learning, consisting of an encoder that compresses input data and a decoder that reconstructs it.

Automated Machine Learning (AutoML): Systems that automate the machine learning pipeline, including feature selection, model selection, and hyperparameter tuning to reduce manual effort.

Average Linkage: A linkage criterion in hierarchical clustering that calculates the distance between clusters as the average of all pairwise distances between points in the two clusters.

B

Backpropagation Algorithm: A supervised learning algorithm used to train neural networks by calculating gradients of the loss function with respect to network weights and propagating errors backward through the network.

Bagging: Bootstrap Aggregating ensemble method that reduces variance by training multiple models on different subsets of data and combining their predictions.

Bandwidth parameter (τ): A critical parameter in LWR that controls the "locality" of the regression; smaller values create very local models while larger values result in smoother fits.

BANG (Balanced Iterative Reduction and Clustering): A grid-based clustering algorithm that uses hierarchical grid structure with balanced partitioning for efficient range queries and multi-level clustering.

Batch Normalization: A technique that normalizes the inputs of each layer in a neural network to have zero mean and unit variance, stabilizing and accelerating the training process.

Batch Processing: A big data processing approach that handles large volumes of data in chunks at scheduled intervals, suitable for historical analysis.

Bayes' Theorem: A fundamental principle in probability theory that describes how to update the probability of a hypothesis based on new evidence, forming the foundation of Bayesian learning methods.

Bayesian Learning: A probabilistic approach to machine learning that uses Bayes' theorem to update beliefs about model parameters as new data becomes available, providing principled uncertainty quantification.

Bayesian Optimization: Model-based sequential optimization approach for hyperparameter tuning that builds a probabilistic model of the objective function.

Bayesian regression: A regression approach that incorporates prior distributions on parameters to make predictions.

Bellman Equations: Fundamental recursive equations in reinforcement learning that express the relationship between the value of a state and the values of its successor states. Forms the basis for many RL algorithms.

Bellman Expectation Equation: Equations that express the expected value of states or state-action pairs under a given policy π.

Bellman Optimality Equations: Equations that define the optimal value functions by expressing the value of a state as the maximum expected return achievable from that state.

Bias Term: An additional parameter in neural networks that allows the activation function to shift, providing more flexibility in fitting the data by adjusting the decision boundary.

Bias-Variance Trade-off: A fundamental concept in machine learning that balances model complexity; high-bias models underfit while high-variance models overfit data.

Binary Classification: A type of classification task where the goal is to classify elements into one of two groups or classes (e.g., spam/not spam, positive/negative).

Big Data: Large volumes of structured and unstructured data that require advanced computational methods for analysis and insights.

Big Data Analysis: The process of examining large, complex datasets to uncover hidden patterns, correlations, and actionable insights.

Biplot: A visualization technique that combines score and loading plots to show relationships between samples and variables in PCA analysis.

Boltzmann Exploration: An exploration strategy that selects actions probabilistically based on their Q-values, with higher-valued actions having higher selection probabilities.

Boosting: Sequential ensemble method that reduces bias by combining weak learners, where each subsequent model focuses on correcting errors of previous models.

Border Point: In DBSCAN, a point that is within the ε-neighborhood of a core point but does not itself have enough neighbors to be considered a core point.

Boundary effects: Performance degradation that occurs near the edges of the feature space in locally weighted methods.

C

Canonical Polyadic Decomposition (CPD): A tensor decomposition method designed to reduce the dimensionality of tensor data while preserving its inherent multi-dimensional structure.

Capacity and Complexity: Measures of a model's ability to fit diverse functions and complex patterns, controlled through regularization and architecture constraints.

Catastrophic Forgetting: The tendency of neural networks to completely forget previously learned tasks when learning new ones, a significant challenge in continual learning scenarios.

Centroid: The geometric center (mean vector) of all data points belonging to a specific class in the feature space.

CLIQUE (Clustering in Quest): A density-based clustering algorithm that operates in subspaces, identifying dense regions in high-dimensional data using a grid-based approach for efficiency.

Coefficient of Determination (R^2) : A statistical measure that represents the proportion of variance in the dependent variable that is predictable from the independent variables.

Complete Linkage: A linkage criterion that defines the distance between two clusters as the maximum distance between any two points in the clusters, resulting in compact, spherical clusters.

Computational Learning Theory: The field that analyzes algorithmic efficiency and learnability, studying sample complexity and computational complexity of learning algorithms.

Computational complexity: The amount of computational resources (time and memory) required to execute an algorithm.

Confusion Matrix: A table used to evaluate the performance of a classification model, showing the counts of true positives, true negatives, false positives, and false negatives.

Cosine Distance: A proximity measure that calculates the angle between two vectors, particularly useful for high-dimensional data and text analysis.

Covariance Matrix: A square matrix that captures the covariance between pairs of variables, fundamental to PCA calculations.

Cumulative Explained Variance: The running sum of explained variance across principal components, used to determine the cutoff for dimensionality reduction.

Curse of Dimensionality: The phenomenon where the difficulty of analysis increases exponentially with the number of dimensions, making dimensionality reduction necessary.

D

DBSCAN: Density-Based Spatial Clustering of Applications with Noise - an algorithm that identifies clusters as regions of high data density separated by regions of low density.

Deep Q-Networks (DQN): An extension of Q-learning that uses deep neural networks to approximate the Q-function, enabling the algorithm to handle high-dimensional state spaces.

Deep Reinforcement Learning (DRL): The integration of reinforcement learning with deep neural networks, enabling agents to handle high-dimensional and complex tasks.

Deep Learning (Missing Data): Advanced neural network approaches for handling missing data that can capture complex non-linear relationships but require large datasets.

Dendrogram: A tree-like diagram that shows the hierarchical relationships between clusters, displaying how clusters are merged or split at different levels of granularity.

Density-Based Methods: Clustering approaches that identify clusters based on the density of data points in different regions of the feature space.

Dimensionality Reduction: An unsupervised learning technique that reduces the number of features in a dataset while preserving important information.

Discount Factor (γ) : A parameter ($0 \leq \gamma \leq 1$) that determines how future rewards are weighted relative to immediate rewards in value function calculations.

Distance Metrics: Mathematical functions used to quantify the similarity or dissimilarity between data points (e.g., Euclidean, Manhattan, Minkowski).

Dropout: A regularization technique that randomly deactivates a fraction of neurons during training to prevent overfitting and improve generalization.

Dynamic Programming: A class of algorithms that solve MDPs by using the structure of the problem to compute optimal policies and value functions efficiently.

E

Early Exaggeration: A t-SNE parameter that encourages cluster formation during the optimization process.

Early Stopping: A regularization technique that halts training when the validation error begins to increase, preventing overfitting by avoiding excessive training.

Elastic Net: A regularization technique that combines both L1 (Lasso) and L2 (Ridge) penalties to balance feature selection and coefficient shrinkage.

Elbow Method: A technique for determining the optimal number of clusters by plotting the within-cluster sum of squares against the number of clusters and identifying the "elbow" point where improvement diminishes.

EM Algorithm: Expectation-Maximization algorithm used for missing data imputation with statistical foundation and efficiency for parametric assumptions.

Environment: The external system with which the reinforcement learning agent interacts, characterized by properties such as observability, determinism, and episodic nature.

Episodic Tasks: Reinforcement learning problems that have clear starting and ending points, with each episode being independent.

Epanechnikov kernel: A kernel function that uses a quadratic function to assign weights within a specified range, setting weights to zero beyond that range.

Euclidean Distance: The straight-line distance between two points in Euclidean space, calculated as the square root of the sum of squared differences between corresponding coordinates.

Exponential weighting: A weighting scheme that assigns weights to neighbors based on an exponential decay function.

Expected SARSA: A variation of SARSA that uses the expected value over all possible next actions instead of the actual next action taken.

Explained Variance Ratio: The proportion of total variance explained by each principal component, used to assess feature importance.

Exploration vs. Exploitation: The fundamental trade-off in reinforcement learning between trying new actions to discover better strategies (exploration) and using known information to maximize rewards (exploitation).

Exploratory Data Analysis (EDA): The process of analyzing data to identify distributions, correlations, and patterns using visualization and statistical techniques.

Explainable AI (XAI) : Techniques and methods designed to make machine learning models more interpretable and their decisions more understandable to humans.

F

F1-Score : The harmonic mean of precision and recall, providing a single metric that balances both measures. Formula: 2 × (Precision × Recall) / (Precision + Recall).

Feature Engineering: The process of selecting, modifying, or creating input variables (features) for machine learning models.

Feature Importance: Measures that quantify the contribution of each feature to model predictions, helping understand which variables are most influential.

Feature Scaling: The process of normalizing or standardizing features to ensure they contribute equally to distance calculations.

Feedforward Neural Networks (FNNs): The simplest form of neural networks where information flows in one direction from input to output without cycles or loops.

Fully Connected Layer: A neural network layer where every neuron is connected to every neuron in the previous layer, typically used in the final stages for classification or regression.

Function Approximation: Using mathematical functions (like neural networks) to approximate value functions when the state or action space is too large for tabular methods.

Fuzzy C-Means: A soft clustering algorithm where each data point can belong to multiple clusters with varying degrees of membership.

G

Gap Statistic: A method for determining the optimal number of clusters by comparing the clustering quality of real data to that of randomly generated data.

Gated Recurrent Unit (GRU) : A simplified version of LSTM with fewer parameters, combining forget and input gates into a single update gate while maintaining comparable performance.

Gaussian Kernel: A kernel function that assigns weights based on squared distance, scaled by a bandwidth parameter, following a normal distribution pattern.

Generalization: The ability of a machine learning model to perform well on previously unseen data, indicating good learning rather than memorization.

Generative Adversarial Networks (GANs) : A framework consisting of two competing neural networks—a generator and discriminator—used for generating realistic synthetic data.

Gradient Boosting : Sequential ensemble method that builds models iteratively, with each new model correcting errors of the previous ensemble.

Gradient Clipping : A technique to prevent exploding gradients by limiting the magnitude of gradients during backpropagation to a predefined threshold.

Gradient Descent : An iterative optimization algorithm used to minimize the cost function by moving in the direction of steepest descent.

Graph Convolutional Networks (GCNs) : Neural networks designed to work with graph-structured data, used in graph embedding for dimensionality reduction.

Graph Embedding: Techniques that map nodes in a high-dimensional graph to a lower-dimensional vector space while retaining structural information.

GRIDCLUS : A grid-based clustering algorithm that uses density-based grid clustering with connected components for simple and efficient processing of large spatial datasets.

H

Hard Clustering : A clustering approach where each data point belongs to exactly one cluster with no overlap between clusters.

Hidden Layers : Intermediate layers in neural networks between input and output layers that process and transform data through weighted connections and activation functions.

Hierarchical Clustering : A clustering method that creates a tree-like structure of clusters, showing relationships at multiple levels of granularity.

Hyperbolic Tangent (tanh) : An activation function that maps input values to the range (-1, 1), often providing better performance than sigmoid due to its centered output.

Hyperparameter Tuning: The process of optimizing algorithm parameters that are not learned from data but must be set before training begins.

I

ID3 (Iterative Dichotomiser 3): A decision tree algorithm that uses information gain as the splitting criterion and is primarily used for classification problems with categorical features.

Imbalanced Data: Datasets where some classes are significantly underrepresented compared to others, potentially leading to biased models.

Incremental PCA: A variation of PCA that processes data in batches, suitable for large datasets that cannot fit in memory.

Inductive Bias : The set of assumptions that a learning algorithm uses to predict outputs for inputs it has not encountered during training.

Information Gain : A measure used in decision trees to determine the effectiveness of a split by calculating the reduction in entropy after splitting on a particular attribute.

Instance-Based Learning: A learning paradigm where predictions are made by comparing new instances to stored training examples.

ISOMAP : A dimensionality reduction technique that extends MDS using geodesic distances to preserve global structure of non-linear manifolds.

J

Jaccard Similarity : A similarity measure for binary attributes and sets, calculated as the ratio of intersection to union of two sets.

K

k-Means: A partitional clustering algorithm that divides data into k clusters by minimizing the within-cluster sum of squares, using centroids to represent cluster centers.

k-Means++: An improved initialization strategy for K-Means that selects initial centroids probabilistically to reduce the likelihood of poor clustering results.

K-Medoids (PAM) : Partitioning Around Medoids - a clustering algorithm that uses actual data points as cluster centers instead of calculated centroids, making it more robust to outliers.

Kernel PCA : An extension of PCA that uses kernel functions to identify non-linear patterns by implicitly mapping to higher dimensions.

Kernel Functions: Mathematical functions used to assign weights to data points based on their distance from a query point.

KL Divergence: Kullback-Leibler divergence, a measure used in t-SNE to minimize the difference between high- and low-dimensional distributions.

L

L1 Regularization (Lasso): A regularization technique that adds a penalty term proportional to the absolute value of coefficients, capable of performing feature selection by shrinking some coefficients to zero.

L2 Regularization (Ridge): A regularization technique that adds a penalty term proportional to the squared magnitude of coefficients, shrinking them toward zero without making them exactly zero.

Lasso Regression : Least Absolute Shrinkage and Selection Operator, a type of linear regression that uses L1 regularization to perform both regularization and feature selection.

Leaky ReLU : A variant of ReLU activation function that allows small gradients for negative inputs, addressing the "dying ReLU" problem.

Learning Rate: A hyperparameter that controls the step size of weight updates during training, determining how quickly a model learns from data.

Linear Discriminant Analysis (LDA) : A supervised dimensionality reduction technique that maximizes class separability by projecting data to maximize between-class variance and minimize within-class variance.

Loading Vectors : Coefficients of original variables in principal components, indicating the contribution of each original feature to each PC.

Locally Linear Embedding (LLE) : A dimensionality reduction technique that preserves local neighborhood relationships by reconstructing each point from its neighbors.

Logistic Function (Sigmoid): A mathematical function that maps any real-valued input to a value between 0 and 1, used in logistic regression to model probabilities.

Logistic Regression : A statistical method used for binary classification that uses the logistic function to model the probability of class membership.

M

Machine Learning (ML): A subset of AI that focuses on developing algorithms that learn patterns from data and make predictions or decisions without explicit programming.

Manhattan Distance : A distance metric calculated as the sum of absolute differences between corresponding coordinates of two points; also called L1 norm or city block distance.

Markov Decision Process (MDP): A formal framework for modeling reinforcement learning problems, defined by a set of states, actions, transition probabilities, reward functions, and a discount factor.

Markov Property : The principle that the future state depends only on the current state and action, not on the sequence of events that preceded it.

Maximum Depth : A parameter in decision trees that controls the depth of the tree to prevent overfitting and improve interpretability.

Mean/Median Imputation : A missing data handling technique that fills in missing values with the mean or median of the feature, preserving distribution characteristics.

Mean Absolute Error (MAE): A regression performance metric that computes the average absolute difference between predicted and actual values.

Mean Squared Error (MSE): A widely used loss function for regression tasks that penalizes large errors by squaring the difference between predicted and actual values.

MinPts : A DBSCAN parameter that specifies the minimum number of data points required in a neighborhood to qualify a point as a core point.

Minkowski Distance : A generalized distance metric that includes Euclidean and Manhattan distances as special cases, controlled by a parameter p.

Model-Based Learning: Reinforcement learning methods that build a model of the environment and use it for planning and decision-making.

Model Compression : Techniques used to reduce the size and complexity of trained models without sacrificing performance, enabling deployment on resource-constrained devices.

Model Deployment: The phase of the ML lifecycle where trained models are integrated into real-world applications and exposed to new data.

Monte Carlo Methods : A family of algorithms in reinforcement learning that estimate value functions by averaging returns from complete episodes of experience.

Multicollinearity : A condition where predictor variables in a regression model are highly correlated, leading to unreliable coefficient estimates.

Multidimensional Scaling (MDS) : A classical linear dimensionality reduction method that aims to preserve pairwise distances between data points.

Multilayer Perceptron (MLP): A type of feedforward neural network consisting of input, hidden, and output layers, commonly used in classification and regression tasks.

Multiple Regression: A linear regression model that predicts a continuous dependent variable using two or more independent variables.

Multivariate Regression: A regression technique used when there are multiple dependent variables to be predicted simultaneously from a common set of predictors.

N

Naïve Bayes : A probabilistic classifier based on Bayes' theorem that assumes strong independence among features, often used in text classification.

Neural Networks : Computational models inspired by the human brain, composed of layers of interconnected neurons used to approximate complex functions.

Noise Point : In DBSCAN, a point that does not belong to any cluster because it lacks sufficient neighboring points within the specified ε radius.

Non-parametric Regression: Regression methods that do not assume a specific functional form for the relationship between features and output, such as LWR and k-NN.

Normality: A statistical assumption that the residuals or errors in a regression model are normally distributed, often required for valid inference.

O

Objective Function : A function that a learning algorithm aims to minimize or maximize, often representing a loss or reward depending on the problem type.

Off-Policy Learning: A reinforcement learning setting where the policy used to generate behavior is different from the policy being learned.

On-Policy Learning : A reinforcement learning setting where the agent learns the value of the policy it is currently following.

Optimization Theory : The mathematical study of methods to find the best solution among a set of possible options, foundational for training ML models.

OPTICS : Ordering Points To Identify the Clustering Structure - a density-based clustering algorithm that addresses the limitations of DBSCAN by identifying clusters of varying densities.

Output Layer : The final layer of a neural network that produces predictions or outputs, typically having one neuron per class in classification tasks.

Overfitting : A modeling error that occurs when a model learns noise or random fluctuations in the training data, resulting in poor generalization to new data.

P

PCA (Principal Component Analysis): A linear dimensionality reduction technique that transforms data into new variables (principal components) that capture maximum variance.

Pearson Correlation : A measure of linear correlation between two variables, ranging from -1 to 1, where 0 implies no linear correlation.

Perceptron : A simple neural network model that learns a linear decision boundary by adjusting weights through an iterative process.

Policy (π) : A function or mapping that defines the agent's behavior by specifying the probability distribution over actions for each state.

Policy Gradient Methods : A class of reinforcement learning algorithms that directly adjust the policy's parameters by maximizing the expected return.

Pooling Layer : A component in CNNs that down-samples feature maps, reducing spatial dimensions and computational complexity while retaining important features.

Precision : A classification metric that measures the proportion of correctly predicted positive observations to the total predicted positives.

Principal Components : New uncorrelated variables formed by linear combinations of original features that capture the most variance in the data.

Q

Q-Learning : An off-policy reinforcement learning algorithm that learns the optimal action-value function by iteratively updating Q-values using the Bellman Optimality Equation.

Q-Table : A tabular representation of Q-values for each state-action pair in Q-learning, used for decision-making.

R

R^2 (Coefficient of Determination): A metric indicating the proportion of the variance in the dependent variable that is predictable from the independent variables.

Random Forest : An ensemble learning method that constructs multiple decision trees and combines their predictions for improved accuracy and robustness.

Recall : A classification metric that measures the proportion of actual positives correctly identified by the model.

ReLU (Rectified Linear Unit): A widely used activation function in neural networks that outputs zero for negative inputs and the input itself for positive inputs.

Regression: A family of supervised learning techniques used to model the relationship between dependent and independent variables for prediction.

Regularization : Techniques used to prevent overfitting by penalizing large model parameters, improving generalization.

Reinforcement Learning : A learning paradigm where an agent learns optimal actions through trial-and-error interactions with an environment to maximize cumulative reward.

Residuals : The differences between actual and predicted values in regression models, used to diagnose model fit.

Reward: A scalar signal received after taking an action in a particular state, representing immediate feedback on the action's success.

Ridge Regression : A type of linear regression that includes L2 regularization to prevent overfitting by penalizing large coefficients.

Root Mean Squared Error (RMSE): A regression metric that measures the average magnitude of errors by taking the square root of the mean squared error.

S

SARSA : State-Action-Reward-State-Action - an on-policy reinforcement learning algorithm that updates Q-values based on the action actually taken.

Scalability : The ability of an algorithm to handle increasing data sizes or dimensions without significant degradation in performance.

SHAP Values: Shapley Additive Explanations - a method to interpret machine learning model predictions by attributing contributions to individual features.

Sigmoid Function : An activation function that maps input values to the range (0,1), commonly used in binary classification problems.

Silhouette Coefficient: A clustering evaluation metric that measures how similar a point is to its own cluster compared to other clusters.

Soft Clustering : A clustering approach where data points can belong to multiple clusters with varying degrees of membership.

State (S): A representation of the environment at a specific time, capturing all necessary information for decision-making.

Stochastic Gradient Descent : An optimization algorithm that updates model parameters using a subset of the data (a mini-batch) rather than the full dataset.

Supervised Learning: A machine learning paradigm where models learn from labeled data, mapping inputs to outputs.

Support Vector Machines (SVMs): Supervised learning models that find the hyperplane that maximizes the margin between different classes.

T

Tabular Data : Structured data organized into rows and columns, commonly used in supervised learning tasks.

Temporal Difference (TD) Learning : A reinforcement learning method that updates value estimates based partly on other learned estimates, combining aspects of Monte Carlo and dynamic programming methods.

t-distributed Stochastic Neighbor Embedding (t-SNE): A non-linear dimensionality reduction technique used for visualization by preserving local relationships in high-dimensional data.

TPOT : Tree-based Pipeline Optimization Tool - an AutoML tool that uses genetic programming to optimize ML pipelines.

Transfer Learning : A technique where knowledge from a pre-trained model is transferred to a new, related problem, reducing training time and data requirements.

Transformer Networks : Deep learning architectures based on self-attention mechanisms, widely used in NLP and increasingly in vision tasks.

Tricube Kernel: A kernel function used in LWR that gives higher weight to points near the query and rapidly decreases to zero beyond a fixed distance.

U

Underfitting : A modeling issue where a model is too simple to capture the underlying patterns in the data, resulting in poor training and testing performance.

UMAP (Uniform Manifold Approximation and Projection): A non-linear dimensionality reduction technique that preserves local and some global structure in high-dimensional data.

Unsupervised Learning : A learning paradigm where the model discovers patterns or structures in data without labelled outputs.

V

Validation Dataset: A dataset used during training to tune model parameters and monitor generalization performance before final testing.

Variance Inflation Factor (VIF): A metric that quantifies multicollinearity by measuring how much a feature's variance is inflated due to correlation with other features.

Visualization : The graphical representation of data and model behavior, aiding in interpretation, debugging, and communication of results.

W

Ward's Method : A hierarchical clustering method that minimizes the variance within clusters at each step, producing compact clusters.

WaveCluster : A grid-based clustering algorithm that uses wavelet transforms to detect clusters of arbitrary shape in spatial data.

Weight Initialization : The process of assigning initial weights in a neural network to break symmetry and promote faster convergence.

Weighted k-NN : A k-NN variant where each neighbor contributes differently to the prediction based on its distance from the query point.

X

XGBoost : Extreme Gradient Boosting - an efficient and scalable implementation of gradient boosting that includes regularization to prevent overfitting.

XOR Problem : A classic challenge for linear models, demonstrating the need for non-linear transformations in neural networks.